PAUL, THE TEMPLE,
AND THE PRESENCE OF GOD

Program in Judaic Studies
Brown University
BROWN JUDAIC STUDIES
Edited by
Ernest S. Frerichs, Wendell S. Dietrich,
Calvin Goldscheider, David Hirsch, Alan Zuckerman

Project Editors (Projects)

David Blumenthal, Emory University (Approaches to Medieval Judaism)
Ernest S. Frerichs, Brown University (Dissertations and Monographs)
Lenn Evan Goodman, University of Hawaii (Studies in Medieval Judaism)
Norbert Samuelson, Temple University (Jewish Philosophy)
Jonathan Z. Smith, University of Chicago (Studia Philonica)

Number 224
PAUL, THE TEMPLE,
AND THE PRESENCE OF GOD

by
David A. Renwick

PAUL, THE TEMPLE,
AND THE PRESENCE OF GOD

by

David A. Renwick

Scholars Press
Atlanta, Georgia

PAUL, THE TEMPLE,
AND THE PRESENCE OF GOD

Library of Congress Cataloging-in-Publication Data

Renwick, David A.
    Paul, the Temple, and the presence of God / by David A. Renwick.
    p. cm. — (Brown Judaic studies ; no. 224)
    Includes bibliographical references and index.
    ISBN 1-55540-615-7 (alk. paper)
    1. Bible. N.T. Corinthians, 2nd, II, 14-III, 18—Criticism,
interpretation, etc. 2. Paul, the Apostle, Saint. 3. Pharisees.
4. Presence of God—Biblical teaching. I. Title. II. Series.
BS2675.2.R46   1991
227'.306—dc20   91-21322
                                          CIP

ISBN 978-1-930675-50-6 (paperback : alk. paper)
Reprinted in paper 2007.

Printed in the United States of America
on acid-free paper
∞

FOR
CURRIE, LALLA, CHARLIE AND MAIRI

Soli Deo Gloria

TABLE OF CONTENTS

ACKNOWLEDGMENTS

There are many people to thank for their support and encouragement in this project. First of all my thanks are due to my professor at Union Theological Seminary in Virginia, Paul Achtemeier. Throughout the years in which this book has developed from thought to dissertation and on to its present form, Dr. Achtemeier has been a constant source of insight and challenge. My thanks are due also to Jacob Neusner, and many other Jewish scholars whose work I came to know in many wonderful hours that sped by all too quickly in the Union Library from 1983-84. I trust that I have represented their thought fairly.

On a more personal level, conversations with Murray Haar, John Blumenstein, and Norman Hutchinson helped to clarify my own thinking in the early stages. The staff of the Union Library have always been exceptional. My own congregation, John Calvin Presbyterian Church, provided the study leave that made a portion of the revision possible, and First Presbyterian Church, San Antonio, provided the facilities. John Blumenstein and Fitz Neal willingly proof-read the manuscript in its final stages.

Last, and above all, my thanks are due to my wife and children, who have patiently born with many hours spent on the project, especially over the past three years. I trust that that time will become theirs again.

ABBREVIATIONS

AHR	*American Historical Review*
Ant.	Josephus, *Antiquities of the Jews*
Ap.	Josephus, *Contra Apion*
ATR	*Anglican Theological Review*
BA	*Biblical Archaeologist*
BAG4	W. Bauer, W. F. Arndt, and F. W. Gingrich, *Greek-English Lexicon of the New Testament*
Bib	*Biblica*
BJ	Josephus, *Bellum Judaicarum (Jewish Wars)*
BJRL	*Bulletin of the John Rylands Library*
BZ	*Biblische Zeitschrift*
CBQ	*Catholic Biblical Quarterly*
CD	Cairo Damascus (Document)
DNTT	*A Dictionary of New Testament Theology*
ExpTim	*Expository Times*
HR	*Historical Review*
HUCA	*Hebrew Union College Annual*
IDB	*Interpreter's Dictionary of the Bible*
IDBS	*Interpreter's Dictionary of the Bible, Supplementary Volume*
Int	*Interpretation*
JBL	*Journal of Biblical Literature*
JES	*Journal of Ecumenical Studies*
JQR	*Jewish Quarterly Review*
JR	*Journal of Religion*
JSJ	*Journal for the Study of Judaism in the Persian, Hellenistic and Roman Period*
JSNT	*Journal for the Study of the New Testament*
JSOT	*Journal for the Study of the Old Testament*
JSS	*Journal of Semitic Studies*
JSSR	*Journal for the Scientific Study of Religion*

JTS	*Journal of Theological Studies*
KJV	King James Version
LXX	The Septuagint
M. Dem.	Mishnah Demai
M. Hag.	Mishnah Hagiga
MT	Masoretic
NEB	New English Bible
NIV	New International Version
NovT	*Novum Testamentum*
NovTSup	Novum Testamentum Supplementary Series
NTS	*New Testament Studies*
OTP1	*The Old Testament Pseudepigrapha*, Volume 1
OTP2	*The Old Testament Pseudepigrapha*, Volume 2
RB	*Révue Biblique*
RelSRev	*Religious Studies Review*
ResSciRel	*Réscherches de Science Réligieuse*
RevExp	*Review and Expositor*
RQ	*Révue de Qumran*
RSV	Revised Standard Version
RTL	*Révue théologique de Louvain*
RTP	*Rabbinic Traditions about the Pharisees*
SBL	Society of Biblical Literature
TDNT	*Theological Dictionary of the New Testament*
TS	*Theological Studies*
VT	*Vetus Testamentum*
WUNT	*Wissenschaftliche Untersuchungen zum Neuen Testament*
ZNW	*Zeitschrift fur die neutestamentliche Wissenschaft*
1QH	Hodayot (Thanksgiving Hymns), Qumran Cave 1
1QM	Milhamah (War Scroll), Qumran Cave 1
1QS	Serek hayyahad (Rule of the Community, Manual of Discipline), Qumran Cave 1
11QTemple	Temple Scroll, Qumran Cave 11 Review

PART ONE

The Quest For The Presence Of God

PART III

The Quest Be... P... Ch...

CHAPTER 1

Paul the Pharisee

I. INTRODUCTION

Wayne Meeks has noted well that there has been no shortage of attempts to set the Apostle Paul against the backround of various types of Judaism, whether as a rabbi, an apocalyptist, a mystic, a gnostic or a Hellenist.[1] Vagueness, anachronism and inappropriate definitions concerning the groups to which Paul has been compared have plagued such studies, and somehow, Meeks suggests, "Paul himself is the clearest proof of their inadequacies."

Inadequate though many such studies may have been, and complex though the endeavor undoubtedly is, nevertheless the attempt to understand Paul in the light of his Jewish background is surely a pursuit that must continue. Indeed the present study is one which attempts to do precisely this: to clarify Paul's thought by setting it in the light of his Jewish background. In particular, the specific background which will concern us is that to which Paul himself refers when writing to the church in Philippi. There he declares that he was not only a member by birth of the tribe of Benjamin and of the people of Israel (a "Hebrew born of Hebrews"), but that he was also by choice, in his understanding of the Mosaic Law, a Pharisee (3:5,6).

Paul was a Pharisee, that much is certain. But this incontrovertible assertion only begs the question as to who the Pharisees were, especially in relation to their religious life and motivation, in the period when Paul was one of them, the period before the destruction of the Jerusalem Temple in the year 70 CE.

---

[1]Wayne A. Meeks, The First Urban Christians: The Social World of the Apostle Paul (New Haven: Yale, 1983), p. 33.

In this study, then, our concern will first of all be to understand the pre-70 CE Pharisees, and to set that understanding against both the broader background of the Biblical witness and the rich faith of Inter-Testamental Judaism. This is the perspective from which the thought of Paul himself will then be examined. Our examination will focus on only one specific Pauline passage, yet one renowned for its complexity, and our aim will be to demonstrate that a clear understanding of the pre-Christian background from which Paul the Christian came does indeed provide *significant* clarification of the development and logic of Paul's thought in one of its most complex forms of expression.

In specific terms, our argument will be that both in the Judaism of pre-70 Pharisaism and in the life of ancient Judaism in general there was a pervasive interest in concepts such as Jerusalem, the Temple, the Priesthood, and other matters relating to the cult, and that this interest was often symptomatic of a deeper interest: the quest for the presence of God. Thus what we ultimately want to argue is that it was the loss of the presence of God which was widely understood in Judaism as the fundamental problematic of life, a problematic for which various expressions of Judaism, including that of the pre-70 CE Pharisees and that of Paul, the Jewish Pharisee-turned- Christian, claimed to have a resolution. This resolution, we shall argue, comes to full expression in Paul within his discussion in II Corinthians 2:14-3:18.

Our study begins, then, by re-emphasizing Paul's assertion that in his pre-Christian days he was "according to the Law a Pharisee," and by asking just who exactly the Pharisees were as they functioned in the mid-first century of the present era.[2]

---

[2]In considering the Jewish background of Paul, E. P. Sanders in Paul and Palestinian Judaism: A Comparison of Patterns of Religion (Philadelphia: Fortress, 1977) refers, but only in a cursory manner, to Paul's background as a Pharisee. In this regard he mentions the difficulty of establishing who the Pharisees of the pre-70 C.E. period were, and provides a useful summary of the debate between Jacob Neusner and Ellis Rivkin on the issue of Pharisaic identity. See especially pp. 60-62, with 50-51, 152-55.

Carol Stockhausen, in her helpful monograph, Moses' Veil and the Glory of the New Covenant (Rome: Pontifical Institute, 1989), also notes that Paul was a Pharisee, and seeks to understand him in the light of his Jewish background. Stockhausen makes no distinction between the pre-70 Pharisees and the much later compilers of the Mishnah and other Jewish literature of the common era. However, her arguments that Paul's thought (specifically in II Corinthians 3, the passage that we shall examine in detail in due course) can be clarified by assuming that he was influenced greatly by traditional rabbinic methods of Scriptural interpretation may neverthelees be valid.

We may also note that whereas Sanders' overall goal is to compare "patterns of religion" -- how getting in and staying in a specific religion are understood (see p. 17) --, and whereas

II. THE PHARISEES

The extent and nature of the sources relating to the Pharisees have, over the past hundred years, spawned an on-going debate concerning the origins, beliefs, practices, general identity and function of Pharisaism within Judaism as a whole.[3] The aspect of this debate on which we shall focus here is represented by two of its recent contributors, Ellis Rivkin and Jacob Neusner.

The rationale for singling out these two scholars from others is both negative and positive. On the negative side the scholarly literature is so vast, and the variety of methodological presuppositions used and conclusions reached by scholars is so broad, that a comprehensive survey of the history of interpretation of Pharisaism could well prove more confusing than enlightening, and thus is not attempted.[4] On the positive side, we would argue that the works of both Rivkin and Neusner have brought Pharisaic studies to a new stage by means of their common concern to clarify the methodological issues behind their conclusions, and consequently behind the conclusions of others before them.

Furthermore, the comparison of the work of these two scholars in particular is of peculiar interest -- and this is crucial to see for our own purposes -- because their methodologies and conclusions are so radically different from each other that they must be viewed as ultimately irreconcileable.[5] That is, in the end, one is forced to choose either the methodology and general conclusions of Rivkin, or of Neusner, or of neither; but not of

---

Stockhausen's comparison focuses on principles of interpretation, our own comparison will focus on another issue, the generative problematic: what is it that is lacking or has been lost which the religion promises to provide or regain? In this framework, we want to seek out the goal of a religion, and will claim that with regard to Pharisaism and at least some other aspects of Judaism, the goal is ultimately neither, for example, forgiveness nor escape from judgment (these being only a means to a greater goal) but to find and live within the presence God, now and always.

[3]M. J. Cook, "Jesus and the Pharisees: The Problem as it stands Today," JES 15 (1978): 441-47, provides an excellent introduction to the confusing array of scholarly views about the Pharisees which have arisen, in his estimation, primarily because of the nature of the sources.

[4]Surveys of the literature can be found in R. Marcus, "The Pharisees in the Light of Modern Scholarship," JR 32 (1952): 153-64; and more recently in J. Neusner, The Rabbinic Traditions about the Pharisees before 70, III, Conclusions (Leiden: Brill, 1971), 320-68. Henceforth cited as RTP.

[5]Sanders. pp. 61-62, seems to be one of the few scholars to have noted the fundamental nature of the difference between the portrayals of the Pharisees by Rivkin and Neusner. He writes (p. 62): "It is evident that Neusner's picture of the Pharisees is almost diametrically opposite that of Rivkin."

both, as if they were complementary. Our own choice, as shall become clear, will lie with Neusner, who argues that the Pharisees before 70 CE were fundamentally interested in the issue of cultic purity.[6] In siding with Neusner, however, our intent is in no way to disparage Ellis Rivkin's scholarship and his numerous significant contributions to the understanding of the ancient world. Rather, the intention is simply to present a viewpoint as clearly and forcefully as possible, with comparison and polemic as the means to this end.

The present study begins with a presentation of the approach of Ellis Rivkin, who argues, among other things, that the Pharisees had no interest whatsoever in the issue of cultic purity the issue which Neusner sees as dominant.[7]

Understanding the Pharisees: The Approach of Ellis Rivkin

Ellis Rivkin's approach to Pharisaic studies has been expressed in numerous articles summarized in his article on the Pharisees in the *Interpreter's Dictionary of the Bible: Supplementary Volume*, and forming the substance of his book, *A Hidden Revolution*.[8] Rivkin's initial presupposition in these latter works is that the only evidence that can be gained about the Pharisees is from documents that refer to them specifically by name -- in Greek as the Φαρισαῖοι or in Hebrew as the *perusim*.[9] On this basis the Psalms of Solomon, used by some as a primary source of Pharisaic thought in the half century before the Christian era,[10] are omitted from the discussion since they simply do not refer to such a group by name. The sources remaining are the works of Josephus, the New Testament Epistles

---

[6]See Neusner's comments in RTP III, pp.301-19 and in "The Pharisees in the Light of the Historical Sources of Judaism," in Formative Judaism: Religious, Historical and Literary Studies, ed. J. Neusner, (Chico, Cal.: Scholars Press, 1982), pp. 77-78.

[7]See, for example, Rivkin's A Hidden Revolution (Nashville: Abingdon, 1978), pp. 84, 86, 97, 135, 152.

[8]Among the articles in which Rivkin's ideas about Pharisaism are developed are "Internal City: Judaism and Urbanization," JSSR 5 (Spring 1966): 225-40; "Defining the Pharisees: The Tannaitic Sources," HUCA 40-41 (1969-70): 205-50; and "Pharisaism and the Crisis of the Individual in the Greco-Roman World," JQR 61 (July 1970): 27-53.

[9]Rivkin, Hidden, p. 31.

[10]The Psalms of Solomon are assumed to be Pharisaic, for example, by J. Jeremias, Jerusalem in the Time of Jesus (Philadelphia: Fortress, 1967), p. 266; M. Black, "Pharisees," IDB, III, pp. 775-81; and recently by W. L. Lane, "Paul's Legacy from Pharisaism: Light from the Psalms of Solomon," Concordia Journal 8 (July 1982): 130-38.

and Gospels, and the Rabbinic literature, each of which mentions the Pharisees by name and is studied by Rivkin individually.

Josephus

With regard to Josephus, Rivkin assumes that the *Jewish Wars*, the *Antiquities*, and the *Vita* present a consistent and complementary picture of those who comprised the Pharisaic movement, and thus are analysed not one by one, but side by side as if they were one and the same source.[11] Furthermore, while recognizing that it was not Josephus' intent to write a history of the Pharisees, but only to mention them in passing as they entered the stage of his history, Rivkin approaches the sources in such a way as to present their information on the Pharisees chronologically, from the appearance of the group in the second century BCE. until the Jewish wars with the Romans in the late first century CE.[12] The picture thus portrayed, argues Rivkin, not only presents the Pharisees throughout the period as believers in both the resurrection and a balance between free will and determinism, but, more particulary, as public, popular and congenial figures with enough support to control the procedures of the temple liturgy. Further, they had enough religious and political authority to determine, and at times to enforce, laws of state based upon their interpretation of a two-fold Mosaic Torah, comprising not only the written scriptures but also the traditions of the Fathers: unwritten oral traditions which, Rivkin argues, enabled the concept of Torah to adapt to the changes of time, and thus to remain alive and relevant to Jewish life, forever changed by the advent of Hellenism in the second century B.C.[13]

Indeed, for Rivkin, it is precisely the Pharisees' relationship with this two-fold Law which provides the essential "core of Pharisaism." Thus, beyond the smaller details of Pharisaic belief and interaction with groups such as the Sadducees and the secular authorities in the land, the Pharisees emerge from the writings of Josephus fundamentally as a scholar class, who introduced to Judaism the revolutionary concept of the two-fold Law, and who defended

---

[11]Rivkin, Hidden, p. 33. References to the Pharisees in Josephus can be found in Ant. XIII.171-3, 288-300, 399-411; XV.2-4, 368-71, XVII.41-46, 148-54; XVIII.2-17, 23; BJ I.107-14, 571; II.118-19, 162-66; Vita 10-12, 21, 189-98.

[12]Rivkin, Hidden, pp. 33-66.

[13]Rivkin, Hidden, pp. 39, 41-42, 53, 55, 67-75, 211-20. See also Rivkin's "Pharisaism and the Crisis of the Individual," JQR 61 (1970): 27-53.

and propagated that Law as binding, not just for themselves, but for every true Jew.[14]

The New Testament

Having established his basic thesis with reference to Josephus, Rivkin proceeds to analyse the documents of the New Testament, choosing to start with the writings of Paul, since Paul, by his own claim, had been, before his conversion to Christ, a Pharisee. In particular, with respect to Paul, Rivkin points out that in Philippians and Galatians Paul refers to his pre-Christian life in Judaism with emphasis on his zeal for the "traditions of the Fathers" (Phil. 3:5-6, Gal.1:13-14); "traditions" to which not only Paul could point as being characteristic of Pharisaim, but, Rivkin notes, to which Josephus pointed, along with the New Testament Gospels as well.[15]

Of the Gospel texts referred to by Rivkin, two in particular can be used to summarize his understanding of the Gospels' Pharisees. The first, Matthew 23:1-2, concerns the Pharisees' authority in legal matters: in this verse Jesus is presented by Matthew as accepting the fact that the Pharisees legitimately "sit on Moses' seat."[16] To be sure, the text also portrays the Pharisees as sharing the seat with the Scribes; yet Rivkin argues that, contrary to common consensus, the Scribes and Pharisees constitute not two groups within Judaism, but one and the same.[17] The second text, Mark 7:3-13, concerns the specific interest of the Pharisees in the "traditions of the elders"[18] -- which to Rivkin, as we have already noted (above, p. 7), is the phrase used to refer to the oral division of the two-fold Law.

These two texts are by no means the only Gospel texts referred to by Rivkin, yet they can certainly be seen to act as the filter through which the

---

[14]Rivkin, Hidden, pp. 68, 72; and the initial summary in IDBS, p. 657.

[15]Rivkin, IDBS, p. 658.

[16]Rivkin, Hidden, pp. 81-83, 87.

[17]Rivkin's argument that the scribes and Pharisees are one and the same is given both in Hidden, pp. 104-23, and in his "Scribes, Pharisees, Lawyers, Hypocrites: A Study in Synonimity," HUCA 49 (1978): 135-42. See also Michael J. Cook, Mark's Treatment of the Jewish Leaders (Leiden: Brill, 1978), pp. 81-97 for a similar view. For the traditional view see J. Jeremias, Jerusalem, pp. 236, 246-47; J. Bowker, Jesus and the Pharisees (Cambridge: University Press, 1973), pp. 40-41; and J. Neusner, "The Formation of Rabbinic Judaism: Yavneh from A.D. 70 to 100," in Aufstieg und Niedergang der römischen Welt, Principat II.19.2., eds. H. Temporini and W. Hasse (Berlin: De Gruyter, 1979), pp. 37-39.

[18]Rivkin, Hidden, pp. 88-91.

other references pass.[19] Thus, while Rivkin acknowledges that many Gospel pericopes involving the Pharisees draw attention to specific issues such as fasting, tithing, purity, divorce, belief in resurrection, and allegiance to the Roman rulers, yet his general argument suggests that these issues themselves are not so important as the issue of legal authority: the question as to who has the right to create and pronounce the law in each specific case -- Jesus or the Pharisees.[20]

The Rabbinic Literature

Throughout his study of Josephus and the New Testament, Rivkin affirms that no evidence whatsoever could be used to suggest that the Pharisees were a closed fellowship concerned primarily with their own welfare and their own cultic purity.[21] The rationale for these disclaimers, and Rivkin's insistence on this point, is clearly polemical: not that Rivkin's polemic is only focused against Jacob Neusner, but rather against the scholarship of the past which had, in Rivkin's opinion, frequently misused the Rabbinic evidence concerning the nature and concerns of the Pharisaic movement.[22]

Two assumptions in particular, according to Rivkin, led to this misuse, assumptions which Rivkin in due course proceeds to refute. The initial false assumption was simply that since the name *perusim* could be translated from Hebrew as meaning (among other things) "separatist," then the Pharisees must have had a concern for separation from something or someone. Far more important however than this observation based on the Pharisees' name, was the second assumption, that the Rabbinic evidence actually supplied the details of that separation -- a separation both from a *group of people*, known as the "Am-Haarez," and from *those things* which the *perusim* regarded as cultically impure.[23]

Indeed, Rivkin indicates that it was the combination of two mishnaic texts in particular, M.Hagigah 2:7 and M.Demai 2:3, which presented this (to him,

---

[19]Rivkin, IDBS, p. 658.

[20]Rivkin, Hidden, pp. 91-104.

[21]E.g., Rivkin, Hidden, pp. 86, 97.

[22]Rivkin's polemic is explicitly made in his introduction, Hidden, pp. 27-28 (see n. 1, pp. 312-16) In which he places himself in opposition to scholars such as Schürer, Herford, Finkelstein, G. F. Moore, and Neusner, for all of whom the Pharisees are attested in the Rabbinic literature as having a fundamental interest in issues of cultic purity.

[23]Rivkin, Hidden, pp. 27-28.

false) picture most clearly.[24] The primary text, M.Hag. 2:7, both drew the contrast between certain *perusim* and the *Am-Haarez*, and pointed as well to the issue at stake as being that of cultic purity -- the key phrase reading as follows: "For Pharisees (*perusim*) the clothes of an *Am-haarez* count as suffering midras-uncleanness; . . ." Furthermore, while the second text, M.Dem. 2:3, made no mention of *perusim* at all, but only of a group of sectarian nature, referred to as the "Associates" (Hebrew, *Haberim*), nevertheless this second text seemed to function as a parallel to that of M.Hag. 2:7 in its concern for purity and its contrast between a certain group (this time, the *Haberim*) and the *Am-haarez*. Indeed, the similarities of the texts seemed to force scholars to the conclusion that the *perusim* and *Haberim* were one and the same; that is, that the Pharisees were a group with a sectarian mentality concerned primarily for their own well-being:

> He that undertakes to be an Associate may not sell to an *Am-haaretz* {foodstuff that is} wet or dry, or buy from him {foodstuff that is} wet; and he may not be the guest of an *Am-haaretz* nor may he receive him as a guest in his own raiment.[25]

In refuting this position, Rivkin not only denies that the name *perusim* (and consequently, its Greek equivalent, Φαρισαῖοι) needs always be translated with the sense of "separatist" -- rather, he regards the title as meaning "heretics," a title uses by the Pharisees' opponents to signify their departure from the "orthodox" position of upholding the single Torah, the written Scripture[26] -- but, of more importance, he denies that the rabbinic texts M.Hag. 2:7 and M.Dem. 2:3, and some other texts as well which refer to the *perusim*, can be used at all as evidence referring to the same group of Pharisees as those mentioned in Josephus and the New Testament in Greek as Φαρισαῖοι.

Indeed, Rivkin's major methodological advance over previous scholarship seems to be the combination of his foundational premise that *only* the texts referring to the Pharisees by name are valid as evidence for historical information about them, with a second premise that not every text in which the word *perusim* appears in the Rabbinic literature provides historical evidence about the group known as Φαρισαῖοι in Josephus and the New Testament. In this second premise, Rivkin acknowledges that he follows the

---

[24]Rivkin, IDBS, p. 657.

[25]The English translation used here is by H. Danby, The Mishnah: Translated from the Hebrew with Introduction and Brief Explanatory Notes (Oxford: Clarendon, 1933).

[26]Rivkin, Hidden, pp. 164-66, 177; "Defining the Pharisees," pp. 247-48.

implicit observation of Solomon Zeitlin that since the word *perusim* can function as a simple adjective describing any group (separatistic, heretical, or whatever), then a control criterion must be used to determine when the word functions specifically as a title.[27] For these scholars, the control is not hard to find, and comprises the presence of the word *Zeduqim* (always used as a title meaning Sadducees) used in contrast to the *perusim*: that is, when found in contrast to the Sadducees (a contrast common in Josephus and the New Testament), the *perusim* are always regarded by Rivkin as Pharisees and not merely as "separatists" or "heretics" of some kind or another.[28]

The initial importance of such a premise is that it leads to the rejection of M.Hag. 2:7 (and thus of M.Dem. 2:3) as a text which provides undoubted historical information about the Pharisees, for in this text no contrast is made between Pharisees and Sadducees, but only between certain *perusim* and the *Am-Haarez*, the "masses." Indeed, argues Rivkin, the case for rejection of the verse as historical evidence is further strengthened by the fact that such a contrast is common neither in the New Testament nor in Josephus, where the Pharisees are actually portrayed not as opposing the masses, but as being freely supported by them.[29]

The rejection of M.Hag. 2:7 is, however, not the only consequence of Rivkin's methodology. Rather, what stands as of equal importance is the fact that the various texts discovered by Rivkin to refer unambiguously to the Pharisees (in which the Pharisees are contrasted with the Sadducees) proclaim a picture of Pharisaism which is quite congruent with that which he derives from Josephus and the New Testament. Indeed, concerning these rabbinic texts, and others to which he finds them related, Rivkin can write:

> In all these texts the Pharisees are, without exception, the source of the Law, never its object. The laws which they expound are oral laws -- laws which are not written down in the Pentateuch. These laws they hold to be binding on all Jews, not simply on themselves. The laws deal with the whole range of legislation: cultic, criminal, and civil. Not one of them pertains to rules for ritual purity binding on the Pharisees, but not on the common people; nor is there any provision made for a legal barrier between the Pharisees and the masses. The picture that emerges from these texts is that of a class of scholars who teach, with authority, the twofold law.[30]

---

[27] In "Defining the Pharisees," pp. 205-6, n.1, Rivkin gives credit to Zeitlin's seminal thinking with regard to this approach to using the Tannaitic sources.

[28] Rivkin, Hidden, pp. 131-32.

[29] Rivkin, Hidden, pp. 167-68; IDBS, pp. 657-58.

[30] Rivkin, IDBS, p. 659.

The only additional remark that need be made to complete the picture of Rivkin's approach and conclusions about the Pharisees concerns his understanding of the historical background of Judaism from which the Pharisees seemed suddenly to emerge in the second century B.C. That is, Rivkin's historical analysis points to the the second century B.C. as an age of radical change in Palestine, which, if Judaism were to survive -- if the Torah were to remain relevant in a world which no longer resembled the world in which the Torah was written -- required an equally radical response to the change from those who held the faith. Quite specifically, what was required was a source of religious authority that not only "updated" the written law, but also maintained the aura of Mosaic authority. In Rivkin's assessment, it was precisely the Pharisees who stepped into the breach as the heroes of the day -- for they alone were bold enough to take the radical and revolutionary step of presenting, defending and developing the traditions of the Fathers as the Oral Law with the claim that it stemmed ultimately not from themselves, but from Moses.[31]

Initial Critique of Rivkin

Before turning attention to the work of Jacob Neusner, three brief observations should be made about Rivkin's analysis of the sources. The first is that there is no evidence in Josephus or the New Testament that the Pharisees regarded the traditions of the elders as Oral Torah and of equal authority to the written Torah. This equation is simply imposed upon the texts by Rivkin on the assumption that the later Rabbinic doctrine of the Oral Torah was developed three centuries or more before the completion of the Mishnah.[32]

The second observation is that it simply does not seem that the argument can be sustained that the Pharisees were the only ones who possessed

---

[31]Rivkin, Hidden, 211-51.

[32]While the assumption that the traditions followed by the Pharisees were oral in nature has been commonly held, for example by J. Z. Lauterbach, "The Pharisees and their Teachings," HUCA 6 (1929), pp. 97-112, and, more recently, M. Simon, Jewish Sects, pp. 34-35, the fact remains, as has been observed by David Ellenson, "Ellis Rivkin and the Problems of Pharisaic History: A Study in Historiography," JAAR 43 (December 1975): 798-801, that "the doctrine of the Oral Law is conspicuously absent from all sources prior to the first century CE." See also, the cogent arguments of Neusner in this regard in "The Rabbinic Traditions about the Pharisees before 70: The Problem of Oral Transmission," in his Early Rabbinic Judaism, (Leiden: Brill, 1975), pp. 73-89. In From Politics to Piety: The Emergence of Pharisaic Judaism (Englewood Heights, N.J.: 1973), pp. 134-37, Neusner argues that the doctrine of the Mosaic nature of the Oral Law was formulated by the Rabbis at Usha, between A.D. 140-170.

"traditions" which enabled the ancient Law to be applied to some aspect of "modern life," nor that the holding of authority appears as a unique attribution defining the Pharisees in distinction to others.[33] For example, in the case of the New Testament it is quite clear that authority in general is a primary issue in Jesus' confrontation with his opponents, whether they be men (including, but not limited to the Pharisees) or demons.[34] That is, what seems unnecessary to conclude, especially in the light of the difficult Matthean text referring to the seat of Moses being shared with the Scribes and implying that the Pharisees exercised *some* authority in Judaism, is that their authority was unique and constituted the bonding factor of their group.

The third observation is that even if Rivkin's methodology in relation to the Rabbinic texts were correct, so that the primary evidence relating to the Pharisees comprised the various texts which refer to the *perusim* as opponents of the *Zeduqim* (or of a related group such as the Boethusians), and that this evidence were historically reliable, it still need not be the case that the unifying factor in these verses concerns the unique Pharisaic authority over legal matters. Indeed, careful analysis of these texts leads Jack Lightstone to conclude quite reasonably that:

> Appeals by either group to general criteria, such as Oral Law versus Written Law, or exegetical versus literal interpretation of Scripture, are conspicuously absent.[35]

To Lightstone, what derives from the texts is only that both Sadducees and Pharisees have their legal traditions, concerning which, especially in relation to matters of purity, they disagree, for reasons not following some explicit general criterion. Furthermore, given the highly formulaic nature of the texts, to Lightstone it seems quite possible that the historical value of the texts is minimal, representing more probably the views of later Rabbis imposing their

---

[33]Lauterbach, HUCA 6 (1929), p. 97, for example, acknowledges that even the Sadducees had their traditions, though these were never given the binding authority attributed by the Pharisees to their own traditions. Furthermore, as Neusner has observed, Early Rabbinic Judaism, p. 79, the Qumran Community also had a corpus of "revelations" external to the Scriptures, and of binding authority -- so that the understanding of authority in ancient Judaism can be seen to be far more complex than Rivkin allows. In the case of Qumran, for example, it would never be claimed that their attitude to authority defined the nature of the group, but, rather, that the content of their authoritative traditions, including their attitude to authority, was what was significant.

[34]See, for example, Mark 1:22, 27, 2:10, 6:7, 11:28.

[35]J. Lightstone, "Sadducees versus Pharisees: The Tannaitic Sources," in Christianity, Judaism and other Greco-Roman Cults, Part 3, ed. by J. Neusner (Leiden: Brill, 1975), p. 216.

own view on an ancient controversy, about which they knew few of the
details.

Thus, in the light of such observations as these, although it is possible to
agree with Rivkin that the evidence of the sources concerning the "traditions
of the elders" is startling, it is still possible to argue against him that it is not
the nature of the authority of those traditions or of those who wielded those
traditions which constituted the defining element of the group; but, rather,
that the definitive factor lay just as probably within the content of those
important traditions -- that there was, despite the seeming lack of focus within
information from Josephus and the New Testament, an over-riding interest
in specific issues which characterized the group as a whole. Indeed, it is
precisely in the provision of a general understanding of the nature of the
content of the Pharisaic traditions that Jacob Neusner's contribution to the
understanding of the Pharisees as they existed before 70 CE becomes so
significant.

Understanding the Pharisees: The Approach
of Jacob Neusner

In assessing the work of Jacob Neusner it is not our intention to provide
a point by point comparison of his work with that of Ellis Rivkin. To be sure,
there are areas both of agreement and disagreement that could be
investigated in depth. However, it seems clear that the ultimate difference
between Neusner and Rivkin lies within the realm of methodology as it
relates both to the study of the Rabbinic literature, and, thus, also to the
conclusions that one draws about the Pharisees from that literature. It is for
this reason that the major concern of this particular section will be with
Neusner's understanding of the Pharisees within the traditions of the rabbis.

Neusner and the Rabbinic Literature

Neusner's search in the Rabbinic literature for historical evidence about
the Pharisees does not, in contrast to Rivkin, begin with a search for texts in
which Pharisees are referred to by the name *perusim*. This is not to say that
Neusner rejects Rivkin's argument that in some of these texts the Rabbis
intended to refer to the group known as Pharisees -- indeed he affirms
Rivkin's basic premise in this regard.[36] Rather, what Neusner affirms

---

[36]Neusner. RTP. I, pp. 2-4.

beyond Rivkin, at least initially, is that relevant Rabbinic texts are far greater in number than Rivkin allows. That is, Neusner assumes that when the Rabbinic literature refers to, or "quotes" specific rabbis such as Hillel or Simon ben Gamaliel, then whether or not the word *perusim* is used becomes irrelevant, for such men can almost certainly be assumed to be Pharisees, and their teaching (or at least the teaching attributed to them) must then be embraced as pertinent for the process of historical enquiry.[37]

It is, however, not only on the issue of the *extent* of relevant rabbinic evidence that Neusner differs from Rivkin, but on the issue of the *reliability* of such evidence. Thus, for example, given that references to Pharisees exist in rabbinic literature, either in texts that refer to *perusim/zeduqim*, or in texts referring to men like Hillel, and given that the earliest compilation of rabbinic literature, the Mishnah, dates from around 200 CE, Neusner questions whether or not the references accurately reflect the historical situation before 70 CE, or whether they reflect a growth and development in the tradition which extended far beyond 70 CE.[38] At this point, indeed, Neusner, who embraces the position of initial doubt, accuses Rivkin of gullability.[39]

The Rabbinic Traditions about the Pre-70 Pharisees

Neusner's investigation, carried out in depth in 1971, in his 3 volume work, *The Rabbinic Traditions About the Pharisees*, popularized in 1973 in his *From Politics to Piety*, and summarized in various articles,[40] begins not with the historical question, "who were the Pharisees?", but with the question of tradition, "what did later rabbis say about who the Pharisees were?"

In answer to this latter question, Neusner concluded that the Rabbinic literature yielded approximately 371 separate stories, sayings, or allusions, in

---

[37]Neusner, "The Pharisees," in Formative Judaism, p. 71. Also, From Politics to Piety, pp. 81-82.

[38]Neusner, Politics, pp. xxi-xxii; Formative Judaism, p. 77.

[39]For example, see RTP I, pp. 2-3, with Neusner's review of Rivkin's A Hidden Revolution, in AHR 85 (October 1980): 863-664. In referring to the general approach to using the rabbinic literature as historically applicable to life in the first century C. E., Wayne Meeks, First Urban, p. 33, note 150, affirms significantly that "however controversial Neusner's work has been and however many corrections of detail it will doubtless have to undergo, these results seem to me irreversible."

[40]We have already referred to Neusner's articles in Formative Judaism, pp. 71-83, and Aufstieg und Niedergang, II.19.2, pp. 3-42; and might also point to "Two Pictures of the Pharisees: Philosophical Circle or Eating Club," ATR 64 (October 1982): 525-38.

various versions, presented in 655 pericopae.[41] Of these items, legal sayings pertaining to such matters as

> adjudication of civil disputes, conduct of the Temple cult, the manner of issuing a writ of divorce, the way to say one's prayers, tithing of food, the preservation of ritual purity, or the purification of something which has been defiled or made unclean[42]

form the great majority, and of these legal sayings, the largest number, 67 percent,[43] refer first to "agricultural tithes, offerings and other taboos, and, second, to rules of ritual purity."[44]

Important as these observations are, Neusner takes pains to emphasize that he is not yet drawing historical conclusions from this portrait, but is merely presenting a collation of traditions which were undoubtedly influenced in some manner by those who brought them together into the documents in which they are found, primarily the Mishnah and Tosefta.[45] Once the traditions are collated, however, the work of historical reconstruction can begin by an examination of the development of those traditions -- the tendencies and additions which the various compilers may have brought to the material they worked with -- and by locating in particular the earliest of those traditions, which, of all traditions, are the ones most likely to be reliable historically.

The issue Neusner faces at this stage, clearly, is that of determining how to assess which traditions are early and which are late. Neusner's approach involves the fundamental assumption that a tradition about a pre-70 Pharisee (or group such as the House of Hillel) that is assigned to the lips of, or is commented on by a certain Rabbi, dates at the latest from the period of the assigned Rabbi. That is, for example, Neusner would say that if R. Eliezer b. Hyrcanus is named as commenting on or quoting a saying of Hillel, a pre-70 Pharisee, then at the least, even if we cannot assume that Eliezer actually made the comment or quote, nevertheless we *can* know that the tradition about Hillel derived from no later than Eliezer's time (late first century).[46]

---

[41]Neusner, RTP, III, p. 303.
[42]Neusner, Politics, pp. 82-83.
[43]Neusner, RTP, III, p. 304.
[44]Neusner, Politics, p. 83.
[45]Neusner, RTP I, p. 4; Politics, pp. 92-93.
[46]Neusner, Politics, pp. 93-94. For a general survey of the methods Neusner has used in his study of rabbinic literature, see his article, "The History of Earlier Rabbinic Judaism: Some New Approaches," HR 16 (1977): 216-36.

On such a premise, Neusner examines the traditions about pre-70 Pharisees that were "Indubitably known and regarded as authoritative and normative at Yavneh,"[47] where not only the process of collation and the formation of what resulted in the Mishnah, and indeed, the whole Talmudic literature, began between 70-125 CE, but where also, for the first time, the attempt was made to preserve the legacy of pre-destruction Pharisaism.[48] On the basis of this examination Neusner concludes:

> Approximately 65 rabbinical traditions about the pre-70 Pharisees are attested at Yavneh. These concern primarily legal questions, and not matters of history, doctrine, or faith. The kinds of law for which Pharisaic derivation is claimed pertain to the Temple cult, tithing, Sabbath, and festival observance, liturgy, uncleanness rules, and family law . . . . We find almost no civil law . . . . There is no criminal law at all.[49]

Analysing the content of the Pharisaic laws further, Neusner finds that the major group of laws pertained to tithing and uncleanness rules, while the next most prominent group pertained to Sabbath and festival observance in which, frequently, the issue related to the preparation of food on such occasions.[50]

With this observation Neusner's conclusions about the nature of Pharisaism clearly begin to part ways with those of Rivkin. Not only does Neusner consider that at this point he has reached the historical situation itself -- an assessment for which he finds confirmation in the similarity of the legal emphases represented by the Rabbis with his understanding of the Gospel representation of the Pharisees -- but Neusner also indicates that the legal content has little to do with either a scholar class or with those responsible for the political legislation of the land. Rather, the picture that Neusner draws from the evidence points to the Pharisees as a group whose primary interest lay in maintaining table-fellowship through the observance of rules for cultic purity and the preparation of food that was properly prepared and tithed, and to this end "legislated" *for themselves* the rules by which their fellowship was governed.[51]

The rationale for maintaining such table fellowship laws was intimately connected with the temple and its priesthood, for, according to Neusner, the purity that the Pharisees required of themselves every day and moment was

---

[47]Neusner, Politics, p. 121.
[48]Neusner, Politics, p. 99.
[49]Neusner, Formative Judaism, pp.
[50]Neusner, Formative Judaism, pp. 79-80; Politics, p. 103.
[51]Neusner, Formative Judaism, pp. 79-80; Politics, pp. 103-4, 122.

that expected of the Temple priests as they carried out the sacrificial service in the Temple, and as they followed that service by eating the Temple food. With regard to those who were not priests, such purity was expected when they went to the Temple, but not for activities that were considered non-cultic. Thus, Neusner concludes:

> But the Pharisees held that even outside of the Temple, in one's own home, the laws of ritual purity were to be followed in the only circumstance in which they might apply, namely at the table. Therefore, one must eat secular meals (ordinary, everyday meals) in a state of ritual purity *as if one were a Temple priest*. The Pharisees thus arrogated to themselves -- and to all Jews equally -- the status of temple priests, and performed actions restricted to priests on account of their status. The table of every Jew in his home was seen as being like the table of the Lord in the Jerusalem Temple. The commandment, 'You shall be a kingdom of priests and a holy people,' was taken literally: Everyone is a priest, everyone stands in the same relationship to God, and everyone must keep the priestly laws.[52]

Neusner's Assessment of Josephus and the New Testament

In order to gain information on the Pharisees of the first Christian century before the destruction of the Temple, Neusner, like Rivkin, not only assesses the Rabbinic literature, but also the literature of Josephus and the New Testament. Furthermore, as with Rivkin, the study proceeds in an orderly fashion by examining Josephus and the New Testament independently of each other.[53]

Two points only need be raised concerning Neusner's work in this regard. The first is negative: it is probably within his assessment of these two sources that the weakest point of Neusner's work lies. In particular, what has been challenged rather forcefully are two of Neusner's conclusions: first, that references in these sources to the Pharisees' political power are generally unhistorical, at least with respect to the Pharisees between 1-70 CE (reflecting instead either the situation before that time, or after, at Yavneh); and, second, that this lack of historicity applies also to Josephus' assertion of the popularity of the Pharisees, a popularity Neusner finds unexpressed in *Jewish Wars* but openly expressed 20 years later in *Antiquities* because, Neusner argues, an emphasis on Pharisaic popularity at that time served

---

[52]Neusner, Politics, p. 83.
[53]Neusner, RTP III, pp. 241-48; Politics, pp. 45-80.

Josephus' purpose of gaining support from the Romans for the cause of the contemporary Pharisees at Yavneh.[54]

The second point is positive, in that, to a certain extent, these weaknesses in Neusner's argument, if they be accepted as such, are irrelevant to his fundamental picture of pre-70 Pharisaism, for Neusner's understanding of the Pharisees can in fact stand by itself on the basis of the Rabbinic evidence without further reference to other sources such as Josephus and the New Testament. That is, for Neusner, whether or not the Pharisees in the first century before the destruction of the Temple were as Josephus and the New Testament describe them -- believing in fate, having traditions from the fathers, amicable, at odds with the Sadducees, concerned with issues relating to various laws and doctrines, at times hypocritical, and perhaps even exercising involvement in political affairs, and popular -- for all that, what remains as of fundamental importance is *not how others viewed them*, but *how they viewed themselves*; what they themselves considered as the issues that distinguished them as Pharisees in contrast to others.[55]

Such information, of course, if such exists, can derive primarily from, of all the sources, only the Rabbinic literature. Moreover, we have already noted that Neusner considers that there does in fact seem to be an issue arising from this literature representing the Pharisees' own traditions which can be seen as providing the most prevalent distinguishing mark of the group: the emphasis on their specific laws, and on an agenda within those laws which reflects a specific concern to maintain priestly purity for the purposes of table-fellowship. Thus, with evidence of such an initial concern in hand, the primary importance of further evidence from Josephus and the New Testament lies for Neusner in its power to corroborate (or fail to do so) this portrait of the Pharisees painted by their heirs, the Rabbis.

In this context, what Neusner concludes is that Josephus provides no such confirmation, since he simply does not provide information at all on the Pharisees' legal agenda, though he does mention an interest in ancestral

---

[54]Neusner's comments on these positions, based on his assessment (following the views of Morton Smith) of the historical worth of Josephus can be found in Politics, pp. 57, 64-65. The strongest criticism of his understanding of Josephus comes from Daniel R. Schwartz, "Josephus and Nicolaus on the Pharisees," JSJ (December 1983): 164-171; and M. J. Cook, Mark's Treatment of the Jewish Leaders, pp. 93-94.

Neusner, in Method and Meaning in Ancient Judaism, Second Series, (Chico, Cal.: Scholars Press, 1981), p. 72, however, seems to pull away from the extreme position with regard to lack of political involvement which seems to be indicated in Politics.

[55]Neusner, Formative Judaism, pp. 74-77.

tradition. Such a lack of confirmation in no way necessarily implies to Neusner that the Rabbinic evidence is any less trustworthy because it stands alone, but only that the aspects of Pharisaism which concerned Josephus were of little concern to the Pharisees as represented by the Rabbis.

On the other hand, Neusner sees the New Testament Gospels as providing evidence that does in fact confirm the rabbinic viewpoint. That is, the Gospels not only speak of Pharisees in terms of their beliefs, behaviour and legal concerns, but, with respect to legal concerns the Gospels actually provide information on the nature of those concerns -- which, in Neusner's estimation, primarily relate to matters of tithing and purity; matters that relate to the maintenance of priestly table-fellowship. Such confirmation from the gospels can only strengthen the sense that the Rabbinic picture as established by Neusner is generally valid.

Summary

What seems to be clear from a brief study of the work of Rivkin and Neusner, whatever one thinks of their peripheral arguments and conclusions, is that their fundamental methodologies and conclusions are not only different from each other, but mutually exclusive. That is, to follow Neusner, for example, is to exclude Rivkin's essential Rabbinic picture of the Pharisees as irrelevant to the historical situation before 70 CE, since the picture merely reflects the concerns of later rabbis at Yavneh.[56] Furthermore, this exclusion is to eliminate from the Rabbinic picture any suggestion that the Pharisees were a scholar class in control of a tradition that had attained the status of "Oral Law," and to allow the re-instatement within the picture of the portrait of the Pharisees as a group with sectarian interest in tithing and purity--the portrait that Rivkin fundamentally opposes.

Indeed, one of Rivkin's critiques of Neusner is that he has not advanced the understanding of Pharisaism one whit from that drawn by other scholars before him on the basis of M.Hag. 2:7 and M.Dem. 2:3.[57] *With regard to*

---

[56]Rivkin, Hidden, p. 315, seems to argue that Neusner has simply side-stepped Rivkin's analysis of the rabbinic Pharisee/Sadducee texts by failing to discuss them. However, Neusner's rationale for such an omission is quite simply that all these texts derive from rabbis of the post-70 Yavnean period, that none can be attributed to pre-70 Pharisees or to pre-70 Pharisaic thought. See Neusner, Formative Judaism, p.74.

[57]Rivkin, Hidden, p. 315.

Neusner's conclusion, this assessment is certainly true.[58] *With regard to methodology,* however, it is quite misleading, for although Neusner might argue that these two Mishnaic texts do indeed represent (at least some of) the pre-70 Pharisees fairly,[59] he does not use them as texts foundational to his study. That is, if relevant they are, it is now because, though deriving from no specified rabbi, they nevertheless reflect similar concerns found in other Rabbinic texts, known, by Neusner's analysis, as early traditions relevant to the pre-70 Pharisees.[60]

My own assessment is that Neusner's methodology and fundamental conclusions are persuasive: that the primary concern of the Pharisees was that "the Temple should be everywhere, even in the home and hearth,"[61] and that the definitive characteristic of the Pharisees was an approach to the law leading them to maintain within the walls of their own homes, beyond the Temple walls, the purity appropriate to the Temple, as if the table in the home were the table of the Lord in the Jerusalem Temple. The rationale provided for such concerns and characteristics stemmed initially, in Neusner's opinion, from a desire to fulfil the admonition of Exodus 19:6, which expressed God's desire that Israel as a whole become a "kingdom of priests and a holy nation."[62]

Thus, simple obedience to the written will of God as expressed in Scripture might appropriately be seen as the basis for the Pharisaic way of life. An emphasis on obedience by itself, however, does not answer the question as to why the Pharisees focused their attention on Exodus 19:6 in particular, out of all the possible verses of scripture, but only raises the question as to what it was about the priesthood and holiness that was so important that the Pharisees were willing to adapt their whole way of life, down to the final detail, in order to attain them. Only a guess can be made to answer this question, for the Pharisees themselves nowhere provide an answer.

---

[58]See, for example, the similarity between Neusner's understanding of the Pharisees and that of J. Jeremias, Jerusalem in the Time of Jesus, pp. 246-67.

[59]For example, M.Hag. 2:7 and M.Dem. 2:3 are referred to by Neusner in Contemporary Judaic Fellowship in Theory and Practice (New York: Ktav, 1972), p. 27, n. 17.

[60]Neusner's procedure for dating un-named sayings is explained in full in From Mishnah to Scripture: The Problem of the Unattributed Saying With Special Reference to the Division of Purities (Chico, Cal.: 1984). See p. 117 for a brief summary.

[61]Neusner, Politics, p. 152.

[62]Neusner, Politics, p. 83.

To be sure, fear of judgment has been adduced as the primary motivation behind the Pharisees meticulous concern for obedience, though such a motive plays no great part in the sources, and simply does not seem to characterize the Pharisees as we know them.[63] Our own suggestion develops from that of Neusner in his book *The Idea of Purity in Ancient Judaism*,[64] where he writes of the Pharisees that:

> The extension of the Temple purity rules to the household might be seen as an expression of extreme piety. As his presence is everywhere, so we should always behave as if we were in the Temple, that is, in his presence.

The direction of Neusner's logic here is not the only one that might be taken, for it might equally be reasoned that since God is everywhere then there is no longer any need for the Temple at all. Clearly, assuming that Neusner is correct in his argument for a fundamental Pharisaic interest in the Temple and its cultic purity, the Pharisees did not follow this latter reasoning, but maintained that the Temple and its laws remained the ideal setting, indeed, the setting ordained by God himself in which his presence would be found. Thus, we would argue, the Pharisees, while undoubtedly acknowledging the reality of the presence of God in the world as a whole, did not take for granted that presence in their lives, but actively sought to ensure its continuation by following the Law in order to maintain the specific atmosphere which God had promised to bless with his presence -- that of the Temple in its purity.

Neusner himself might agree with this slight alteration of his understanding, for he quotes with approval the words of Baruch Levine about Israel's religion as a whole:

> The process of expiation bore a practical relationship to the covenant. It was to ensure the continued residence of Yahweh in the Israelite community by

---

[63]For example, Emil Schürer in his section "Life Under the Law," pp. 90-91, in A History of the Jewish People in the Time of Jesus Christ, 2.II, trans. by S. Taylor and P. Christie (New York: Scribner's, 1891), writes:

"But what were the motives, whence sprang this enthusiasm for the Law, what means whereby it obtained this enormous sway over minds? To answer briefly: it was faith in Divine retribution, and that a retribution in the strictest juristic sense."

Sanders's book, Paul and Palestinian Judaism, is in part an attempt to refute this kind of understanding of Rabbinic Judaism, which, he points out, has so often been equated with "Pharisaism." See pp. 33-59, in particular, for his survey of scholarship.

[64]Neusner, The Idea of Purity in Ancient Judaism (Leiden: Brill, 1973), p. 69.

enforcing the basic precondition for such residence, that is, the purity of Yahweh's surroundings.[65]

Just how concerned the Pharisees were with the Israelite community as a whole may remain unanswered. However, what was at least possible, assuming that God was everywhere, and that He was to be found "in a special way" anywhere that the atmosphere of the Temple could be maintained, was that the Pharisees themselves could now fulfil the vision of Exodus 19:6, and become by behaviour, if not by birth, a kingdom of priests. This behaviour, we would argue, they attempted to attain and maintain through the Law, believing that in the face of such purity, especially when they gathered to eat, even in the home, God would sanctify them with his presence, or, to paraphrase Revelation 3:20, would "come in and eat with them and they with him." No greater blessing than to have such a Guest could ever be found.

Paul was a Pharisee. If the analysis above is correct, then access to the presence of God, not merely forgiveness (though forgiveness, and the removal of any defilement, was certainly a necessary means to the end), was what Paul the Pharisee sought. A sense of access to God through obedience to the Law (through being righteous with respect to the Law, Phil. 3:6,9) was no doubt part of his Pharisaic experience -- a certain measure of salvation. What we want to claim, however, is that through faith in Jesus as Messiah, the salvation Paul found was a mode of access to God that provided perfectly what the Law promised, and thus both fulfilled the Law and made it redundant. In this sense, in connection with access to God's presence, to Paul the Pharisee Christ became the end of the Law (Rom. 10:4).

Before proceeding with our study of Paul, however, one aspect of our argument needs further discussion: the connection between the Pharisees' interest in matters legal and cultic and their interest in establishing and maintaining the presence of God. That is, we need to review the broader context of religious life in ancient Judaism, and to ask what general interest there was, if any, in this pursuit.

---

[65]Neusner, Purity, p. 10, for a brief summary.

CHAPTER TWO

The Quest for the Presence of God in Paul's Judeo-Christian Heritage

I. INTRODUCTION

"Where is God?" Such a question may seem almost irrelevant to many in twentieth century western society: both to those who no longer believe there is a God in the first place, and to those who believe there is a God and yet assume that by definition God is everywhere. "Does God exist?"; or "What is God like?"; or "Will God forgive me?"[1] may seem to be more pertinent questions, though in the face of human tragedy the question may still be heard from friend or foe "Where is God now?"[2] Even here, however, the unspoken assumption is still surely that of God's omnipresence: that God is not so much absent (if God does indeed exist) but silent, somehow failing in his duty.

The ancients made no such assumptions.[3] That is, while not necessarily denying God's omnipresence, they believed deeply in the possibility of establishing exact locations where significant encounters between God and human beings had, and perhaps could still, take place: places where God was present; and conversely, where God might be absent. Two scholars among a vast array of others who discuss this interest in the paradoxical, or elusive, presence of God, are Ronald Clements in *God and Temple*, and Samuel

---

[1] See, for example, Stephen Westerholm's description of the influence of Luther and Augustine in this regard, Israel's Law and the Church's Faith: Paul and His Recent Interpreters (Grand Rapids: Eerdmans, 1988), p. 67.

[2] With the Psalmist, Psalm 42:3.

[3] See, for example, Baruch Levine, "On the Presence of God in Biblical Religion" in J. Neusner, ed., Religions in Antiquity (Leiden: E.J. Brill, 1968), p. 71.

Terrien in *The Elusive Presence: The Heart of Biblical Theology*.[4] Ronald
Clements writes,

> The question of the divine presence was not patent of an obvious solution
> in early times, and, in the Ancient Near East various ways were adopted by
> men in an effort to make the presence of the gods accessible.[5]

What was true of the Ancient Near East in general was also true, argues
Clements, of Israel in particular.

While Clements' intention in *God and Temple* is to provide a history of
religions approach to the development of the understanding of God's presence
in Israel (within Israel's Canaanite context) that of Samuel Terrien in *The
Elusive Presence* is to formulate a theology of "presence" from the Christian
Bible as a completed unit. Indeed, Terrien sees the quest for God's presence
as dominant enough in the Biblical literature as a whole to argue that it
should be the organizing theme for a new Biblical Theology.[6]

To be sure, the details of both theses, that of Clements as well as of
Terrien, may certainly be challenged.[7] Nevertheless, for our purposes it can
be said that both scholars demonstrate convincingly that interest in locating
and maintaining the divine presence, if not central, is at least one prominent
and remarkably frequent issue in the life of the people who gave rise to the
Biblical literature.

The following brief study is, then, merely intended to be suggestive of
this pervasiveness. Furthermore, no attempt is deemed necessary to deal with

---

[4]Ronald Clements, God and Temple (Philadelphia: Fortress, 1965). Samuel Terrien, The
Elusive Presence: The Heart of Biblical Theology (San Francisco: Harper & Row, 1978). On
the theme of God's presence, see the extensive bibliography provided by Terrien, p. 54, note
131.

[5]Clements, p.1.

[6]Terrien, pp. xxviii-xxvix.

[7]See, for example, Menahem Haran's review of Clements in "The Divine Presence in the
Israelite Cult and the Cultic Institutions," Biblica 50, 1969, pp. 251-67. Also, the reviews in in
God and His Temple -- Reflections on Professor Terrien's "The Elusive Presence: Toward a
New Biblical Theology," Lawrence E. Frizell, ed. (S. Orange, N.J., Seton Hall University, 1980).
One criticism in particular, which could of course also be directed to this present work, is that
the pursuit of a theme directs attention to aspects of Biblical literature which are supportive,
while glossing over those which are not (Frizzell, p. 34), thus leading to the "imposition" of a
system on the evidence (Haran, p. 253). It must be said that this danger is almost unavoidable
when dealing with a vast body of diverse literature. Nevertheless, the attempt is still worth
making, so long as the claims of accomplishment are not overstated. Terrien, for example, calls
his work a "prolegomenon." The same word would be fitting for the work presented here.

the references in terms of their origin or strict chronological development within the life of Israel. A simple thematic presentation, generally following the order of the Biblical history as given, will suffice for our purposes before referring in addition to some of the Jewish extra-canonical and Christian New Testament literature.

II. THE PRESENCE OF GOD IN THE BIBLICAL LITERATURE

The issue of God's presence (or absence) arises in the earliest chapters of Genesis, in the narrative of the Garden of Eden. Into this garden God placed the man and the woman whom he had created. There in the garden the Lord God could be found "walking . . . in the cool of the day." This natural communion with God was not, however, to last long. According to Genesis, disobedience in the man and the woman affected their relationship with the creator so that they "hid themselves from the presence of the Lord" (RSV, Gen. 3:8).[8] This desire to hide from God's presence on the part of the humans was followed by a parallel act by God himself, who, having found the couple, then dismissed them from his presence by casting them out of the garden. There, their son Cain committed murder and "went away from the presence of the Lord, and dwelt in the land of Nod, east of Eden" (4:16).

The lost or obscured presence of God experienced by the original couple and their descendants, provides part of the background for the story of Israel's Patriarchs, to whom the promise of a restored "presence" was linked with the promise of a special covenant relationship with God. In the story of Abraham the promise of God's presence is not explicit. However, the promise that "God will be his God and the God of his descendants" is seen by Clements, for example, as being closely related to that in Lev. 26:11,12, in which the two promises (to be "their God," and to be "with them") are indeed explicitly tied together: God promises that obedience to his statutes and commandments will lead him to "set my tabernacle in your midst . . . and I will walk among you and be your God (RSV)."[9]

The connection between covenant and "presence" re-appears in the story of Jacob, where Jacob finds the covenant promise to Abraham re-affirmed

---

[8]Unless otherwise indicated, translations of biblical passages in this chapter are from the Revised Standard Version.

[9]Clements, pp. 110-12, states that "The divine promise 'I will be their God' must be interpreted here, not merely in the sense of a formal covenant relationship, but in a sense that is of crucial importance to the priestly authors, that Yahweh himself will dwell in the midst of Israel."

at a place he names Bethel (Gen. 28:10-22). Fleeing from his brother Esau, he spends a night at this place where he dreams of a ladder reaching from earth to heaven with God standing above. In re-affirming the covenant promise, God this time gives explicit assurance of his presence, declaring that "I am with you and will keep you wherever you go" (28:15). On waking, Jacob declares that "Surely the Lord is in this place, and I did not know it." This sense of God's presence causes him fear, and leads to the statement made with awe that the location to which Jacob happened to come "is none other than the house of God, this is the gate of heaven."

This same covenant is re-affirmed by God, this time to Moses, at another location, Horeb (that is, Sinai).[10] There, from an unconsumed burning bush, God calls Moses and commissions him as Israel's leader (Exod. 3:4). The theme of fear and awe noted in previous incidents is found in this one too: though summoned to the bush, Moses is not to approach without care, nor is he to approach too near, for "the place on which you are standing," says the Lord, "is holy ground" (3:5).[11]

The same sort of care is to be taken by the people of Israel as a whole when after the exodus from Egypt God calls Moses to prepare the people to meet with God at Mount Sinai.[12] In cloud, smoke and thunder God appears (Exod. 19:1-25), and not surprisingly, perhaps, God's presence once again evokes fear. Indeed, God declares that his presence can actually be life-threatening, necessitating Moses to warn the people "lest they break through to the Lord and perish"(Exod. 19:21).

Though God's presence at times may be dangerous, nevertheless to Moses life without it was scarcely worth living. However, vital as it was, God's presence was by no means guaranteed. Thus in an incident involving idolatry by the people with a golden calf (Exod. 33:1-23), Moses' fear was that God's presence would depart, leading him to plead on their behalf and his own for such a departure not to take place. God hears Moses' plea and reassures him, saying, "My presence shall go with you, and I will give you rest" (Exod. 33:14). Moses expresses his concern further by declaring that without God's presence Israel has no distinguishing mark from the other nations, and that without God being with them, further progress in the

---

[10]On the relationship between Horeb and Sinai, see s.v "Sinai, Mount," IDB IV, p. 376.
[11]If Moses and the people met God at Horeb, so too did the prophet Elijah (I Kings 19:7-18).
[12]On the relationship between Sinai and Horeb, see Terrien, pp. 133-34.

wilderness would be futile. Furthermore, he actually requests to see God's "glory," and in response God partially grants what is asked: "you shall see my back; but my face shall not be seen" (Exod. 33:23).

The promised presence of God with the people as they moved through the wilderness was symbolized in the portable tabernacle which was filled with "the glory of the Lord" (Exod. 40:34,35). In the promised land, the temple in Jerusalem, obviously, yet by way of contrast, was stationary. Not surprisingly, then, the establishing of the temple in Jerusalem provoked much debate in Israel, both positive and negative.[13] Israel's cultic poets spoke positively of the movement of God from Sinai to dwell in Zion's Temple -- another "holy place," yet prominent above every other:

> With mighty chariotry, twice ten thousand,
> thousands upon thousands,
> the Lord came from Sinai into the holy place.
> Thou didst ascend the high mount,
> leading captives in thy train,
> and receiving gifts among men,
> even among the rebellious,
> that the Lord God may dwell there. (RSV, Ps. 68:17-18)

This choice of Zion as God's dwelling place was intimately linked with the election of David:

> The Lord swore to David a sure oath
> from which he will not turn back:
> "One of the sons of your body
> I will set on your throne.
> If your sons keep my covenant
> and my testimonies which I shall teach them,
> their sons also for ever
> shall sit upon your throne.
> For the Lord has chosen Zion;
> he has desired it for his habitation:
> "This is my resting place for ever;
> here I will dwell, for I have desired it." (RSV, Ps. 132:11-14)

Indeed, the Psalmists could think of no better place to be than on this holy hill of the Lord:

---

[13] See Clements, pp. 23-49.

Oh send out thy light and thy truth;
let them lead me,
let them bring me to thy holy hill
and to thy dwelling! (RSV, Ps. 43:3)

This declaration of Zion (held in intimate association by the Psalmist with
the temple, e.g. in 48:9-11) as God's dwelling place was not without its
detractors. According to 2 Samuel 5:4-11 David's own desire to build a
temple on Zion was thwarted by the prophecy of Nathan who declared,

"Thus says the Lord: Would you build me a house to dwell in? I have not
dwelt in a house since the day I brought up the people of Israel from Egypt
to this day, but I have been moving about in a tent for my dwelling."

The tension between the moving (tabernacle/tent) presence of God, and
the stationary (Zion/temple) presence was only one tension related to
defining the location and nature of God's presence. Another was that between
God as the God of heaven, and God as the God of *any* specific locale on
earth.[14]

The Psalmist ties the two themes together with little sense of tension in
Ps. 11:4:

The Lord is in his holy temple
The Lord's throne is in heaven.

The tension, however, is clearly seen in Solomon's temple dedicatory
prayer in I Kings 8:23-53. Verses 27-29, RSV, are as follows:

But will God indeed dwell on earth? Behold, heaven and the highest heaven
cannot hold thee; how much less this house which I have built! Yet have
regard to the prayer of thy servant and to his supplication, O Lord my God,
hearkening to the cry and to the prayer which thy servant prays before thee
this day; that thy eyes may be open night and day toward this house, the
place of which thou hast said, 'My name shall be there,' that thou mayest
hearken to the prayer which thy servant offers towards this place."

It was in this temple at Jerusalem, in the face of an overwhelming
experience of God's presence that Isaiah's call to ministry came (Isaiah
6:1-13). Far from there being a "still small voice," as was the case, for
example, when the prophet Elijah was confronted by God's presence at

---

[14]See Clements, p. 68.

Horeb (see I Kings 19:7-18), the voice heard by Isaiah shook the foundations
of the threshold, and sent fear through the prophet-to-be:

> And I said: Woe is me! For I am lost; for I am a man of unclean lips, and
> I dwell in the midst of a people of unclean lips; for my eyes have seen the
> King, the LORD of hosts!" (RSV, Is. 6:5)

The prominence given by Isaiah to the Jerusalem temple on Mt. Zion is
nowhere more clearly seen than in Isaiah 2:2-3, RSV:

> It shall come to pass in the latter days
>   that the mountain of the house of the Lord
> shall be established as the highest of the mountains,
>   and shall be raised above the hills;
> and all the nations shall flow to it,
>   and many peoples shall come, and say:
> "Come let us go to the mountain of the Lord,
>   to the house of the God of Jacob;
> that he may teach us his ways
>   and that we may walk in his paths."
> For out of Zion shall go forth the law,
>   and the word of the Lord from Jerusalem.

Jeremiah, too, speaks of a time when "Jerusalem shall be called the
throne of the Lord, and all nations shall gather to it, to the presence of the
Lord in Jerusalem" (Jer. 3:17). However, whereas Isaiah (31:4,5) can speak
of God's sure, almost guaranteed, defense and protection of Jerusalem, for
Jeremiah this defense and protection was clearly conditional, intimately
related to the people's obedience or disobedience.

This link between obedience and presence has already been observed in
the wilderness story of Israel's idolatry. However, the nature of the tension
in Jeremiah is specifically between the call to moral response and the value
of the temple in and of itself. That is, for Jeremiah, the presence of the
temple, important as it was, was no guarantee of God's presence and thus of
deliverance from danger (see Jer. 7:1-15).

> "Do not trust in these deceptive words: 'This is the temple of the Lord, the
> temple of the Lord, the temple of the Lord.' For if you truly amend your
> ways . . . then I will let you dwell in this place, in the land which I gave of
> old to your fathers for ever. (RSV, Jer. 7:4,5)

Without moral response, God's presence could be lost, either by God's
departure from Jerusalem, or by the forced departure of the people

themselves (presumably with God remaining, see Ezek. 11:15). Without moral response, Jerusalem could only expect to follow in the steps of Shiloh, "where I made my name dwell at first" (but presumably do no longer, Ezek. 7:12), and the people expect that God "will cast (them) out of my sight" (through exile from Jerusalem and from its surrounding land, Ezek. 7:15).

According to Ezekiel, what happened to Shiloh did indeed happen to Jerusalem: in the days of the exile the "glory" which marked God's presence departed (Ezek. 11:22-23). God's presence, however, was by no means lost. The God who once moved with his people in the wilderness could just as easily move with his people into the land of exile, and, according to Ezekiel, God did in fact choose to do this by being "a sanctuary to them for a while in the countries where they have gone" (Ezek. 11:16). Furthermore, in an age to come, God would:

> make a covenant of peace with them; it shall be an everlasting covenant with them; and I will bless them and multiply them, and will set my sanctuary in the midst of them for evermore. My dwelling place shall be with them; and I will be their God, and they shall be my people. Then the nations will know that I the Lord sanctify Israel, when my sanctuary is in the midst of them for evermore. (RSV, 37:26-28)

The last eight chapters of Ezekiel comprise a vision of a rebuilt temple (or sanctuary, 44:9), culminating in the description of both land alloted to the various tribes of Israel, and a city: "And the name of the city henceforth shall be, The Lord is there" (48:35).

Following the exile the prophet Haggai spurred on the rebuilding of the temple, in which, when completed, God would appear in his glory (Hag. 2:7). Similarly, Haggai's contemporary Zechariah called on the people to sing and rejoice,

> For lo, I come and I will dwell in the midst of you, says the Lord. And many nations shall join themselves to the Lord in that day, and shall be my people; *and I will dwell in the midst of you*, and you shall know that the Lord of hosts has sent me to you. (RSV, Zech. 2:10,11; italics mine)

With regard to wisdom literature, which finds only an awkward place, if any, in some proposed Biblical theologies,[15] Samuel Terrien, and not

---

[15] See the positive comments of Walter Brueggemann on this aspect of Terrien's thesis in Frizell, God and His Temple, p. 31.

alone,[16] has argued that the search for wisdom is at the same time a search for God's presence. For example, concerning Job, Terrien states,[17]

> It is the theology of presence, not the problem of suffering which lies at the core of the poem (p. 362) . . . Modern critics who discern on Job's part an abject surrender show they do not understand the depth of the holy, "I had heard of thee by the hearing of the ear, but now my eye sees thee (42:5);" . . . an all-sufficient gift: the immediacy of God himself.

This concern for the presence of God stretches beyond the Biblical literature, influencing, for example, works such as those of Ben Sira, I Enoch, Jubilees, Psalms of Solomon, and IV Ezra, as well as the literature of the Qumran Community and the early Christian church.[18]

III. THE PRESENCE OF GOD IN THE EXTRA-CANONICAL JEWISH LITERATURE

Our survey here is once again cursory. However, our intent is to demonstrate no more than the constant repetition of our theme at different times and in diverse groups within ancient Judaism.

The work of Ben Sira is perhaps most noted for chapters 40-50, commonly called "the Praise of the Fathers." This section reaches its climax as the high priest Simon emerges from the temple, shining gloriously, as Moses had once done when descending from God's presence on Mount Sinai:[19]

> How glorious he was as he came out of the inner sanctuary!
> Like the morning star among the clouds . . .

---

[16]See James L. Crenshaw, "In Search of Divine Presence: Some Remarks Preliminary to a Theology of Wisdom." RevExp 74, (July 1977): 353-69.

[17]Terrien, The Elusive Presence, pp. 371-72.

[18]Clearly the literature of the extra-canonical Jewish literature is vast. For the sake of convenience, the literature represented here simply corresponds with that selected for study in E. P. Sanders's prominent work, Paul and Palestinian Judaism: A Comparison of Patterns of Religion (Philadelphia: Fortress, 1977).

[19]James Crenshaw, Old Testament Wisdom: An Introduction (Atlanta: John Knox, 1981), p. 154, argues that the details and glowing account of the priestly duties and privileges, along with the excitement such thoughts engendered, "show clearly the precise point at which Sirach's heart beats excitedly."

Like the sun shining upon the temple of the Most High . . . (Sir. 50:5-7)[20]

Furthermore, the commonly accepted pivotal chapter of Ben Sira,[21] chapter 24, portrays "wisdom" descending from heaven to take up residence among God's people in Zion:

> and the one who created me assigned for me a place for my tent.
> And he said, 'Make your dwelling in Jacob,
>   and in Israel receive your inheritance.'
> From eternity, in the beginning he created me,
>   and for eternity I shall not cease to exist.
> In the holy tabernacle I ministered before him,
>   and so I was established in Zion.
> In the beloved city likewise he gave me a resting place,
>   and in Jerusalem was my dominion.
> So I took root in an honored people . . . (Sir. 24:8-12)

If "wisdom" can be understood here as a manifestation of God's presence (see above, p. 33), then Maurice Gilbert is surely correct in regarding Ben Sira as presenting "une théologie de la Présence":[22]

In the Book of Jubilees there is general agreement that the theme of God's covenant with Israel is of paramount importance.[23] In this context, E. P. Sanders has pointed out that the covenant made between God and Israel is portrayed not only as the means of forgiveness and blessing, but as

---

[20]The translation here is from the Revised Standard Version (Oxford: Oxford University, 1957).

[21]The programmatic value of Sir. 24 (along with Sir. 1:1-10) is the specific assertion, for example, of J. Marbock, Weisheit im Wandel: Untersuchungen zur Weisheitstheologie bei Ben Sira, (Bonn: Peter Hanstein Verlag GMBH, 1971), part II, chapter 2, pp. 15-96. Furthermore, Sir. 24 is regarded by Martin Hengel, Judaism and Hellenism: Studies in their Encounter in Palestine during the Early Hellenistic Period, trans. J. Bowden (Philadelphia: Fortress, 1974), p. 134, as "the hymn which forms the center and climax of his work." For similar views, see also W. Roth, "On the Gnomic Discursive Wisdom of Jesus Ben Sirach," Semeia 17 (August 1980):71; R.A.F. MacKenzie, Sirach (Wilmington, Del.: Glazier, 1983), p.100; George Nickelsburg, Jewish Literature between the Bible and the Mishnah: A Historical and Literary Introduction (Philadelphia: Fortress, 1981), p. 59.

[22]Maurice Gilbert, "L'éloge de la Sagesse," RTL 5 (3, 1974): 348.

[23]This is the conclusion of, for example, E. P. Sanders, Paul, pp. 370-71. This connection between covenant and presence has also been noted by Annie Jaubert, La Notion d'Alliance Aux Bords de l'Ère Chrétienne, (Paris: Éditions de Seuil, 1963), pp. 89-115; and by Michel Testuz, Les Idées Réligieuses du Livre des Jubilées (Paris: Libraire Minard, 1960), p. 72.

the means of providing God's presence to the people.[24] Thus, for example, Abraham's sacrifice is understood as effecting not so much forgiveness, but that "God should be with him and not forsake him all the days of his life" (Jub. 13:9). Furthermore, the eschatological hope in Jubilees, that God's presence would finally be manifest with his people for ever, is similar:[25]

> And he said to the Angel of the presence, "Write for Moses from the first creation until my sanctuary shall be built in their midst for ever and ever. And the Lord will appear in the sight of all. And everyone will know that I am the God of Israel and the father of all the children of Jacob and king upon Mount Zion for ever and ever. And Zion and Jerusalem will be holy." (Jub. 1:27-28)[26]

In the varied literature of I Enoch, George Nickelsburg has observed the interest in the issue of God's presence within Chapters 1-36. For example, Nickelsburg notes that the prelude to Enoch's prophetic commissioning involves a remarkable journey into God's presence (14-16), a journey in which God does not descend to earth, but in which Enoch ascends to heaven "where God dwells in a temple of psychedelic construction and proportions," and where "Paradoxically in this account the inaccessible God summons a mortal man into his presence."[27]

> And I entered into the house which was hot like fire and cold like ice, and there was nothing inside it; so fear covered me and trembling seized me. And I saw and observed inside it a lofty throne . . . And the Great Glory was sitting upon it . . . None of the angels was able to come in and see the face of the Excellent and Glorious One . . . And the Lord called me with his own mouth and said to me, "Come near to me, Enoch, and to my holy Word." (I Enoch 14:13, 18, 20, 24)[28]

Furthermore, Nickelsburg notes that in I Enoch 13:7 ("And I went and sat down upon the waters of Dan -- in Dan which is on the southwest of

---

[24]See, for example, E. P. Sanders, Paul, pp. 366-67, 379-80. This connection between covenant and presence has also been noted by Annie Jaubert, La Notion, p. 98; and by Michel Testuz, Les Idées, pp. 49-50.

[25]See Gene Davenport, The Eschatology of the Book of Jubilees (Leiden: E. J. Brill, 1971), p. 66, who argues that the final redactor of Jubilees was "sanctuary oriented," and whose interest in the sanctuary is especially prominent in the eschatological texts of 1:4b-26, 27-28, 29c; 23:14-31.

[26]The translation used for Jubilees is that of O. S. Wintermute in OTP2, pp. 35-142.

[27]Nickelsburg, "Enoch, Levi, and Peter: Recipients of Revelation in Upper Galilee," JBL 100 (December 1981): 581.

[28]The translations of I Enoch are those of E. Isaac in OTP1, pp. 5-89.

Hermon -- and I read their memorial prayers until I fell asleep") the location of the place at which the vision was received is clearly indicated. This observation, with others, leads him to suggest that I Enoch 12-16 as a whole represents a polemic deriving from circles in upper Galilee who view the Jerusalem priesthood as defiled, and who claim that the proper location for obtaining true access to God is the ancient holy place of Dan rather than Jerusalem.[29]

In another section of I Enoch, the Similitudes (37-71),[30] David Suter points to numerous texts which lead him to argue that for the Similitudes, to dwell in the presence of God represents "the essence of salvation."[31] The following reference is illustrative:

> Those who do not slumber but stand before your glory, did bless you. They shall bless, praise, and extol (you), saying, "Holy, Holy, Holy, Lord of the Spirits; the spirits fill the earth." And at that place (under his wings) my eyes saw others who stood before him sleepless (and) blessed (him), saying, Blessed are you and blessed is the name of the Lord of the Spirits forever and ever." And my face was changed on account of the fact that I could not withstand the sight. (I Enoch 39:12-14)

---

[29]Nickelsburg, "Enoch," p. 586.

[30]D. Suter, "Masal in the Similitudes of Enoch," JBL 100 (June 1981): 209-10. Both Suter and James Charlesworth note that the consensus of scholarship now rejects the view of J. T. Milik that the Similitudes are a Christian writing of the third century, and agree instead that they date from the latter part of the first century (and are thus admissible as evidence of the environment within which the Christian movement arose). See D. Suter, "Weighed in the Balance: The Similitudes of Enoch in Recent Discussion" RelSRev 7 (July 1981): 217-18; and J. H. Charlesworth, "The SNTS Pseudepigrapha Seminars at Tübingen and Paris on the Books of Enoch," NTS 25 (April 1979): 315-23.

[31]Suter, "Masal," pp. 209-10, is worth quoting extensively here:

"The concept of dwelling or dwelling place, one of the topics of the pattern outlined above, is central to the comparison in the Similitudes between the reward of the righteous and the punishment of the wicked. In I Enoch 41:2 and 61:2, the dwellings of the righteous are mentioned. In 41:4; 45:4; 51:5; 61:12; and 70:4, these dwellings are on earth. In 39:5, they are with the angels (cf. Ps. 73:24). In I Enoch 39:6; 45:4; 49:3; 62:8, 14; and 71:16 (cf. 39:8), the righteous dwell in the presence of the messiah (the Elect one or that Son of Man). Several times the notion of dwelling is associated with the praise of God (see 39:4-14; 47:2; 48:5; 51:4-5; and 61:12). While the concept is used with a certain degree of ambiguity, it is clear that, in the Similitudes of Enoch, to dwell in the presence of God represents the essence of salvation.

"The fate of the sinners or kings and mighty of the earth is contrasted to this notion of salvation. They are to be excluded from heaven (I Enoch 45:2) and driven from the face of the earth (38:1; 45:2, 5-6; 53:3-5; 54:1-2; 56:8; and 69:27), from the presence of the righteous (38:3; 41:2; 56:8; and 62:13), and from the presence of the messiah (62:11; 63:9,11) .... If the essence of salvation is dwelling in the presence of God, the essence of damnation is exclusion from that presence."

With regard to the remainder of I Enoch, the only passage to be quoted directly comes from the second of the two dream visions of I Enoch 83-90, in which the vision of God's people finding a home in the eschatological temple, God's house, is clearly of critical importance:

> I went on seeing until the Lord of the sheep brought about a new house, greater and loftier than the first one, and set it up in the first location which had been covered up -- all its pillars were new, the columns new; and the ornaments new as well as greater than those of the first, (that is) the old (house) which was gone. All the sheep were within it . . . . and the Lord of the sheep rejoiced with great joy because they had all become gentle and had returned to his house. (I Enoch 90:29, 33)

The Psalms of Solomon were written as a response to the desecration of the temple by Pompey in 63 BCE.[32]

   In connection with our study of the Pharisees (see above, pp. 5-23) it is interesting to note that since the late nineteenth century, especially following Wellhausen's work, *Die Pharisäer und die Sadducäer*, written in 1874, the Psalms of Solomon have generally been regarded as a classic source for the understanding of Pharisaism, a view espoused wholeheartedly by scholars such as G. B. Gray, *APOT*, II, p. 630; H. E. Ryle and M. R. James, *Psalmoi Solomontos: Psalms of the Pharisees Commonly Called the Psalms of Solomon* (Cambridge: Cambridge University Press, 1891), pp. xliv-lii; H. Braun "Von Erbarmen Gottes über den Gerechten: Zur Theologie der Psalmen Salomos," *ZNW* 43 (1950): 1 (although his position in "Salomo-Psalmen," *RGG3*, 1961, was more moderate); M. Black, "Pharisees," *IDB*, III, p. 777; A. M. Denis, *Introduction aux Pseudepigraphen Grecs d'Ancien Testament* (Leiden: E. J. Brill, 1970), p. 64; and, recently, J. Schupphaus, *Die Psalmen Salomos: Ein Zeugnis Jerusalems Theologie und Frommigkeit in der Mitte des vorchristlichen Jahrhunderts* (Leiden: E. J. Brill, 1977), p. 132. The importance of this view in formulating past understanding of this aspect of ancient Judaism is best illustrated by quoting Matthew Black, p. 777, who writes that "Fortunately there is no doubt about the Pharisaic authorship of the Psalms of Solomon (ca. 60 B.C.), doctrinally one of the most important of the Pharisaic and anti-Sadducean documents of this century, since it supplies our main evidence for the Pharisaic messianic hope."

---

[32]Ryle and James, Psalmoi Solomontos, pp. xxxvi- xliv, provide a thorough analysis of the possible dating of the Psalms, arguing for a range stretching from 70-40 B.C., and encompassing the era of the Roman general Pompey. This dating has been accepted by almost all recent scholars; J. Ephron (see U. Rappaport, "Solomon, Psalms of," Encyclopedia Judaica 15, col. 116.), who regards the Psalms as Christian, seems to be the only notable exception. R. B. Wright, "Psalms of Solomon: A New Translation and Introduction," in OTP2, pp. 640-41, presents a more recent defense of this position.

Otto Eissfeldt, *The Old Testament: An Introduction Including the Apocrypha*, trans. P. Ackroyd (New York: Harper & Row, 1965), p. 612, however, could find no specific Pharisaic-Sadducaic polemic in the work, and in recent years, even though some have indicated a possible connection between the Psalms and "Pharisaism" as a broad movement -- for example, G. W. E. Nickelsburg, *Jewish Literature*, 203; E. P. Sanders, 388; L. Rost, *Judaism Outside the Hebrew Canon: An Introduction to the Documents*, trans. D. E. Green (Nashville: Abingdon, 1976), p.119 -- others have specifically rejected the Pharisaic option, either looking toward other Jewish movements from which the literature might have arisen, or simply being skeptical about the possibility of defining such a group precisely: e.g Jerry O'Dell, "The Religious Background of the Psalms of Solomon (Re-evaluated in the Light of the Qumran Texts)," *RQ* (May 1961): 241-7; A. Jaubert, *La Notion d'Alliance*, 254; M. Delcor, "Psaumes de Salomon," *Dictionnaire Biblique*, Sup. Vol.9 (1979), col. 236-44; and J. H. Charlesworth, review of *Die Psalmen Salomos*, by J. Schupphaus, *JAAR* 50 (1982), 292-93.

To be sure, the desecration of the Temple by the Romans was deemed in the Psalms of Solomon to be an appropriate judgment on God's own people who had defiled the temple with their "profane offerings and lawless acts" (Ps.Sol. 2:2-5, 8:11-15). Nevertheless, the Psalmist could still cry to God concerning a fear of worse judgment to come, the fear that God's presence, and consequently God's protection, should actually leave them:[33]

Do not move away from us, O God,
   lest those who hate us without cause should attack us.
While your name lives among us, we shall receive mercy
   and the gentiles will not overcome us. (Ps.Sol. 7:1, 6)[34]

The Book of IV Ezra was also written as a response to the destruction of the temple, this time, though, in the first century of the common era.[35] Ezra's desolation over this destruction, described in a series of seven visions, is the theme of the book. Scholars agree that the pivotal vision is the fourth, a vision of the eschatological restoration of Zion.[36] No common consensus

---

[33]With Adolf Büchler, <u>Types of Palestinian Piety from 70 BCE to 70 CE: The Ancient Pious Men</u> (New York: Ktav, 1966), pp. 174-75.

[34]Translation by R. B. Wright, <u>OTP2</u>, p. 658.

[35]On the dating of IV Ezra, see H. C. Kee, <u>SBL 1981</u>, pp. 199-200; Nickelsburg, <u>Jewish Literature</u>, pp. 287-88; Michael A. Knibb, <u>The First and Second Books of Esdras</u>, (Cambridge: University Press, 1982), pp. 101, 104.

[36]References to the importance of the fourth vision can be found in E. Brandenburger, <u>Die Verborgenheit Gottes im Weltsgeschehen: Das literarische und theologische Problem des 4. Esrabuches</u> (Zurich: Theologische Verlag, 1981), pp. 60-84; Earl Breech, "These Fragments Have I shored Against My Ruins: The Form and Function of 4 Ezra," <u>JBL</u> 92 (September

exists as to how exactly this vision functions within the book as a whole;[37] nevertheless, the conclusion of the vision is clear. The angel Uriel addresses Ezra in terms of his extraordinary access to God's presence:

> Therefore do not be afraid, and do not let your heart be terrified; but go in and see the splendor and vastness of the building, as far as it is possible for your eyes to see it, and afterward you will hear as much as your ears can hear. For you are more blessed than many, and you have been called before the Most High, as but few have been. (IV Ezra 10:55-57, RSV)

The blessing of God's presence is notable too in the diverse literature from Qumran. While Bertil Gärtner and others have noted that the Qumran Community came to conceive itself as a temple,[38] E. P. Sanders has added that the members of the community seem to have felt intensely that they were living in the presence of God and that this feeling was connected with the crucial moment of entry into the sect, a moment in which they were "brought near to God" and from then on, like the angels, live "before Him" for ever.[39]

The following quotations, taken from a broad range of Qumran literature, bring together aspects of the community's understanding of cultic, legal and presence issues:[40]

1973), pp. 272-73; Alden Thompson Responsibility for Evil in the Theodicy of IV Ezra (Missoula, Mont.: Scholars Press, 1977), p. 218; Nickelsburg, Jewish Literature, p. 291; and Michael Stone, "Reactions to the Destruction of the Second Temple: Theology, Perception and Conversion," JSJ 12 (December 1981), p. 203, who comments not only on the pivotal nature of the vision, but calls it "perhaps the most lyrical lament in the apocryphal literature."

[37]For examples of diversity of understanding, see Thompson, p. 231; Breech, p. 272; Stone p. 203.

[38]See Bertil Gärtner, The Temple and the Community in Qumran and the New Testament (Cambridge: University Press, 1965), pp. 15, 21-46; Carol Newsom, Songs of the Sabbath Sacrifice (Atlanta: Scholars Press, 1985), pp. 21-22; Michael Newton, The Concept of Purity at Qumran and in the Letters of Paul (Cambridge: University Press, 1985), 8-10. Georg Klinzing Die Umdeutung des Kultus in der Qumrangemeinde und im Neuen Testament (Göttingen: Vandenhoeck & Ruprecht, 1971), p. 89, accepts the general validity of this view while warning against using the Qumran documents as if there were no theological differences between them.

[39]Sanders, Paul, pp. 314-15.

[40]All translations below are from Geza Vermes, The Dead Sea Scrolls in English (New York: Penguin, 1962). The only exception is the quotation from the Temple Scroll, translated by J. Maier, The Temple Scroll: An Introduction, Translation and Commentary (Sheffield: JSOT Press, 1985).

The common names of the texts quoted are usually given as the Damascus Document (CD), the Temple Scroll (11Q Temple), the Manual of Discipline (1QS), the War Scroll (1QM), and the Hymns (1QH).

Hear now, all you who know righteousness, and consider the works of God; for He has a dispute with all flesh and will condemn those who despise Him. For when they were unfaithful and forsook Him, He hid His face from Israel and His Sanctuary and delivered them up to the sword. (CD1:1-4)

The Books of the Law are the *tabernacle* of the king. (CD 7:15,16)

And you shall make an embankment around the sanctuary, one hundred cubits wide, so that it divides the holy sanctuary from the city, and they shall not enter unprepared into my sanctuary, and they shall not profane it, but shall keep my sanctuary holy, and conduct themselves respectfully toward my sanctuary, where I dwell in their midst. (11Q Temple 46:9-12)

It shall be that tried wall, that precious corner-stone, whose foundations shall neither rock nor sway in their place. It shall be a Most Holy Dwelling for Aaron, with everlasting knowledge of the Covenant of justice, and shall offer up sweet fragrance. It shall be a House of perfection and Truth in Israel that they may establish a Covenant according to the everlasting precepts. And they shall be an agreeable offering, atoning for the land and determining the judgement of wickedness, and there shall be no more iniquity. (IQS 8:5-10)

Blessed art Thou, my God,
  who openest the heart of Thy servant to knowledge!
Establish all his deeds in righteousness,
  and as it pleases Thee to do for the elect of mankind,
grant that the son of Thy handmaid
  may stand before Thee for ever. (IQS 11:15-17)

Furthermore, Moses taught us, 'Thou art in the midst of us, a mighty God, and terrible, causing all our enemies to flee before {us}.' He taught our generations in former times saying, 'When you draw near to battle, the priest shall rise and speak to the people saying, "Hear, O Israel! You draw near to battle this day against your enemies. Do not fear! For your God goes with you to fight for you against your enemies that He may deliver you."' (IQM 10:1-4)

Thou hast caused {the straying spirit} to return
  that it may enter into a Covenant with Thee,
and stand {before Thee for ever}
in the everlasting abode,
  illumined with perfect Light for ever,

Key passages used by Klinzing and Gärtner to link the community with the concept of temple also include I QS 5:4-7, 9:3-6, 11:8; CD 3:18-4:10; 4QFlor 1:1-7; 4QpIsa, frag.1; and IQpHab 12:1-4.

with {no more} darkness,
   {for un}ending {seasons of joy}
and un{numbered} ages of peace. (IQH 18:28-30)

IV. THE PRESENCE OF GOD IN THE NEW TESTAMENT

If, as we have tried show, the issue of establishing God's presence was commonplace in the literature and experience of ancient Judaism, the question remains as to whether the same issue reflects the thought of those Jews who became followers of Jesus of Nazareth in the decades surrounding the destruction of the Jerusalem Temple in 70 CE. A cursory review of the New Testament literature would indicate that for at least some early Christians this was indeed an issue.[41]

In this regard, for example, familiarity with the New Testament might lead one immediately to the thought of the writers of the Book of Revelation and of Letter to the Hebrews who wrote of access to God and of God's dwelling with people in glowing terms (italics mine):

> [2]And I saw the holy city, *new Jerusalem*, coming down out of heaven from God, prepared as a bride adorned for her husband; [3]and I heard a great voice from the throne saying, "Behold, the dwelling of God is with men. He will dwell with them, and they shall be his people, and God himself will be with them; . . .
> [22]And I saw no temple in the city, for *its temple is the Lord God Almighty and the Lamb.* (Rev. 21:2, 3, 22, RSV).[42]

> [19]Therefore, brethren, since we have confidence *to enter the sanctuary* by the blood of Jesus, [20]by the new and living way which he opened for us through the curtain, that is, through his flesh, [21]and since we have a great high priest over the house of God, [22]*let us draw near* with full assurance of faith, . . .
> (Heb. 10:19-22a, RSV)[43]

---

[41]See also Terrien, The Elusive Presence, pp. 410-440, and Clements, God and Temple, pp. 138-40.

[42]See further, M. Rissi, The Future of the World: An Exegetical Study of Revelation 19:11-22:15 (London: SCM Press, 1972), pp. 39-61.

[43]William Barclay, in The Letter to the Hebrews (Philadelphia: Westminster, 1955), p. xiii, writes:

> "To some men religion is access to God. It is that which brings them into the very presence of God. It is that which removes the barriers, which takes away the estrangements, and opens the door to the living presence of the living God. That is what religion is to the writer of the Letter to the Hebrews."

In the Letter to the Hebrews it is in part the priesthood of Christ which is stressed as the means through which access to God is granted (for example, see 4:14-16; 6:19-20; 9:24). In Revelation and I Peter the authors point to access to God gained also through the priesthood of individual believers, specifically as expressed in Exodus 19:6 (the verse we have previously noted, p. 21 above, as being of great importance to the Pharisees):

> To him who loves us and has freed us from our sins by his blood and made us a kingdom, priests to our God and Father, to him be glory and dominion for ever and ever. (Rev. 1:5,6, RSV)

> But you are a chosen race, a royal priesthood, a holy nation, that you may declare the wonderful deeds of him who called you out of darkness into his marvellous light. Once you were no people but now you are God's people; . . . (I Peter 2:9,10, RSV) [44]

While the quest for God's presence represented by these texts is couched clearly in terms of temple and priest, the same concern in more general terms can also be found in a casual reading of Matthew's Gospel, which emphasizes God's presence through Jesus Christ both at its beginning and its end, in what Samuel Terrien calls "a poetic *inclusio* on a grand scale":[45]

> [23]"Behold a virgin shall conceive and bear a son, and his name shall be called Emmanuel" (which means, God with us). (Matt. 1:23, RSV)

> [20]. . . and lo, I am with you always, to the close of the age. (Matt. 28:20b, RSV)

In addition, we might add, Matthew also relates Jesus' promise of ongoing presence in the heart of his gospel, that where two or three are gathered in his name, there he is in their midst (Matt. 18:20).[46]

Our major interest in the New Testament literature is, of course, with the letters of the Apostle Paul and with the theology expounded within them. The text we shall turn to shortly, II Corinthians 2:14-3:18, is not one that is patently concerned with God's presence. Other texts in Paul, however, clearly are. In I Corinthians 3:16, for example, Paul describes the church as the

---

[44]See Lev. 26:11-13.

[45]Terrien, The Elusive Presence, p. 430.

[46]The Matthean emphasis on presence is certainly not limited to these points, which serve only to indicate the importance of the concept throughout the Gospel. On the significance of the "saving presence" of Jesus with his disciples see Jack D. Kingsbury, Proclamation Commentaries: Matthew (Philadelphia: Fortress, 1977), pp. 80-81.

temple of God in which God's spirit (God's presence?) dwells. The same cultic image is applied to the individual believer three chapters later in 6:19, and to the church and/or individuals in II Corinthians 5:16.

Furthermore, as we shall note below, themes relating to God's presence occur at crucial junctures in Paul's letter to the Romans: at 5:1 Paul speaks of access to God gained by Christ; at 8:38-39, he speaks of the inability of anything to separate the believer from God; and at 12:1 he speaks of the appropriate manner of the Christian life as being that of a holy sacrifice -- a sacrifice, of course, being something brought into and laid before God's presence in the temple.

V. SUMMARY AND DEVELOPMENT

Our review of the Biblical and extra-Biblical material in connection with the issue of God's presence has been cursory. For the sake of brevity, we have not always attempted to discuss in depth the contexts from which our evidence has arisen, though we would argue that we have not done injustice to those contexts. Our purpose, however, has not been to provide a definitive understanding of all of Judaism. Rather, what we have attempted to establish is that the issue of finding God's presence and living within it was a recurrent, and at times central, passion in the broad literary background and experience of faithful Jews in the first century of the common era, and in the scriptures of the early Christian Church, including some of the writings of Paul himself.

In this context, then, we hope also to have shown that it is by no means idiosyncratic to suggest that the overarching concern of the Pharisees of the first century was with the issue of finding, establishing and maintaining the presence of God in their midst. Indeed, the matter is undoubtedly worth pursuing in its possible ramifications for understanding the thought of Paul, the Pharisee-become-Christian. This we shall do after two matters of clarification.

First, the specific question that we want to ask in this endeavor is not merely whether Paul was interested in this theme -- we have already observed that to some extent he certainly was. Rather the issue at stake is whether or not the assumption of an over-riding interest in finding and maintaining God's presence can cast light on the structure of Pauline thought as a whole, and/or on specific aspects of his thought in particular (for example, Paul's use of juridical and participationist categories for salvation, or his view of the "Law").[47] Merely surveying different texts at this point will not provide an answer. Only detailed examination of specific sections of Paul's writing in context will suffice.

Second, danger lurks even with this procedure, for the imposition on the text of a prior assumption may well seem forced, leading to eisegesis (a "reading into" the text) rather than a faithful exegesis (a "reading out of" the text). The danger, however, is worth facing: to read the text with a twentieth century mindset without some sort of assumption such as the present proposal might just as easily be a forcing of the text, a forcing to which we are blind and leading in its own way to eisegesis.[48]

The issue of eisegesis is a difficult one to deal with fairly. Undoubtedly, in the pages which follow we will at times open the door to the suggestion of eisegesis, by "pressing our text" to the fullest. In the end, however, it is surely another issue, the issue of results, which must determine the validity of the approach: does the bringing of the assumption to the text bear fruit? does it help explain and unravel Paul's thought? These are the questions to keep in mind in turning now to a specific passage in the Pauline literature, II Corinthians 2:14-3:18, a passage renowned for its complexity.

Our discussion of Paul turns to this particular passage primarily because of an initial observation concerning the frequent use within it (eleven times) of the word δόξα, a word which in the Septuagint and elsewhere often refers

---

[47]With regard to the debate concerning how Paul connects juridical/forensic and participationist categories in his understanding of salvation, see Sanders, Paul and Palestinian Judaism, pp. 497-511. We believe that salvation understood in terms of the presence of God is a critical model for understanding the (necessary) interconnection between these ideas.

With regard to the issue of "Law," our exegesis barely mentions it explicitly. However, if to the Pharisees, as we have argued, the purpose of the law was to create and maintain the atmosphere in which God was pleased to be present, then clearly our thesis makes an implicit contribution to the debate on Paul's complex and varied use of the term. For recent literature, see Stephen Westerholm, Israel's Law; Frank Thielman, From Plight to Solution: A Jewish Framework for Understanding Paul's View of the Law in Galatians and Romans, NovTSup 61, (Leiden: E. J. Brill, 1989); and Brice L. Martin, Christ and the Law in Paul, NovTSup 62, (Leiden: E. J. Brill, 1989), especially, pp. 21-23.

[48]Sanders's Paul and Palestinian Judaism, pp. 2-59, for example, attempts to destroy a legalistic works-righteousness view of Judaism which has affected the interpetation (i.e., led to eisegesis) of Paul for the past century. Krister Stendahl's famous essay, "The Introspective Conscience of the West," in Paul Among Jews and Gentiles (Philadelphia: Fortress, 1976) also focuses on the problem of eisegesis in Paul, filtering our understanding of Paul and the Law through our "introspective western consciences."

to some kind of manifestation of God's presence.[49] Furthermore, in this connection Paul's self-designation in II Cor. 2:17, as one who, in Christ, lives and speaks as κατέναντι θεοῦ (as before, or in the presence of God) becomes manifestly intriguing. Indeed, these two observations not only serve to define the section of II Corinthians with which we shall be mainly, though not exclusively, concerned[50] -- 2:14-3:18 -- but also suggest a possible focus for the varied criticisms of Paul by his opponents in Corinth:[51] that Paul was a man who did not stand in God's presence, and therefore could not impart salvation, understood as God's presence or the manifestations of it, to others.[52]

---

[49]See, for example, Exod. 33:18, Wis. 9:10 and 2 Macc. 2:8. Many other references are provided by G. von Rad and G. Kittel, TDNT, s.v. "Δόξα," 2: 232-55. Including two verbal forms, the word occurs 13 times in II Cor.3.

[50]It is not our intention to enter any debate on the unity or otherwise of II Corinthians 1-13. Two assumptions, however, need be indicated in this regard: first, with scholars such as V. P. Furnish (The Anchor Bible: II Corinthians {Garden City, N.Y.: Doubleday, 1984}, p. 35), and Ralph P. Martin (Word Biblical Commentary, Vol. 40, 2 Corinthians {Waco, Tx.: Word, 1986}, pp. xl-xlvi), against, for example, Bultmann (The Second Letter to the Corinthians, trans. Roy A. Harrisville, {Minneapolis: Augsburg, 1985}, p. 18), that II Cor. 2: 14-7:4 belongs to the context in which it is presently found and is not an editorial insertion; second, with, for example, D. Georgi (The Opponents of Paul in Second Corinthians {Philadelphia: Fortress, 1986}, pp. 13-14), J.-F. Collange (Énigmes de la Deuxième Epître de Paul aux Corinthiens {Cambridge: University Press, 1972}, p. 15), and M. Rissi ("The Brighter Splendor: Paul and the Old Testament according to II Corinthians 3," Affirmation 1 {July 1967}: 60), that even if the letter as it now stands is an editorial composition by someone other than Paul, nevertheless the opponents and general circumstances giving rise to the whole are virtually the same, thus making it legitimate to draw on evidence from various parts of the letter to aid in the explanation of specific sections of the argument. For example, it is clear from the epistle as a whole that Paul's discussion stems in large measure from the presence in Corinth of those who publicly oppose him (cf. 6:8; 10:10-12), and that the general nature of the opposition is consistent throughout (see Rissi, p. 61, Furnish, p. 53).

With Thomas Provence, "'Who is sufficient for these Things?': An Exegesis of 2 Cor. 2:15-3:18," NovT 24 (January 1982): 69; C. J. A. Hickling, "The Sequence of Thought in II Corinthians Chapter Three," NTS 21 (April 1975): 380; and A. T. Hanson, "The Midrash in II Corinthians 3: A Reconsideration," JSNT 9 (October 1980): 23, we believe that Paul's thought is not greatly clarified by attempting to understand his opponents' background in the Greco-Roman world in depth (as, for example, Georgi has attempted to do). However, against Hickling's thesis, we do believe that it is important to see the passage as basically polemical and to make some inferences from the text about Paul's opponents, while agreeing with Furnish, p. 44, that Paul remains in full control of his argument in II Corinthians.

[51]For examples of these criticisms, see Furnish, p. 52.

[52]To my knowledge, such a suggestion has not been made elsewhere, and certainly seems to be absent, for example, from the recent commentaries of Victor Furnish and Ralph P. Martin on II Corinthians. However, Walter Brueggemann, in "The Crisis of Promise and Presence in Israel," Horizons in Biblical Theology 1 (1980): 65, clearly notes the importance of God's presence as the legitimating factor in Moses' authority to mediate the covenant in Exod. 33, and indicates in passing that the thought is paralleled by Paul in II Corinthians: "the issue of

Our procedure, then, shall be both *to establish the possibility* of Paul's vital concern for God's presence -- examining further our initial understanding of Paul's use of words such as δόξα and κατέναντι, as well as his use of other words and concepts related generally to the cult -- and *to apply the hypothesis* to the development of Paul's argument in II Cor. 2:14-3:18 as a whole, to see if any significant clarification of the sense and logic becomes apparent.[53] We begin with a summary of our understanding of the passage.

Yahweh's presence is enmeshed in the issue of Moses' vocation."

[53]As Joseph Fitzmyer has observed, "Glory Reflected in the Face of Christ (2 Cor. 3:7-4:6) and a Palestinian Jewish Motif," TS 42 (December 1981): 630, our chosen passage in II Corinthians is "very complicated." Fitzmyer, p. 634, suggests that Paul's thought must be understood as developing on the basis of "catch-word bonding," while Alfred Plummer A Critical and Exegetical Commentary on the Second Epistle of Paul to the Corinthians (New York: Scribner's, 1915), p. xlii, has suggested that Paul had no great concern for logical consistency. Indeed, Morna Hooker, "Beyond the Things that are written? St. Paul's Use of Scripture," NTS 27 (April 1981): 304, claims that Paul's thought is filled with contradictions and non-sequiturs--a claim echoed by James McDonald, "Paul and the preaching Ministry: A Reconsideration of 2 Cor. 2:14-17 in its Context," JSNT 17 (February 1983): 43.

The complexity of the passage is beyond dispute. On the other hand, it is hoped that the exegesis presented here will demonstrate that Paul's logic, though complex, is nevertheless consistent and rational, and, as far as we can ascertain, devoid of non-sequiturs.

CHAPTER THREE

The Outline of Paul's Argument in
II Corinthians 2:14-3:18

I. THE CORINTHIAN CONTEXT OF II COR. 2:14-3:18

Paul begins the Second Epistle to the Corinthians by informing his readers of the almost unbearable suffering which had confronted him in Asia (II Cor. 1:3-11). Before informing the Corinthians of a second occasion in which he had suffered extensively, this time in Macedonia (7:5), Paul launches into a lengthy theological defence of his apostleship in 2:14-7:4, with the primary aim being to counteract the accusation that his suffering was evidence that his claim to apostleship was invalid.[1]

---

[1]See Furnish, p. 54. The clearest texts in II Corinthians in which Paul's sufferings seem to be regarded as the major obstacle to his opponents' acceptance of his apostolicity are 6:3-10 and 11:23-12:13.

In stressing the importance of this inverse connection between suffering and the validity of apostolic ministry, we by no means intend to deny that the charge against the validity of Paul's apostolic status was based on other reasons as well. For example, it seems that the charge was placed against Paul that his taking up of a collection for the Jerusalem church was pursued out of a concern for personal financial gain (2:17 with 7:2, 12:16-17); that Paul did not love the Corinthians as a true apostle ought to have done (3:2 with 2:1-4, 12:15); that Paul could well be an impostor (6:8 with 11:13-15) because he possessed no written evidence such as "letters of reference" to support his claim that his apostolicity was valid (3:1-3); and that consequently his "gospel" and ministry were unable to impart God's richest blessings to those to whom he ministered (3:17-18 with 4:3).

It cannot be doubted, then, that a variety of charges was levelled against Paul. However, it still seems reasonable to conclude on the basis of Paul's repeated concern to speak openly about his suffering in connection with his ministry (e.g., 1:3-11, 4:7-11, 6:3-10, 7:5, and especially 11:23-30) that this constant suffering was the crowning objection -- the seeming God-given evidence -- used by Paul's opponents to denounce the validity of his apostolic status.

The inability of Paul's opponents to conceive of suffering as characteristic of apostolic life derived from their use of the Biblical story of Moses in Exodus 32-34,[2] in which Moses functions in his role as the bearer of God's word, and thus as a possible paradigm for apostleship. In the Exodus narrative Moses is presented as one who was summoned into God's presence (both on Mt. Sinai and in the tent of witness). There alone he received God's word, and from there he returned to the people with divine authority to speak for God. Moreover, the evidence that Moses' authority was valid was written, as it were, on his face and general appearance. That is, his true experience of God's presence (God's presence being referred to by the word δόξα in II Cor. 3:7-11, for example) had so transformed his appearance that his face shone.

Paul's opponents' argument against him, therefore, was as follows: A valid apostle is one who has access to God's presence. There alone God's word can be received to be imparted to God's people. The evidence that the word of God's messenger does in fact derive from God himself is to be found in the appearance of God's messenger, whose face (and general appearance), if the messenger has truly been granted access to God's presence, should shine as did Moses' (though, presumably, figuratively; see II Cor. 5:12). It was, however, in no way possible to think of a man such as Paul as one whose face or appearance "shone"; for Paul's personal appearance and mode of preaching was not only generally unimpressive (see I Cor. 2:1-5; II Cor. 10:10) but was also crowned with constant suffering and affliction. Paul, therefore, was not a person to whom God had granted access to His presence. Consequently, Paul was not an apostle.

II Cor. 2:14-17 serves as the basic introduction to Paul's defence against such an argument, and lays bare his fundamental position.[3]

---

[2]The story of Exod. 34:29-35 is explicitly referred to in II Cor. 3:7 and 13, while allusions to the story are also made in 3:14-18. Walter Brueggemann, Horizons in Biblical Theology, 1, pp. 65-70, 84, n. 55, has demonstrated Paul's great familiarity with Exod. 33, and has argued for the importance of understanding Paul's use of the chapter (for example, in II Cor. 4:6, Rom. 9:14-18, and I Cor. 13:12) within its Exodus context, consisting of Exod. 32-34. We simply wish to affirm his observation by claiming the reverse to be true as well, that Paul's use of Exod. 34 can be understood only by affirming Paul's familiarity with Exod. 32-33.

[3]The introductory nature of 2:14-17 has been observed frequently. See, for example, M. Thrall, "A Second Thanksgiving Period in II Corinthians," JSNT 16 (1982): 117-18; Collange, p. 40; and Furnish, p. 185.

II. II CORINTHIANS 2:14-17

Paul's claim in II Cor. 2:14-16 is that his ministry is effective (and therefore valid) because it imparts salvation to some and confirms others in their own condemnation. This power to impart salvation (and its opposite, condemnation), Paul implies, derives from the intimate identity of his life with the sacrifice of Christ. That is, Paul claims that his suffering is certainly not punitive, nor is it accidental, but is, in accordance with God's will, so intimately associated with Christ's sacrifice that God embraces it within his salvific work and uses it to spread the fragrance of Christ's sacrifice (ὀσμή and εὐωδία) to those with whom he, Paul, comes in contact.[4]

Paul believed, therefore, that to embrace his message and life, despite its deathly appearance, was to embrace what pertains to salvation. On the other hand, to reject his message and life, as if it were merely deathly and not redemptive, as his opponents implied, was to embrace death.

The nature of apostolic ministry as Paul conceived it, then, was sacrificial. To question Paul's sufficiency (2:16b) for the apostolic task, as Paul's opponents did, was, in this light, to play into his hands: for a major criterion of sufficiency for sacrificial ministry had to be one's willingness to suffer -- which, by common consensus, Paul was doing. Furthermore, in this light any criticism that Paul was hawking the gospel (καπηλεύειν, 2:17a), using his status for financial gain, and thus divorcing his personal life from the message he proclaimed, was rendered meaningless. That is, even to contemplate the idea that Paul's proclamation of the Gospel was for financial gain was patently absurd: in comparison with the suffering that Paul was experiencing no amount of financial gain could ever act as adequate compensation.[5]

---

[4]With Collange, p. 41; Martin p. 45; and C. K. Barrett, The Second Epistle to the Corinthians, (London: A. & C. Black, 1973), pp. 98-100, we shall defend below the sacrificial interpretation of Paul's use of ὀσμή and εὐωδία. Such a defence, given our understanding of Paul's broad concern with God's presence, need not signify the absence from Paul's mind of the connection of these words with God's presence, as indicated, for example, in Sir. 24, and emphasized by, among others, Furnish, pp. 176-77; Plummer, p. 70; Bultmann, p. 63; Rissi, p. 65; and J. Hering, The Second Epistle of Saint Paul to the Corinthians, trans. A. W. Heathcote and P. J. Alcock (London: Epworth, 1967), p. 18.

[5]Scott Hafemann's thorough examination of the word καπηλεύειν, Suffering and the Spirit (Tübingen: J.C.B.Mohr-Paul Siebeck, 1985), pp. 106-26, has convincingly demonstrated that the evidence is lacking in the ancient literature for its understanding as "water-down" or "adulterate," but that there is widespread support for its understanding as "to sell," frequently with the pejorative connotation of to "traffic" or "hawk."

Moreover, in providing such a conception of apostolic ministry Paul was levelling a severe blow at the fundamental objection to his status. That is, in portraying the apostolic life as sacrificial service, Paul was providing a Biblical paradigm for a way of life that could be lived in the presence of God and which, at the same time, positively embraced suffering: sacrifices, by definiton, suffered, and such suffering, when acceptable to God (as the effectiveness of Paul's ministry proved his suffering to be), were necessarily cultically pure and were offered in one place only -- on the altar, in the tabernacle or temple, in the presence of God (κατέναντι Θεοῦ, 2:17). From such a location as this, in God's presence, Paul claimed to exercise his ministry. His life, therefore, filled with suffering as it was, fulfilled at least one of the criteria for valid apostolic ministry decreed by his opponents and with which Paul would have had no quarrel: a valid apostle must have access to God's presence.

Such is the thrust of Paul's discussion in the introductory verses, 2:14-17. What must be noted, however, is that in these verses Paul merely makes assertions without proof -- either Scriptural or experiential. Proof-less assertions, though, would undoubtedly be challenged by his opponents as amounting to no more than mere self-commendation (3:1). Paul, therefore, now had to provide the necessary evidence to substantiate his introductory claims.

III. II CORINTHIANS 3:1-3

In defending his claims in 2:14-17, Paul first of all presents experiential evidence for the validity of his apostleship. This evidence did not consist of letters of recommendation but of the working of God himself in the lives of the Corinthian Christians through Paul. In specific terms, Paul stresses that it was through his loving ministry alone that the life-giving Spirit had been imparted to the Corinthians.[6] No one could deny this fact. Consequently,

---

[6]In the present study there will be no detailed exposition of II Cor. 3:1-3. The only comment that need be made here to supplement those readily available in commentaries concerns 3:2. That is, we follow the better attested reading of "ἡμων" rather than "ὑμων" with Wm. Baird, "Letters of Recommendation: A Study of II Corinthians 3:1-3," JBL 80 (June 1961): 166-72, and Furnish, p. 181 (who also cites Plummer, Kummel, Allo, and Collange against Barrett, Bultmann, Rissi, and the RSV). In context, as Baird indicates, this reading implies that Paul is declaring that he carries the Corinthians (his letter of recommendation) around with him in his heart, as one who loves them. Such an understanding fits well with Paul's use of καρδία in 6:11, 7:2, and 8:16, and also re-emphasizes the point that Paul tries to drive home elsewhere in the epistle, that all his actions towards the Corinthians stem from love, unlike those of his

therefore, no one could deny that at least at one point in Paul's life God had placed his seal on the ministry which Paul had conducted, thus confirming his status as one whom God had at one time welcomed into his presence.

Whether Paul still remained an apostle was, however, another question, for it could at least be argued by some that Paul's suffering was a divine indication that his freedom of access to God and his status as an apostle, convincingly demonstrated by his former ministry among the Corinthians, had been revoked. A major issue at stake, then, in the argument which develops from 3:1-3 must be assumed to be related not just to the question of apostolicity but to the broader question as to whether or not suffering was any indication of God's displeasure, indicating the consequent exclusion of a person from God's presence.[7]

IV. II CORINTHIANS 3:4-6

In 3:4 Paul affirms that God's imparting of the Spirit through his ministry -- the Spirit's function, in part at least, being to confirm the belief that a new covenant through Christ had been inaugurated[8] -- gave him the confidence which he needed to claim that he had access to God (and thus, implicitly, to

---

opponents (see 1:6; 2:4; 5:12; 11:7-21; 12:14-18).

This assertion of Paul's love for the Corinthians is, as are the claims of 2:14-17, "mere assertion." Thus, the crucial verse in 3:1-3, as far as Paul's defence of his apostolicity is concerned, is 3:3, which focuses on the Corinthians' own experience--an experience of the Spirit which they cannot deny.

[7]The concern for establishing the proper reasons for excluding someone with a natural right to approach God and serve him at his altar (i. e., the priests) from doing so was both a Biblical and a contemporary concern in Paul's era. In the Bible, the concern of Leviticus 21-22 is with precisely this issue: physical blemishes as well as uncleanness caused, for example, by contact with death, would lead to such an exclusion of the priests in question.

In the era surrounding the first Christian century the concern within Judaism for maintaining the proper purity for such priestly service can be seen in the Qumran literature, CD 5:6-7, 11:19-22. See also Pss.Sol. 2:3-5; 8:11-12, and I Enoch 6-11. Concerning this section of Enoch, David Suter, "Fallen Angel, Fallen Priest: The Problem of Family Purity in I Enoch 6-16," HUCA 50 (1979): 123-24, writes that the exclusion of angels from heaven for inappropriate marital relationships in the Enochic narrative serves as a paradigm indicating the necessary exclusion from service in the presence of God at his altar of those priests who also enter inappropriate relationships. So also Josephus, Ap. I.36 and Ant. XI.308.

In Paul's case, the question would be whether his suffering should be viewed either as punishment from God for sins, or as indicative of the fundamentally "blemished" nature of his life, either one of which would indicate sufficient impurity within his life to render him excluded from God's presence.

[8]With Rissi, p. 71.

claim that his apostolic status was valid). Indeed, Paul affirms in 3:5-6 that the access to God which he enjoyed had not been granted to him because of any worthiness within his life, but was linked entirely with the working of God in establishing this new covenant.[9]

The introduction of the theme of covenant (see, e.g., 3:2-3, 3:6) is crucial to Paul's argument as it now develops.[10] By contrasting the new covenant with the old, as he does throughout the rest of II Corinthians 3, Paul is first of all able to demonstrate that his opponents' paradigm of the kind of life that characterizes a person who has access to God's presence is invalid, and, second, that access to God's presence has been opened up to all Christians, including those who suffer.

Furthermore, by means of this covenantal contrast Paul provides the basis on which he can rest the argument to be developed in Chapters 4 and 5, that the most appropriate paradigm for the life of a person who has gained access to God through the covenant established by Christ is sacrificial (see, for example, 4:10). That is, Paul argues in II Cor. 4-5 that Christ himself must be the Christian paradigm of one who lives in God's presence, and, in particular, that it is Christ's ministry on the cross -- as a sacrifice -- which must function, at least until the final judgment, as the visual image of the appearance of those who have entered God's presence through the new covenant.[11]

V. II CORINTHIANS 3:7-11

The paradigm used by Paul's opponents to illustrate the valid characteristics of the life of someone who had experienced, and was experiencing, the presence of God, becomes explicit in II Cor. 3:7, and comprises the visible appearance of Moses in the incident related in Exod.

---

[9]Thus we regard "τοιαύτην" in 3:4 as referring to the new covenant referred to implicitly by reference to the spirit in 3:3, and explicitly in 3:6. See below, p. 243.

[10]Rissi, p. 71, is correct in declaring that:

"The antagonists of Paul do not understand him because they do not understand the eschatological significance of his apostleship. It is of the greatest importance that it is the new covenant announced already by Jeremiah which is administered by Paul."

[11]With Paul J. Achtemeier, The Quest for Unity in the New testament Church (Philadelphia: Fortress, 1987), pp. 80-82:

"Life and theology are one for Paul, and to understand them in different terms is simply to misunderstand Paul. To say that a theology of the cross precedes a theology of glory in Paul is as much to describe the life he lived as the theology he proclaimed."

34:29-36: his face shone. The key word in the passage is "δόξα," which is used by Paul in II Corinthians 3 to express both the idea of God's presence itself as well as the visible effect of that presence on the lives of those who experienced it.

Within 3:7-11 Paul's discussion has a three-fold emphasis. The first comprises a *qal-wahomer* argument which seems to develop the conclusion that there should be more "δόξα" in the new covenant than in the old. It is most unlikely that Paul's opponents would have had any objection to such an argument. Indeed, it could well be insisted (as, perhaps, the opponents really did insist) that the natural consequence to follow from such a conclusion could only work against Paul and his suffering. That is, it could be argued that if in the old covenant Moses' face shone as a result of being in God's presence, then in the new covenant the appearance of God's servants must also shine, and do so with more brilliance (more evidence of δόξα) than that which was given to Moses and the Israelites -- not less, as seemed to be the case with Paul.[12]

We shall argue below, however, that Paul's thrust in these verses is not that *in the present there is* more δόξα in the new covenant than in the old (with δόξα understood as visible evidence for the presence of God), but that *there will be in the future*. Thus, for Paul, the visible manifestation of δόξα as some sort of radiant light can only be conceived as "hope" (3:12), and not as a present possibility or necessity.[13]

Paul's second emphasis, made in 3:10, is that in the present the visible evidence of God's presence, at least as portrayed in the appearance of Moses, is of no worth at all. For Paul to expect that his opponents would even contemplate such radical conclusions as these -- both that the concern for δόξα must be oriented toward its future manifestation, and that the Mosaic conception of δόξα as some sort of radiance (literal or otherwise) was worthless in the present -- there must have been biblical warrant which Paul's opponents could not deny. Our discussion below intends to demonstrate that

---

[12]Following Rissi, p. 74.

[13]Paul's emphasis on the future aspect of δόξα in II Cor. 3:7-12 has also been noted, for example, by J. Koenig, "The Motif of Transformation in the Pauline Epistles" (Ph.D. dissertation, Union Theological Seminary, New York, 1971), p. 155, n. 139.

such warrant is to be found in Haggai 2, a passage which also confirms the eschatological thrust of Paul's argument about δόξα in 3:7-11.[14]

Paul's third emphasis in these verses is to convey his basic understanding of the old covenant in contrast to the new. That is, in 3:7-11 Paul asserts that the old covenant is one that leads to death (Θάνατος, 3:7) and condemnation (κατάκρισις, 3:9) and is being abolished (καταργέω, 3:11), while, with the fear of death and condemnation removed, the new covenant is one of the Spirit (πνεῦμα, 3:8) who imparts a new relationship of righteousness with God (δικαιοσύνη, 3:9) which is secure for ever (τό μένον, 3:11).

VI. II CORINTHIANS 3:12-18

In 3:7-11, Paul neither explains why he makes the claims that the old covenant was a covenant of death and condemnation, nor does he provide proof to substantiate them, but merely asserts them, offensive as they must have been to his opponents.[15] In 3:12-18, on the other hand, the explanation becomes apparent, and a biblical example justifying them is provided.

Paul wishes now to argue that access to God's presence under the old covenant was in fact generally not beneficial but actually dangerous. That is, whereas under the new covenant which abolished death and condemnation and assured the hope of the future manifestation of δόξα, Paul knew that he was free to approach God and to lead others into God's presence with confidence (3:12), under the old covenant Moses knew of no such confidence (3:13). Rather, knowing that the old covenant manifestation of God's δόξα could just as easily kill sinners as bless them, Moses, for the sake of Israel's very life, hid the δόξα on his face from those who wished to fix their gaze upon it (II Cor. 3:13 with Exod. 34:33).

---

[14]Koenig, p. 156, n. 139, quotes H. Ulonska (Evangelische Theologie 26 {1966}, p. 348) as declaring that the proof of Paul's assertions in 3:7-11 lies only in the eschaton. Our position is that while Paul's opponents would have required some sort of proof that his argument was valid, they certainly would not have been willing to wait until the eschaton for that proof to be provided.

[15]While F. F. Bruce, 1 & 2 Corinthians (London: Oliphants), p. 190; Furnish, p. 201; and Barrett, II Corinthians, p. 113, each point out that Paul's understanding of the law as bringing death ran directly counter to the prevailing Jewish understanding, none of them comment on the revulsion and the inevitable rejection with which Paul's opponents would have received Paul's words unless they realized that within Paul's comments there also lay some solid (Scriptural?) evidence for his position.

The Biblical warrant for such an understanding of the old covenant and its δόξα as dangerous derives from the narrative section of Exodus (Exod. 32-34) in which the paradigmatic story of Moses is found (Exod. 34:29-35). Thus, for example, one clear warning in the narrative is that no one can see the face of God and live (Exod. 33:20).[16] The Israelites, however, fascinated by the appearance of Moses and the glimpse of the manifestation of God's presence which his appearance seemed to promise them, failed to remember that the lasting result, or "τέλος," of beholding such δόξα under the old covenant was death (3:13b),[17] and so they continued to pursue it, with Moses and the books which bore his name (3:14-15) as the respective paradigm and means for attaining it.[18]

Paul's argument, however, in claiming that the same veil (τό αὐτό κάλυμμα, 3:14) which Moses used in the days of the exodus still remained over the reading of the old covenant, was that the sentence of death and condemnation that characterized the covenant at that time still remained on those who pursued the experience of God's presence which it offered. On the other hand, Paul argued, a new covenant had been inaugurated by Christ, and within this covenant the veil -- and consequently the sentence of death and condemnation -- had been abolished (3:14b), and thus a new possibility of access to God had been opened wide.

In this new context, with the veil of death and condemnation abolished, it might well have been argued that people could now seek the kind of δόξα as portrayed on Moses' face with immunity. Paul on the other hand argues that the Mosaic paradigm properly understood no longer calls upon God's people to gaze upon his δόξα "second-hand" -- as did the Israelites in gazing at Moses -- but, rather, summons new covenant believers actually to join Moses in entering God's presence, as if on Sinai itself or in the tent of witness

---

[16]See also, Exod. 19:21, 33:3, 5, with 33:14-16. The tension between the presence of God as both blessing and curse in Exod. 19:16-22 is described well by Jon Levenson, Sinai and Zion (Minneapolis: Winston, 1985), p. 15, who writes that the passage speaks of "a barrier between God and Israel, which if transgressed, will turn the moment of destiny into one of disaster."

Georgi, p. 256, sees clearly the wonder expressed by Josephus, Ant. III:75-82, that "Moses does not perish in the presence of the divine." Georgi does not, however, seem to see that Paul's concern is also focused on the connection between "presence" and death, and in particular with the fact that the Mosaic experience of God is simply not generally applicable to others within the context of the Old Covenant.

[17]See below, pp. 135-45, for our discussion on this understanding of Paul's use of τέλος in II Cor. 3:13.

[18]On the close association of Moses with the covenant and Scriptures associated with him see Georgi, p. 250, and Fitzmyer, pp. 637-38.

(3:16).[19] The freedom to approach God's presence with such boldness, Paul argues, was made possible through the gift of the Holy Spirit (3:17), whom the Corinthians themselves had received (3:3), and who provided for new covenant believers the very same degree of God's presence as Moses experienced on Sinai and in the tent of witness (3:17).[20]

The Spirit's task, however, was not to draw the gaze of believers to Moses to be transformed by his radiant appearance -- a transformation which would provide evidence of their standing in the presence of God. Rather, the Spirit's task was to draw the gaze of believers to the transforming image and δόξα of God himself (3:18), as represented, at least until the last judgment, when one manifestation of δόξα would give way to another (3:18b), by Christ crucified (see, for example, 4:5-12, and 5:14-15). The new covenant evidence, therefore, that a life was being lived in the presence of God was transformation into the sacrificial image of Christ. Paul's life of suffering fit the pattern, and consequently it could not be argued that his suffering was evidence of his expulsion from God's presence and the loss of his apostolic status.

VII. THE ARGUMENT OF II CORINTHIANS 2:14-3:18 CONTINUING AND DEVELOPING IN II CORINTHIANS 4 AND 5

Although our study will not pursue Paul's argument beyond II Corinthians 2:14-3:18, except to make reference to Paul's thought as it illumines our major section of interest, nevertheless, we would claim that his fundamental argument as introduced in 2:14-17, and as defended in 3:1-18 is expanded in chapters 4-6. For example, in 4:1-6 Paul explains how it is possible for some people to reject both his life and the image of Christ crucified as the valid representation of the glory of God. In 4:7-12 he explains the exact nature of the relationship between his life and that of Christ crucified. In 4:13-5:10 he expands upon the eschatological nature of the experience of God which the new covenant brings, and so explains further why the present apparent lack of glory does not cause him to despair. In

---

[19]Héring, p. 27, n. 21, writes that "Every Christian has become a Moses, . . ."

[20]We do not intend to enter the debate on Paul's use of "κύριος" in 3:16-18. Our own understanding is that the fundamental referent is God rather than Christ, though this is not to deny that there is an intimate relationship in the passage between the two. See the helpful discussion in Furnish, pp. 212-14, 234.

5:11-21 he explains why it is Christ crucified ("the love of Christ," 5:14)[21] which controls his understanding of Christ, and why, consequently, it is to be as ambassadors of his death that apostles are to function. In 6:1-7:4 he calls the Corinthians to abandon all shame and repulsion at what they see occuring in the life of Paul, and to abandon as well their association with those who reject his cultic interpretation of Christian experience, and to do so in order to re-unite themselves with their true apostle, who had suffered only because he loved them (see II Cor. 2:4; 11:7-11).

VIII. II CORINTHIANS 2:14-3:18: SUMMARY

In II Cor. 2:14-3:18, then, Paul has argued with his opponents on their own ground in assuming that the ability to stand in God's presence was necessary for apostolic ministry to be valid. Nevertheless, in directing the thrust of his argument to the ability of all Christians, not just apostles, to stand where Moses stood, and to do so as those being transformed into the sacrificial image of Christ, Paul has clearly imposed themes reflecting independent theological insights of his own upon his opponents' thought.

It must not be thought, however, that Paul's present concern with God's presence in relation to the lives of Christians in general was developed merely to meet the need of the present debate. Rather, in arguing as he does in II Corinthians, Paul is drawing upon his fundamental understanding of the gospel of Christ. For example, in Romans the concern for God's presence is expressed at crucial junctures in the development of Paul's argument (5:1-5; 8:38-39; 12:1). Thus, Paul can claim that the fruit of the righteousness supplied by Christ to all Christians is access to God's presence (5:1), from which nothing can separate them (8:39); that the present Christian experience of suffering has been embraced by God in his salvific work (5:2-4), which is to be understood both as a call to transformation ("μεταμορφοῦσθε") and, in cultic terms, as a call to live as a "living sacrifice" (12:1-2); and that in the midst of suffering the Christian is to be characterized by the future hope of the δόξα of God (5:3-5, 8:18-26).

Indeed, we would suggest that an excellent summary of Paul's apostolic defence in II Corinthians, against the accusation that the suffering and general lack of impressiveness which characterized his life was indicative of his exclusion from God's presence, can be found in Rom. 8:35-37, a passage

---

[21]We understand the genitive here to be subjective, with for example, Bultmann, p. 150; Bruce, p. 207; and Barrett, II Corinthians, p. 167; against Héring, p. 42.

which refers to Paul's understanding of the significance of the new covenant for all Christians. In these verses Paul asks the question as to who can separate God's elect from the love of Christ -- the presence of God as made possible and made manifest in Christ crucified -- and answers his own question by affirming that nothing in all creation can cause such a separation:

> [35]"Shall tribulation, or distress, or persecution or famine or nakedness, or peril, or the sword? [36]As it is written,
>
>> "For thy sake we are being killed all the day long;
>> we are regarded as sheep to be slaughtered."
>
> [37]No, in all these things we are more than conquerors through him who loved us.[22] (RSV)

This understanding of Paul's argument in II Corinthians 2:14-3:18, as summarized above, is, then, the one that we intend to defend now, and to do so by examining the text and its vocabulary in some detail. We shall begin with an examination of II Cor. 2:14-17, and, in particular, with the preposition "κατέναντι," a rare word but of critical importance for a proper understanding of Paul's conception both of valid apostolic ministry and of the Christian experience of God's presence in general.

---

[22]The connection between the vocabulary of Rom. 8:35b and the vocabulary which Paul uses to describe his life in II Corinthians is remarkable. That is, every word in Rom. 8:35b except μάχαιρα appears in II Corinthians: θλῖψις 6:4, 7:4; στενοχωρία, 6:4, 12:10; διωγμός, 12:10; λιμός, 11:27; γυμνότης 5:3; κίνδυνος 11:26.

PART TWO

EXEGESIS OF II CORINTHIANS 2:14-3:18

CHAPTER FOUR

II Corinthians:14-17

I. THE IMPORTANCE OF THE PRESENCE OF GOD IN II CORINTHIANS 2:14-17: THE USE OF Κατέναντι IN II COR. 2:17

Possible Meanings of Κατέναντι: Figurative or Literal?

The reason for beginning our exegesis of II Cor. 2:14-3:18 with a study of the preposition "κατέναντι," which Paul uses in the phrase "κατέναντι θεοῦ" both in II Cor. 2:17 and in II Cor.12:19, is that if it can be established that in all likelihood the apostle is using the word in the literal sense of "opposite, before, in the presence of, in the sight of,"[1] then a foundation will have been laid for affirming Paul's continuing interest in the subject of God's presence throughout the passage. Only three times in the extant letters of Paul is the word κατέναντι used.[2] Two of the occasions, to which we have just referred, are in II Corinthians -- 2:17 and 12:19 -- while the third is in

---

[1]W. Bauer, A Greek-English Lexicon of the New Testament and Other Early Christian Literature, 4th ed., trans. and ed. W. F. Arndt and F. W. Gingrich (Chicago: University of Chicago Press, 1955), p. 422.

[2]In both II Cor. 2:17 and 12:19 the variant reading of κατενώπιον for κατέναντι is attested by some witnesses. The unanimous consent of scholarly opinion is that the reading of κατέναντι, supported in both 2:17 and 12:19 by P46, ℵ*, A, B, etc., is correct. We should note, however, that in the two other uses of κατενώπιον in the wider Pauline literature, Eph. 1:4 and Col. 1:22, the use is literal, referring to the Christian's entering the presence of God in heaven on the day of judgment. Furthermore, in the seven possible LXX usages of κατενώπιον, Lev. 4:17, Josh. 1:5, 3:7, 21:44, 23:9; Ps. 43:16; and Dan. 5:22, the literal understanding dominates, with the only pentateuchal reference, Lev. 4:17, being a cultic reference concerning the priestly sprinkling of blood "ἔναντι κυρίου κατενώπιον τοῦ καταπετάσματος τοῦ ἁγίου" -- before the Lord in front of the holy veil.

Romans 4:17, within the grammatically difficult phrase referring to Abraham, "κατέναντι οὗ ἐπίστευσεν θεοῦ." Although we shall refer in the course of the following discussion to the understanding of κατέναντι in the latter two references, II Cor.12:19 and Rom.4:17, the main concern of this section will be to assess its probable meaning in II Cor.2:17, which reads as follows:

οὐ γάρ ἐσμεν ὡς οἱ πολλοί καπηλεύοντες τὸν λόγον τοῦ θεοῦ,
ἀλλ' ὡς ἐξ εἰλικρινείας, ἀλλ' ὡς ἐκ θεοῦ
κατέναντι θεοῦ ἐν Χριστῷ λαλοῦμεν.

For we are not like so many, peddlers of God's word;
but as men of sincerity, as commissioned by God,
in the sight of God we speak in Christ. (RSV)

The RSV here has chosen to translate κατέναντι by the phrase "in the sight of," which is one of the options presented by Bauer-Arndt-Gingrich (*BAG4*); the other options, as we have noted above, being "opposite" (the most common meaning in the NT, as in Matt. 21:2 and parallels; Mark 12:41 and 13:3) or "in the presence of"/"before" (as in Matt. 27:24, Rom. 4:17). While the use of "opposite" can only have a locative sense if applied to II Cor. 2:17 (assuming Paul is not saying that he is "opposing" God!) the other possible senses given by *BAG4* can also have a figurative sense.

In this latter case, for example, Paul's declaration that he speaks κατέναντι θεοῦ ἐν Χριστῷ would amount either to an assertion of his willingness to defend the integrity of his character *even before God himself*, that is, even before the court of God's estimation, or to his general sense of openness and responsibility towards God rather than people -- the person of God being more important to him than people and acting as a determining factor in his relationships with all others. In either event, although Paul might well have sensed that God's presence was a reality, and not merely hypothetical, the major thrust of this use of κατέναντι in both cases would not have been to assert that reality, but to defend his integrity.[3]

---

[3]Van Unnik, "'With Unveiled Face': An Exegesis of 2 Corinthians 3:12-18," NovT 6 (July 1963): 158, and Plummer, p. 74, understand κατέναντι in terms of Paul's stressing God's presence as witness to his sincerity. Hering, p. 20; Rissi, p. 67; Bultmann, p. 70; Barrett, II Corinthians, p. 104; and Furnish, p. 179, consider Paul to be describing the fact that the presence of God is of more importance to him than that of humans when it comes to his sense of responsibility. Martin, p. 50, without further comment, adopts the literal translation, "in the presence of God."

Bultmann's comments are worth quoting to illustrate the general scholarly thrust which, while not denying the literal sense of God's presence, nevertheless feels that Paul is not merely (or primarily) attempting to assert the literal fact that he is a man who stands in God's presence

The appeal of this figurative interpretation has influenced the great majority of commentators, and would seem to find support in two further observations. The more general observation would be that Paul elsewhere appeals to the court of God's judgment, albeit in other words, in precisely this kind of way. Thus, for example, in II Cor. 1:23, Paul calls God to witness against him concerning the truth of his explanation to the Corinthians as to why he did not visit them as previously promised ("Έγὼ δὲ μάρτυρα τὸν θεὸν ἐπικαλοῦμαι ἐπὶ τὴν ἐμὴν ψυχήν . . .").Similar oath formulae and assertions of the unimportance of human opinion in comparison with God's can easily be found elsewhere in Paul: for example, in I Cor. 4:2-4, II Cor. 11:31 and Gal. 1:20.

The more immediate observation on which the figurative interpretation of κατέναντι might be based is that in 2:17 the issue does in fact seem at first glance to be one in which Paul's integrity, as in II Cor. 1:23 above, is being challenged; so that a reference to God as judge or witness would seem to be highly appropriate. Specifically, the question at issue seems to be whether or not Paul has acted "ὡς ἐξ εἰλικρινείας," as from sincerity -- *sincerity* being the sense of εἰλικρίνεια given by the majority of translations and commentators.[4] In this interpretation of Paul's use of εἰλικρίνεια, the phrase "ἐκ θεοῦ, κατέναντι θεοῦ," would serve to guarantee or to affirm the nature of his sincerity: open to God's view to be assessed by him if need be (in line with the first figurative possibility suggested above).

The Cultic Significance of Εἰλικρίνεια as a Possible Key to Translating Κατέναντι

The word "εἰλικρίνεια," however, can have a sense other than *sincerity*. Indeed, Friedrich Büschel points out that the noun originally signified *purity*,

---

by his claims in 2:17: "The κατέναντι θεοῦ denotes the apostle as speaking before God's eyes, answerable to God . . . . The ἐν Χριστῷ is used in a locative sense, as in verse 14 and denotes a new creature belonging to the new world of Christ." What we wish to stress as remarkable, and what Bultmann's comments hint at without making the connection (like many others), is that being "in Christ" in a locative sense results in being κατέναντι θεοῦ in a literal sense: the new world which Christ has made possible is a world which "is full of the knowledge of the glory (the presence) of God" (Hab. 2:14).

[4]The interpretation of εἰλικρίνεια as sincerity can be seen, for example in the KJV, RSV, NEB, NIV, and GNB; as well as in the commentaries of Martin, p. 50; Furnish, p. 179; Barrett, II Corinthians, p. 104; Plummer, p. 74; and Bruce, p. 189.

while the adjective, "εἰλικρινής" meant *pure* or *spotless*.[5] To be sure, the word is never used at all in the canonical LXX,[6] and thus, among other reasons, it may never have occurred to Paul to use the word in its *original sense*. Paul's own use elsewhere, however, infrequent as it may be, points strongly to this particular emphasis, and leads us, we shall argue, to consider the possibility that Paul may in fact be using κατέναντι not figuratively at all, but quite literally.

Paul uses the noun three times and the adjective once. In this latter case, the reference is in Paul's letter to the Christians in the church in Philippi in connection with their imminent appearing before the presence of Christ as those who are "εἰλικρινεῖς καὶ ἀπρόσκοποι" -- "pure and blameless" (RSV, Phil. 1:10). In this context the issue of sincerity (though sincerity or integrity may be one aspect of purity or blamelessness) is clearly not central to Paul's thought.

In the case of Paul's use of the noun, εἰλικρίνεια, its only occurrence outside II Corinthians is in I Cor. 5:8, and its context is that of moral admonition: in I Cor. 5:1-8, Paul is lamenting the tolerance of sexual immorality in the Corinthian congregation, and is telling the Corinthians how they ought to respond to such an evil. The moral admonitions which Paul provides, however, and the rationale supporting them, are clearly couched in terms of the responsibilities of cult and temple. Thus, Paul attempts to persuade the Corinthians to change their ways by arguing that the appropriate manner of the Christian life is to live without the "old leaven" of malice and evil, but to live instead with the unleavened bread of "εἰλικρινείας καὶ ἀληθείας." The RSV translates εἰλικρινεία here by "sincerity," and yet the more general cultic sense of the word, "purity," is undoubtedly more appropriate in the context of Paul's argument.

---

[5]F. Büschel, "εἰλικρίνεια," TDNT 2, pp. 397-98.
[6]Εἰλικρινής, however, does occur in Wis.Sol. 7:25, in the phrase "τῆς . . δόξης εἰλικρινής" which refers to the purity (not sincerity!) of God's glory. In both Josephus and Philo the word is used, and though it is used to describe generally moral behavior, the association with the word "καθαρωτής" (cleanness, purity) in both writers indicates, along with other contextual evidence, the cultic framework within which the word finds meaning. In Josephus, see BJ II. 345; in Philo, see De Somnis Liber II. 20, 74, 134; Quis Rerum Divinorum Heres 308; Legum Allegoriae 88; De Specialibus Legibus I. 99.

The comments of Michael Newton on Paul's understanding of the relationship between cult and morality in this passage are clearly pertinent. Newton writes:[7]

> Windisch, commenting on ζύμη (leaven) in I Corinthians 5:6, describes Paul here as changing the cultic command into a moral injunction and sees this as "an important example of the translation of cultic concepts into ethical." This is not the case; for there is a cultic element still in the forefront of Paul's thinking. He is dealing with what he considers to be the Temple of God, the Church, and as such it has cultic demands, namely the necesssity of purity within its precincts. To point out the fact that the purity Paul calls for stems from what the modern mind sees as moral questions (sexual immorality, greed, etc.) only clouds the issue. Such a division between the realm of cult and that of morality would never have occurred to the semitic mind. The important thing was that vice, in any form, was seen to be impure, and thus inappropriate for the household of God.

The remaining two occasions in which Paul uses εἰλικρίνεια both occur in II Corinthians, the second occurrence being in our own text, 2:17, while the first is in 1:12. In this first occurrence, 1:12, the cultic thrust of the use observed in I Corinthians 5:8 seems to be maintained, for Paul speaks of εἰλικρίνεια in conjunction with a clearly cultic term, ἁγιότης, meaning "holiness."

To be sure, some scholars are in ageement with the Nestle Greek text in choosing a variant for ἁγιότης, "ἁπλότης," a word which signifies generosity, frankness, simplicity or sincerity.[8] However, the reasons for such a choice according to Metzger and Furnish, for example, are certainly not based on the external witness of the ancient texts, which strongly favors ἁγιότης (P46 ℵ* A B C K P Ψ, etc.). Rather the case is argued on the basis of the internal evidence that Paul nowhere else uses ἁγιότης, but does use ἁπλότης, and, furthermore, that the context seems to require a word meaning simplicity or candor, not only because Paul here is defending his frankness with the Corinthians, but also because ἁπλότης would then

---

[7]M. Newton, The Concept of Purity at Qumran and in the Letters of Paul (Cambridge: University Press, 1985), p. 92. See also n. 78, p. 143.

[8]So, BAG4, p. 85. Among those adopting the alternate reading, "ἁπλότης," are Furnish, p. 127; Barrett, II Corinthians, p. 71, Metzger A Textual Commentary on the Greek New Testament (London: United Bible Societies, 1975), p. 575; Martin, p. 18. Preferring ἁγιότης are Bultmann, p. 33; Newton, p. 143, n. 78; and Thrall, "2 Corinthians 1:12: ΑΓΙΟΤΗΤΙ or ΑΠΛΟΤΗΤΙ?" in Studies in New Testament Language and Text, NovTSup 44, ed. J. K. Elliott (Leiden: Brill, 1976), p. 372.

function as a term somewhat parallel to εἰλικρίνεια, understood as sincerity.

As Margaret Thrall has indicated, however, the lack of Pauline use of ἁγιότης elsewhere might just as easily have provided a reason for a scribe to change the text from the unfamiliar to the familiar as vice versa.[9] Moreover, to argue from the context to determine that ἁγιότης was a word that Paul would have been unlikely to use is quite possibly to prejudge the intent of the context, especially when the manuscript evidence for ἁγιότης is so impressive. Thus, for example, although it cannot be denied that the immediate context is one in which Paul needed to assert his consistent frankness and lack of vacillation (see II Cor. 1:12-2:1), and is thus one in which Paul could well have chosen to use a term of general moral connotation such as ἁπλότης, yet, if, as Newton argues, Paul's understanding of his own life and of the moral life of the Church were conceived by him not merely for convenience but fundamentally in terms of cult, then both ἁγιότης, "holiness," and εἰλικρίνεια, in the sense of "purity," would have been terms which would have been entirely appropriate to use in describing the integrity of his character: for the cultic attributes of holiness and purity were ones that also described the *essential* qualities of those who could gain valid access to and who were allowed to live within the church, which, to Paul, was the "temple of God," the dwelling place of God by his Spirit (see I Cor. 3:16-17).[10]

In attempting to assess the significance of εἰλικρίνεια in its only remaining occurrence in the New Testament, II Cor. 2:17, then, it seems reasonable to claim that the cultic association of the word in other contexts may well be a factor in its continued employment. Thus, if, as seems certain, Paul is using the word here in the immediate context of defending the morality of his behavior in the face of a charge that in some way his behavior was unacceptable (to people or to God), then it could well be argued that he is doing so in a way that intends to affirm not merely his sincerity and general moral character, but much more his cultic purity, and thus his continued right to live within the sphere of God's presence, a presence which, as in the Temple, demands such purity.

---

[9]Thrall, "2 Corinthians 1:12," p. 368.

[10]Newton's comments on the text, p. 143, n. 78, are precisely to the point: "In 2 Cor. 1:12 (Paul) describes his life in the world and before the Corinthians as being enacted with holiness ἁγιότης (cf. Heb. 12:10) and εἰλικρίνεια τοῦ θεοῦ. . . . Paul has behaved as befits one who is in God's service, with both holiness and purity. He has been set apart for this service like the priests who performed their duties in the Temple."

Indeed, this possible understanding of εἰλικρίνεια in terms of cultic purity draws us back to the original discussion concerning the use of κατέναντι in II Cor. 2:17, and does so with the conviction that it is by no means impossible that the word is *not* functioning figuratively, or not merely functioning figuratively (we do not need to deny the possibility of a double emphasis), but rather quite literally, as part of a declaration by Paul that God is not only his witness, but that God is the one in whose presence he lives; a standing before God (κατέναντι θεοῦ) which is inviolate -- for, however he is perceived to have behaved, he remains as one who is pure, and thus acceptable to God.

The question that must be raised now is whether there is any evidence outside II Cor. 2:17 for believing that not just εἰλικρίνεια but κατέναντι as well had for Paul an inherent association with cultic matters, signifying, for example, that when one stood "κατέναντι θεου" then, as in a cultic location such as the temple or Mount Sinai, one was literally standing "opposite, before, in the sight of," and thus in some sense "in the presence of" God. To attempt to answer this question we shall consider the use of the word both in the LXX, in the New Testament in general, and in Pauline passages other than II Cor. 2:17.

Before proceeding further, however, three aspects of our discussion need to be emphasised or re-emphasised. First, it is obvious that no amount of evidence from other use can "prove" that Paul's use of κατέναντι in II Cor.2:17 is literal rather than figurative. Paul is not necessarily bound by use elsewhere. Rather, our intention is to see if the evidence from other use simply opens the door to this literal possibility in Paul. Our study, consequently, does not need to be exhaustive of all uses of κατέναντι everywhere![11]

Second, to repeat ourselves, our argument is not necessarily for an exclusively literal interpretation of the phrase κατέναντι θεοῦ. Clearly we

---

[11]A computer search of 46 Hellenistic authors (including, for example, Dio Chrysostom, Epictetus, and Galen) found κατέναντι in only eight (Clement of Alexandria, Clement of Rome, Irenaeus, Joseph and Aseneth, Lucian, Sibylline Oracles, Origen, and Theophilus of Antioch). In these eight, the word occurs 29 times. Twenty are quotes from usage in the LXX or New Testament (nineteen of these are in works by Origen). All but four occurrences were concerned with defining location (opposite, before, to the east of, etc.). These four occurrences, two each in Joseph and Aseneth, 28:3-5, and in Irenaeus, Fragmenta, 23.2; 44:2, have the meaning unattested in BAG4 of opposite in the sense of "against" or "contrary to." See, for example, the translation of the Joseph and Aseneth passage by C. Burchard in OTP1, pp. 245-46.

believe that such an interpretation could stand. However, if Paul intended a double understanding, figurative and literal, or figurative because literal, then our purposes will still have been served.

Third, we are not arguing that Paul uses κατέναντι in the sense of "in the presence of" *as opposed to* the sense of "opposite" or "before" or any other variation. As we have already noted, *BAG4* provides a variety of possible meanings. We use the phrase "in the presence of" merely as the one most clearly expressing the thrust of our argument: if Paul intended to say that he was in God's presence as one actually "opposite" (that is, facing) God, or as "before" God, then such an understanding is, once again, sufficient for our purposes.

The Use of Κατέναντι in the LXX

In contrast to εἰλικρίνεια, which appears nowhere in the LXX, κατέναντι occurs there on approximately eighty occasions. Of these cases some carry the sense of "against" (e.g., Ezek. 3:9, Sir. 29:13), while others specify a direction to the east (e.g., Gen. 2:14, II Chr. 4:10, Ezek. 11:1). The great majority, however, have the the range of meanings represented by "in front of," "facing," "opposite," "before," "in sight of," and "in the presence of." Of this latter group, on approximately fourteen occasions (nearly twenty per cent of the total use) connection is made in the text, or in the close context, with matters of cult.

Thus, for example, the desire of Isaiah (38:20) is to sing Psalms all the days of his life "κατέναντι τοῦ οἴκου τοῦ θεοῦ"; while Daniel (3:3, 7) will not not worship κατέναντι the image of Nebuchadnezzar, but prays κατέναντι Jerusalem (6:11). Furthermore, Ezekiel (44:4) finds himself brought κατέναντι the eschatological Temple, from which point he can see that it was filled with glory (δόξης).The Psalmist, on the other hand, uses κατέναντι to describe the lot of the lawless (5:6, LXX) as those who cannot stand κατέναντι God's eyes -- not that the sense is figurative, for the contrast is immediately made with the Psalmist himself who, unlike the lawless, has the right to enter God's house and worship before God's presence there (Ps. 5:8, LXX).

The only two occurrences of a possible figurative use of κατέναντι are also in the Psalms (25:3, 43:16, LXX), where the Psalmist speaks of God's mercy as κατέναντι his eyes, and his own humiliation as always κατέναντι him. In this latter case, however, there is something almost concrete and visible about the Psalmist's humiliation -- as if he cannot get it out of his sight --, and in the former case, where "*mercy* is before his eyes," the reference seems to be to the fact that the Psalmist spends his day at the altar (θυσιαστήριον, Ps. 25:5) in the Temple -- where God's *mercy* in the form of atoning sacrifice is quite literally to be seen.

This connection between κατέναντι and the altar (θυσιαστήριον) in the Jerusalem Temple is apparent not only in the Psalter, but in the writings of the Chronicler (II Chr. 6:12, 22; 32:12), who regards this position (κατέναντι τοῦ θυσιαστηρίου) as significant precisely because a sacrifice (or prayer, 6:12; or oath, 6:22) made there is made κατέναντι God himself. Furthermore, a similar understanding is apparent in the use of κατέναντι in Exod. 32:5 and 32:11 (Alexandrian text), a section of the Old Testament which, as we shall argue later, seems to have been in Paul's mind as he wrote to the Corinthians (see below, p. 143). In this Exodus narrative Aaron builds an altar κατέναντι the golden calf, the emphasis being entirely literal, as if the altar was placed immediately in front of the idol. In contrast to, and to counter such worship, Moses' immediate response, on the other hand, is to plead for mercy for the Israelites κατέναντι κυρίου τοῦ θεοῦ, "before the Lord God."

Only four further occurrences of κατέναντι appear in the Pentateuch. Three of these are in Genesis and can be translated by the phrase "to the East of" (Gen. 2:14; 4:16; 50:13). The other occurrence is in Num. 17:4 (17:19, LXX) in which Moses is told to confront a rebellion against his authority by taking twelve rods and placing them in the tent of testimony before the testimony (κατέναντι τοῦ μαρτυρίου), where God would make himself known. What is noteworthy about this particular situation is that the "testimony" is clearly understood as the location of the manifestation of the presence of God himself (cf. Num. 17:7, 9; LXX, 17:22, 24): thus to be in the tent of testimony is to be, as in Exod. 32:11, κατέναντι κυρίου τοῦ θεοῦ.[12]

The evidence from the LXX for the figurative use of κατέναντι, then, is almost non-existent, with no evidence at all of its use within an oath formula to indicate the presence of God as a witness, or as the one to whom one considers oneself accountable. Indeed, of the five references in *BAG4*,

---

[12]According to Martin Noth, Numbers: A Commentary (Philadelphia: Westminster, 1968), p. 131, the "testimony" here refers to the "ark" of the covenant.

other than in II Corinthians, supposedly indicating a figurative sense of κατέναντι, three are clearly literal (Judith 12:15,19; Sib.Or. 3:489-98, where the expression is κατέναντι θεοῦ, one is literal and associated with cult (Sir. 50:19); leaving only one which is in some sense figurative (Sir. 28:26). Thus, the overwhelming use in the LXX is literal and locative in one way or another (i.e., "before," "in front of," etc.), and its frequent occurrence in relation to the cult refers specifically to the literal position of a person in front of, facing, and in the presence of holy space, such as the Temple with its altar, and consequently, in the presence of God himself.

Non-Pauline New Testament Use of Κατέναντι

In the New Testament, outside of the Pauline literature, κατέναντι is used six times. Three are gospel parallels (Matt. 21:2, Mark 11:2; Luke 19:30) and refer to a request by Jesus that his disciples, having come near to the Mount of Olives, go into the village "opposite." Another occurrence is in Matt. 27:24 which refers to Pilate's washing his hands "before" a crowd of people. The final two references, in Mark 12:41 and 13:3, are to Jesus sitting "opposite" or "facing" the treasury and temple respectively. In each of the six cases the sense is literal: the issue is location, with proximity (in these cases, visual) being assumed.

Paul's Use of Κατέναντι in Romans 4:17

The only use of κατέναντι by Paul outside II Corinthians occurs in Rom. 4:17, a verse which, with its context, is grammatically complex. The RSV of Rom. 4:16-17 reads as follows:

> [16] That is why it depends on faith, in order that the promise may rest on grace and be guaranteed to all his descendants--not only to the adherents of the law but also to those who share the faith of Abraham, for he is the father of us all, [17] as it is written, "I have made you the father of many nations" -- in the presence of (κατέναντι) the God in whom he believed, who gives life to the dead and calls into existence the things that do not exist.

The above translation is sufficiently accurate to enable us to assess the basic issue involved in interpreting κατέναντι: the issue being to determine whether the word refers to what precedes it or to what follows. In the former case, for example, κατέναντι would refer back to the words "descendants" or "father of us all" in v.16, to imply that Gentiles and Jews together are descendants of Abraham "in the sight of God" (in God's judgment or estimation).[13] In the latter case, κατέναντι would refer forward to the position in which Abraham stood in relation to God when he chose to exercise faith (he was in God's presence).[14] Among the scholars adopting the latter interpretation are Ernst Käsemann and Matthew Black who both argue cogently against the former view by claiming that the flow of the grammar leads far more naturally to the connection of κατέναντι with what follows (οὗ ἐπίστευσεν) than with what precedes.[15] Furthermore, Sanday and Headlam observe that this understanding would be quite comprehensible in the light of the Genesis account of Abraham's faith, which did indeed find expression in God's presence (see, e.g., Gen. 17:1).[16]

While it might seem hard to see why Paul would want, either in reference to Gen. 17:1-27 or to Gen. 15:1-21 (the passage to which he clearly refers in Rom. 4:3), to emphasize the position of Abraham as being "in the presence" of God as he believed (unless, as we have suggested, it was of general importance for Jews, and for Paul in particular, to emphasize that the righteous life was conceived fundamentally as living in God's presence), nevertheless it seems possible that some indication of Paul's rationale might be provided by the adoption of a tentative proposal made by C.K. Barrett.[17] Barrett's proposal is that in Rom. 4:17 Paul had in mind not only, or primarily, the faith of Abraham expressed in Gen. 15 or Gen. 17, but rather the faith of Abraham as expressed in Gen. 22:1-19, the story of Abraham's willingness to sacrifice Isaac on Mount Moriah. Our own observation based on this proposal would be that Jewish tradition as embodied, for example, in II Chronicles 3:1, explicitly equated Mount Moriah with Mount Zion and the Jerusalem Temple, God's dwelling place on earth (cf. II Chr. 5:11-6:2),[18] so that it would not be impossible that the phrase

---

[13]So, e.g., C. E. B. Cranfield, A Critical and Exegetical Commentary on the Epistle to the Romans, vol. 1 (Edinburgh: T. & T. Clark, 1975), p. 243; J. Murray, The Epistle to the Romans, vol. 1 (Grand Rapids: Eerdmans, 1959), p. 146; J. Calvin, The Epistles of Paul to the Romans and Thessalonians, trans. Ross Mackenzie (Grand Rapids: Eerdmans, 1973) p. 95; C. K. Barrett, The Epistle to the Romans (New York: Harper & Bros., 1957), p. 96; and the NEB.

[14]So, for example, Wm. Sanday and A. C. Headlam, A Critical and Exegetical Commentary on the Epistle to the Romans (Edinburgh: T. & T. Clark, 1911), p. 113; Matthew Black, Romans (Greenwood, S. C.: Attic Press, 1973), p. 79; Ernst Käsemann, Commentary on Romans, trans. G. Bromiley (Grand Rapids: Eerdmans, 1980), pp. 117, 121; and C. H. Dodd, The Epistle to the Romans (London: Hodder & Stoughton, 1932), p. 67.

[15]Käsemann, p. 121; Black, p. 79.

[16]Sanday & Headlam, p. 113.

[17]Barrett, Romans, pp. 97 and 99.

[18]See von Rad's comments on the significance of Mount Moriah in Genesis 22:2 in his Genesis: A Commentary, trans. J. H. Marks (Philadelphia: Westminster, 1961), p. 235.

"κατέναντι οὗ" in Rom. 4:17 could have been intended by Paul as a reference to Mount Moriah, thus pointing to the incident with Isaac as one in which Abraham exercised faith in the resurrection power of God, who, according to the writer of Hebrews at least, in providing an alternative sacrifice for Isaac, figuratively raised Isaac from the dead (cf. Heb. 11:19).

Whether or not this latter argument has any validity, the possibility, and, indeed, the probability, remains that Paul's use of κατέναντι in Rom. 4:17 was literal, and referred to his physical location in relation to God.

Paul's Use of Κατέναντι in II Cor. 12:19

The remaining occurrence of κατέναντι outside II Cor. 2:17 is in II Cor. 12:19, where, as in Romans, the two approaches to interpretation, literal and figurative, are both conceivable. II Cor. 12:19 reads as follows:

Πάλαι δοκεῖτε ὅτι ὑμῖν ἀπολογούμεθα
κατέναντι θεοῦ ἐν Χριστῷ λαλοῦμεν·
τὰ δὲ πάντα, ἀγαπητοί, ὑπὲρ τῆς ὑμῶν οἰκοδομῆς.

Have you been thinking all along that we have been defending
   ourselves before you?
It is in the sight of God that we have been speaking in Christ,
and all this for your upbuilding, beloved. (RSV)

The immediate impression given by the RSV could well be that the contrast that Paul makes between the first and second halves of the verse is between the Corinthians and God, as if Paul were primarily arguing that he was accountable to God rather than to the Corinthians. In this event κατέναντι would function figuratively, which is, in fact, the understanding of the majority of commentators.[19]

Victor Furnish's discussion of the passage,[20] however, stands in clear distinction from the interpretation of the majority (although he is by no means alone in his assessment, which is shared, for example, by Bultmann and Martin).[21] That is, Furnish completely by-passes any discussion of the

---

[19]Bruce, p. 251; Plummer, p. 365; Barrett, II Corinthians, p. 328; Bultmann, p. 237; P. E. Hughes, Paul's Second Letter to the Corinthians (Grand Rapids: Eerdmans, 1962), p. 469.
[20]Furnish, pp. 566-67.
[21]Bultmann, p. 237: "The motive behind Paul's statement is not self-defense but the edification or furtherance of the community." Also Martin, p. 452.

possibility that Paul was attempting to clarify the issue as to who it is before
whom he speaks, and insists instead that Paul's concern was rather to attempt
to clarify the *type of writing* that he had just laid before the Corinthians --
whether he had been writing a "self-defense" or *apologia*, or whether he had
been writing in full apostolic authority with the effect that through his words
it was in fact the voice of Christ which could be heard. The argument
provided by Furnish in defense of this view is mainly based on the context,
which is connected with the Corinthian demand made explicit in II Cor. 13:3
for Paul to demonstrate that Christ is speaking through him -- a demand in
the light of which any type of self-defense, whether "before the Corinthians"
or "before God" would seem more like petty self-interest than apostolic
concern.

Furnish's position seems to be basically sound, although he does not deal
explicitly with the positive function of κατέναντι within the verse. In this
regard, our main observation would be that his argument makes the figurative
use of κατέναντι to be unlikely, and opens the door to the possibility that
Paul's intent is quite literal -- claiming that when he speaks he does so
"κατέναντι θεοῦ ἐν Χριστῷ," as one who literally, through Christ, stands
in God's presence, and who thus speaks with apostolic authority.

Indeed, one further observation of our own should be added: that a
specific connection between cult and the use of κατέναντι in II Cor. 12:19
cannot be ruled out, for Paul here employs the word "οἰκοδομή,"
"upbuilding," a word used in the LXX in reference to the building and
structure of the Temple.[22] To be sure, it might be futile to press this
observation too far, for οἰκοδομή used in the sense of "edification" certainly
need have no necessary connection to a literal building, let alone a
temple,[23] and was used in Jeremiah to describe the prophet's task in
general.[24] Nevertheless it is surely pertinent to observe that Paul himself
in corresponding with the Corinthians (I Cor. 3:9-17) makes the connection
between the church conceived both as building (οἰκοδομή) and as temple

---

[22]See I Chron. 26:27; 29:1; and Ezek. 40:2. The only other occurrences of οἰκοδομή in the
LXX are in Ezek. 16:61 where it means "household," and Ezek. 17:17, where it means the
process of building. Paul also uses the verb οἰκοδομέω (Rom. 15:20; I Cor. 8:1, 10; 10:23; 14:4,
17; Gal. 2:18; I Thess. 5:11), which is used more frequently in the LXX, often in association
with the building of the temple or of altars. For example, see, Gen. 8:20; 13:18; 22:9 (the
building of the altar at Moriah. See note 17 above); I Kings 8:13-20; Ps. 77:69, LXX; Dan. 9:25.
[23]See BAG4, p. 561.
[24]Furnish, p. 467, claims that Paul's use of οἰκοδομή probably derives from Jeremiah. See
LXX Jer. 1:10; 24:6, etc.

(ναός), thus making it more than possible that he might have chosen this particular word, "οἰκοδομή," quite deliberately as a key word to describe the nature of the apostolic task (see, for example, II Cor. 10:8, 13:10):[25] the task being to *build a building* -- the Temple, the church of God -- in which one could live "κατέναντι θεοῦ," in the presence of God.

The Possible Meaning of Κατέναντι: Summary

The use of κατέναντι both in the LXX and in Pauline texts other than II Cor. 2:17, have shown us that the literal sense is far more dominant than the figurative. Indeed, although the latter cannot be ruled out as a possibilty, the association of κατέναντι with cultic matters, including the presence of God, makes it highly probable that when Paul speaks as one "κατέναντι θεοῦ," he is thinking of himself as standing literally in God's presence, as in the Temple or in a similar holy location. To draw this conclusion is not, however, to rule out utterly the figurative possibilities so commonly suggested in interpreting κατέναντι. Rather, it is to argue, as does Michael Newton, that the literal and cultic pattern of thought must not be considered as secondary or as merely useful, but as fundamental: that existence itself for Paul functions within a framework that is fundamentally cultic in orientation.

With such a conclusion we can now return to the remarks with which our study of κατέναντι began. That is, in our introduction we suggested that if it could be established that in all likelihood the apostle is using "κατέναντι" in its literal sense, to refer to his location "in the presence of" God, then a foundation would have been laid for suggesting Paul's broader interest in the subject of God's presence elsewhere in the passage. The question that arises now is whether the context of II Cor. 2:17 can sustain such a possibility. Consequently, it is with this question in mind that we need now to examine the context of II Cor. 2:17, II Cor. 2:14-17, verses regarded by some as introductory to much of the section which follows (II Cor. 2:14-7:4).[26]

---

[25]The importance of the words "οἰκοδομή" and "οἰκοδομεῖν" in describing the apostolic task is emphasized by Martin, pp. 310, 460; Furnish, p. 561. See also, P. Vielhauer, Oikodome (Munich: Kaiser Verlag, 1979), pp. 72-88. Vielhauer, pp. 81, 108, however, rejects any suggestion that the use is completely determined by the cultic connection (although he recognizes some connection as undeniable).

[26]For example, Thrall, JSNT 16, pp. 117-18; Collange, p. 40; and Furnish, p. 185.

II. CONFIRMATION OF THE IMPORTANCE OF THE PRESENCE OF GOD IN II CORINTHIANS 2:14-17: THE CULTIC ORIENTATION OF Ὀσμή AND Εὐωδία

Introduction

The text of II Cor. 2:14-17 is as follows:

[14]Τῷ δὲ θεῷ χάρις τῷ πάντοτε θριαμβεύοντι ἡμᾶς ἐν τῷ Χριστῷ καὶ τὴν ὀσμὴν τῆς γνώσεως αὐτοῦ φανεροῦντι δι' ἡμῶν ἐν παντὶ τόπῳ: [15]ὅτι Χριστοῦ εὐωδία ἐσμὲν τῷ θεῷ ἐν τοῖς σῳζομένοις καὶ ἐν τοῖς ἀπολλυμένοις, [16]οἷς μὲν ὀσμὴ ἐκ θανάτου εἰς θάνατον, οἷς δὲ ὀσμὴ ἐκ ζωῆς εἰς ζωήν. καὶ πρὸς ταῦτα τίς ἱκανός; [17]οὐ γάρ ἐσμεν ὡς οἱ πολλοὶ καπηλεύοντες τὸν λόγον τοῦ θεοῦ, ἀλλ' ὡς ἐξ εἰλικρινείας, ἀλλ' ὡς ἐκ θεοῦ κατέναντι θεοῦ ἐν Χριστῷ λαλοῦμεν.[27]

---

[27]In the body of our text we shall be arguing for the overall cultic significance of II Cor. 2:14-17. No mention will be made of the opening words, "Τῷ δὲ θεῷ χάρις," or of the possible significance in 2:14 of "πάντοτε" and "ἐν παντὶ τόπῳ." Some brief comments need to be made now, which, though not crucial to our argument, should nevertheless strengthen it.

With regard to the phrase "Τῷ δὲ θεῷ χάρις," the liturgical "flavor" of the wording has often been noted. For example, see Furnish, p. 186 (concerning vv. 14-17); Bultmann, p. 62; Martin, p. 45; Collange, p. 22.

With regard to "πάντοτε" and "ἐν παντὶ τόπῳ," some commentators ignore the words (Héring, Martin, Bruce), while Bultmann, p. 66, simply declares that they "correspond to the liturgical-hymnal character of the verse." Collange, p. 23 and Barrett, II Corinthians, p. 99, suggest that they reflect an affirmation of the absolute validity of the apostle's ministry, always and everywhere, while Collange adds that this clarification would be necessary in the face of opposition questioning.

While there is no reason to question the correctness of Barrett and Collange, the idiomatic use of the word "place" to refer to the synagogue, as mentioned by Furnish, p. 176, is an idea worth noting and developing. In particular, Helmut Koester, TDNT 8, pp. 193-200, has observed the technical association of "τόπος" as used in the LXX with the place in which God's name is present (e.g. Deut. 12:5,11), the place of justice (Deut. 17:8-9) worship and sacrifice (16:16; Lev. 4:24, 6:9, 18), and thus the Temple (I Kings 8:29). We should also note that Mt. Moriah, in the story of the sacrifice of Isaac (see above, p. 70), is called the "τόπον, ὃν εἶπεν αὐτῷ ὁ θεός" (LXX Gen. 22:3b).

What we want to suggest on the basis of this evidence is that whereas in Jerusalem-oriented Judaism, "every place" outside Jerusalem could be considered the place of exile, death, and abandonment by God (see LXX Jer. 8:3, ἐν παντὶ τόπῳ, and Ezek. 34:12, ἀπὸ παντὸς τόπου), and whereas there were explicit laws forbidding sacrifices in every place (ἐν παντὶ τόπῳ, LXX Deut. 12:12); and whereas the cult was regulated according to specific times and seasons (Deut. 16:16; Lev. 16:29), then Paul's comments in II Cor. 2:14, referring to the effect of his ministry "always" and "in every place" should not be read merely as indicating the permanent validity of his apostolic ministry, but as emphasizing the fundamentally cultic nature

Our main interest in turning now to II Cor. 2:14-17 is to find intial confirmation for the hypothesis that the presence of God is a theme of great importance for Paul in the context surrounding II Cor. 2:17, a verse in which Paul describes himself as a man who lives and speaks "in the presence of God." Such confirmation is itself important in that, if such can be found, the further hypothesis can then be made with confidence that the theme of God's presence can be understood to function as an interpretive key to Paul's argument not only in II Cor. 2:14-17, the immediate context of II Cor. 2:17, but also in II Cor. 3:1-18 and other passages in II Corinthians which function as the greater context.

In general, the issues which surround the interpretation of II Cor. 2:14-17 are exceedingly complex, focusing in particular on the reason for the shift in theme -- if such there be -- between 2:13 and 2:14;[28] on the understanding of θριαμβεύω (2:14);[29] on the significance of Paul's use of ὀσμή and

---

of that ministry, and its contrast, both in time and space, with the old cultic ministry associated with the Mosaic covenant.

[28]C. K. Barrett, II Corinthians, p. 96, sums up the problem of understanding the relationship between II Cor. 2:13 and 2:14 in writing as follows:

> That the epistle as we read it in the MSS here takes a sharp turn is beyond doubt.
> The story of Paul's anxious wait for Titus is abruptly dropped, and we hear no more
> of it until it is taken up, in language similar to that of 2:12 f., at 7:5.

While the abruptness and sense of discontinuity between 2:13 and 2:14 have led scholars such as Weiss and Bultmann to argue that 2:14-7:4 formed an originally distinct epistle, Matthias Rissi, pp. 63-65, on the other hand, has argued that there is less continuity between 2:13 and 7:5 than most scholars allow, and more continuity between 2:13 and 2:14, which he regards as being united by the common theme of Paul's love for the Corinthians. While we do not see that Paul's particular concern to demonstrate his love for the Corinthians is dominant in 2:14, nevertheless we agree with Rissi that the theme continues past 2:13, and can be found, for example, in 3:2.

The majority of scholars take a mediating position, rejecting the interpolation theory of 2:14-7:4, but without satisfactorily explaining the abrupt transition between 2:13 and 2:14. Margaret Thrall, JSNT 16, pp. 101-124, provides the best survey of scholarship on the problem (especially pp. 102-11). Our own proposed solution is given below, p. 87.

[29]An excellent summary of scholarship relating to the understanding of θριαμβεύω (2:14), a word which occurs elsewhere in the New Testament only in Col. 2:15, is provided by Furnish, pp. 174-75. The options which scholars and translations have provided in translating the word are roughly as follows:

a. Causeth us to triumph. So, KJV.

b. Leads us in triumph, as if Christians were Christ's triumphant soldiers. So, e.g., Barrett, II Corinthians, pp. 97-98.

c. Triumphs over us ("conquered by God"). So, Vulgate.

d. Leads us as captives in his triumphal procession. So, Lamar Williamson, "Led in Triumph: Paul's Use of θριαμβεύω," Int. 22 (July 1968): 317-32; NEB; GNB.

e. Puts us on display (no military connotation). So, R. Egan, "Lexical Evidence on Two Pauline Passages," NovT 19 (January 1977): 34-62.

εὐωδία -- odor and fragrance (2:14-16);[30] and on the understanding of the question, "Who is sufficient for these things?"(2:16b).[31] Given the diversity of scholarly opinion on the possible resolutions to each of these issues, it is clear that to discuss them all in any detail here would be to risk losing sight of our main interest. Our procedure, therefore, will be to focus on only one, with the intention of applying the results from our discussion to the other issues in only a very general manner. In this regard, the issue that will draw our initial and primary attention is the one that concerns the reason for Paul's employment of words relating to the sense of smell -- ὀσμή and εὐωδία -- to describe the manner in which he spreads the knowledge of God.

Although the words "ὀσμή" and "εὐωδία" appear quite frequently in the LXX, their occurrence in the broader Pauline literature is limited to our passage of particular interest, II Cor. 2:14-16, as well as Phil. 4:18 and Eph. 5:2. In these passages neither word appears without the other, and in the latter two the words are intimately connected in the genitival phrase, "ὀσμήν εὐωδίας," meaning "fragrant offering" (RSV), or more literally, "odor of fragrance."

---

f. Leads us in shame and humiliation. So, P. Marshall, "A Metaphor of Social Shame: θριαμβεύειν," NovT 25 (October 1983): 302-17.

In addition to these positions which Furnish surveys, two other suggestions need to be mentioned. First, Scott Hafemann, Suffering and the Spirit, p. 39, argues that the term means being led to death. Second, George Findlay (see Egan, p. 35) suggests the understanding of being led in festal or choral procession. While Egan is not particularly impressed with Findlay's suggestion, James I. H. McDonald, JSNT 17, pp. 37-40, gives it a measure of credit:

"In 2 Cor. 2:14, Paul bursts into a song of thanksgiving . . . . He has also a temple theology: 'we are the temple of the living God' (6:16) . . . . I find this an attractive idea: θριαμβεύω as 'lead in celebration' fits the context well and may have been linked in Paul's mind with his temple theology. But the lexical difficulty remains."

The lexical difficulty concerns the lack of explicit evidence, rather than merely circumstantial evidence, for the use of θριαμβεύω in this manner.

On the other hand, we would add, there can be no doubt that Plutarch's use of θριαμβεύω, Plutarch's Lives: Aemilius Paulus, XXX-XXXVI (late first century, early second century), in the context of a triumphant military procession demonstrates clearly not only that the procession was a political event, but a religious one as well (see especially, XXXII.2; XXXIII.1). The use, then, of this essentially military image (if θριαμβεύω is understood as such) in a passage (2:14-17) which is fundamentally cultic would not have been surprising or out of place. While we do not intend to espouse any one position just now, nevertheless we would suggest that (c), (d), (e), in any combination, along with Scott Hafemann's position, would fit the context well (see below, pp. 88).

[30]On the significance of ὀσμή and εὐωδία (2:14-16), see below, pp. 78 -86.

[31]On the question of "sufficiency," (2:16c) see Bultmann, pp. 70-71; Barrett, II Corinthians, p. 102; Furnish, p. 190; Rissi, pp. 65-66.

The Case for Interpreting ὀσμή
and Εὐωδία in terms of Cult

Paul's Use of ὀσμή and εὐωδία outside II Corinthians. The context
of both occurrences of the words in the Pauline literature outside II
Corinthians implies that their usage is linked to the cult. Thus, in writing to
the Philippians, for example, Paul describes a gift sent to him by the
Christians in Philippi not only as a "fragrant offering" (ὀσμήν εὐωδίας), but
as a "θυσίαν δεκτήν, εὐάρεστον τῷ θεῷ" -- a sacrifice acceptable and
pleasing to God" (4:18, RSV). Moreover, in the Ephesian context the same
sacrificial terminology is apparent in the description of Christ as "θυσίαν τῷ
θεῷ εἰς ὀσμὴν εὐωδίας" -- "a fragrant offering and sacrifice to God" (5:2,
RSV).

The Use of ὀσμή and εὐωδία in the LXX. That the Pauline use of the
words "ὀσμή" and "εὐωδία" should occur in the context of terms which are
manifestly associated with the cult should not be surprising in the light of
their use in the Old Testament (LXX).[32] Indeed, of the approximately
fifty-seven occurrences of εὐωδία, and seventy-five occurrences of ὀσμή in
the LXX (including the apocrypha), no less than on forty-seven occasions
(that is, in all but two occurrences of εὐωδία in the Hebrew canon) the two
words appear together in the same genitival relationship as in Phil. 4:18 and
Eph. 5:2, referring in these forty-seven cases *without exception*, and, indeed,
in the remaining two canonical occurrences of εὐωδία as well, to the odor
of an offering or sacrifice offered to God, placed on the alter
(θυσιαστήριον) to be burned by fire before God ("before" frequently
translating ἔναντι, cf. Lev. 1:3-17; LXX 6:17-23/MT 6:24-30; Num. 15:1-25).

In the light of such evidence from Paul's own use and that of the LXX,
some scholars, such as C. K. Barrett,[33] for example, have concluded that in
II Cor. 2:14-16 as well, Paul must have intended to use the words ὀσμή and

---

[32]The texts in which οσμή and εὐωδία occur together in the canonical books are as follows:
Gen. 8:21
Exod. 29:18,25,41
Lev. 1:9,13,17; 2:2,9,12; 3:5,11,16; 4:31; 6:15,21; 8:21,28; 17:4,6; 23:13,18
Num. 15:3,5,7,10,13,14,24; 18:17; 28:2,6,8,11,13,24,27; 29: 2,6,8,11,13,36
Ezek. 6:13; 16:19; 20:28,41
Dan. 4:37a.
The remaining two canonical occurrences of οσμή are in Ezra 6:10 and Dan. 2:41.

[33]Barrett, II Corinthians, p. 99.

εὐωδία in a sacrificial sense, to refer to his life as "the smoke that arises from the sacrifice of Christ to God, diffusing as it ascends the knowledge of God that is communicated in the cross."[34] Not all scholars by any means would accept this cultic and specifically sacrificial interpretation of the use of ὀσμή and εὐωδία in 2:14-16, and the arguments of some of these scholars will be considered in due course below.[35] At present, however, our concern is to further strengthen the case for holding to the view expressed above by Barrett, and this we shall attempt to do by referring to Paul's similar cultic thought (describing Christian life and activity in terms of the life and activity of the cult) elsewhere in his epistles in general, and in II Corinthians in particular.

Strengthening the Case for Interpreting Paul's Use of Ὀσμή and Εὐωδία in terms of Cult

Paul's Interest in Cult outside II Corinthians. We have already noted that in I Cor. 5:1-8 Paul discusses morality from a cultic perspective (see above, p. 64, 65). We may also note that beyond the confines of the Corinthian correspondence Paul can speak of the Christian life in general as a matter of presenting one's body to God as a living sacrifice (θυσίαν ζῶσαν, Rom. 12:1); and of his own ministry, and that of Epaphroditus, as that of a λειτουργός, a priest or minister of the tabernacle (Rom. 15:16; Phil. 2:25).[36] Furthermore, Paul also portrays himself as one being poured out like sacrificial blood (σπένδομαι) on the sacrifice (θυσία) and in the sacrificial service (λειτουργία) of the Philippians' faith (Phil. 2:17).

---

[34] Acknowledging the sacrificial association of ὀσμή and εὐωδία are Collange, p. 41; Martin, p. 45; Maurice Carrez, "Présence et Fonctionnement de L'ancien Testament dans L'annonce de L'évangile," ResSciRel 63 (Jl-Sept. 1975): 137; M. Thrall, The First and Second Letters of Paul to the Corinthians (Cambridge: University Press, 1965), p. 130. See also the recent work of Scott J. Hafemann, Suffering and the Spirit, 1986, pp. 41-51.

[35] While not necessarily rejecting the sacrificial connotations of ὀσμή and εὐωδία, emphasis is placed on the relationship of these words to the presence of God in, for example, Sir. 24, by Furnish, pp. 176-77, 188; Plummer, p. 70; Bultmann, p. 63; Héring, p. 18; McDonald, p. 40; and Rissi, p. 65. What, perhaps, should be noted now is that whether the focus of the words is cultic or not, the association of the words with God's presence in some sense is virtually unchallenged (though Bruce, pp. 187-88, following T. W. Manson, et al)., suggests a possible medicinal and pharmacological understanding of the words, pointing to Christ as the "life-giving remedy against sin and death").

[36] BAG4, p. 472.

The only confusion in this varied use of cultic imagery lies in the fact that sometimes the Christian is viewed by Paul as the one serving at the altar as priest, while at other times the Christian is actually regarded as the sacrifice being offered up to God on the altar itself.[37] However, what remains quite clear throughout, given the LXX background of the terms which Paul employs, is that his imagery speaks of activity and service occurring in one place only -- in the Temple, Tabernacle or Tent, in the presence of God.

Paul's Interest in Cult within II Corinthians. This interest of Paul, to express the intimate association of his life with cultic activity, can be seen not only outside II Corinthians, but also within it. In particular, Paul's interest in cultic matters within II Corinthians centers largely on his emphasis on Christ's death as a death "for others" (5:14-15) which brings reconciliation and salvation (5:18-21; 1:5-6). In this regard, what is important to note immediately is that Paul views this sacrificial death as providing salvation not only as an event which occurs in time and space outside himself, but also as an event in which he somehow participates and which is therefore determinative for the very shape of his ongoing existence.

Moreover, this emphasis on personal participation in the sacrifice of Christ cannot be regarded as of only passing significance for Paul, for he refers to the theme on a number of occasions throughout the letter (e.g., 1:5; 4:7-12; 5:14-16) -- making it quite conceivable that in 2:14-16, where the connection between Paul's existence and Christ's salvific work is also clearly in view, Paul's implicit intention in employing the words ὀσμή and εὐωδία was to use them in their cultic sense, as indicative of the intimate connection between his own life and the life of Christ given in sacrifice (as it were, on the cultic altar in the presence of God) for himself and for others.[38]

---

[37]Our argument and conclusions here are in complete agreement with those of Michael Newton, The Concept of Purity, pp. 70-78. Newton presents a detailed exegesis of the relevant passages throughout his book. See especially pp. 52-116.

[38]Our argument here is rather similar to that of Collange, p. 33, and Barrett, II Corinthians, p. 100, who both acknowledge the connection between Paul's use of ὀσμή and εὐωδία in 2:14-16 with his sense of identity with the sacrifice of Christ, expressed explicitly in 4:10. Correctly, Barrett explains, "Here, as regularly, Paul applies the language of cultus to life and preaching; . . ." However, his next comment is fundamentally misleading: "priests, sacrifices, incense in the conventional cultic sense, are of little or no interest to him." To be sure, this is true when it comes to literal practice and participation. On the other hand, the possible further implication of Barrett's comments, that cultic thought-patterns are of only secondary importance to Paul, is the very implication that we would wish to refute.

The strongest support for such a suggestion comes from II Cor. 4:7-12 and the verses immediately preceding, 4:1-6, verses which not only explicitly emphasize the connection between the character of Paul's existence and the death of Christ, but also display a remarkable similarity of vocabulary to that of 2:14-16: the words φανερόω, ἀπόλλυμι, ζωή, θάνατος and πάντοτε, occur in both 2:14-16 and 4:7-12 (cf. ἐν παντὶ τόπῳ and περιφέρω as well), while φανερόω, γνῶσις, and ἀπόλλυμι occur not only in 2:14-16, but also in 4:1-6. The extent of this overlap in vocabulary cannot be merely coincidental, but suggests rather that the latter passage may have been intended to function as a development of some of the themes introduced in the former.[39] Thus, for example, it can be observed without much difficulty that the work of the "god of this world" (4:3-6) to keep those who are perishing (ἀπολλυμένοις, 4:3) from embracing the gospel of Christ, functions as an explanation of the paradoxical fact that to the perishing (ἀπολλυμένοις, 2:15) the knowledge of Christ imparted by Paul is nothing more than the smell (ὀσμή) of death.

Assuming that such a connection between II Cor. 2:14-17 and II Cor. 4:1-12 does in fact exist, what must now be determined in order to cast further light on the earlier passage, is the thrust of Paul's thought within the latter, or at least within the second half of it, 4:7-12.

Paul's Thought in II Cor. 4:7-12. A cursory reading of II Cor. 4:7-12 would indicate that the focus of Paul's thought there is to be found in his insistent testimony to the fact that his life bears witness to the Gospel of Christ even in the midst of tribulation. Such a testimony by Paul is necessary, it would seem, because of the appearance of his life as one which is always characterized by tribulation, and even by death and destruction--to such an extent, in fact, that some had come to suggest that his life was a testimony not to salvation but to despair (ἐξαπορούμενοι), forsaken (ἐγκαταλει-πόμενοι) by God (4:8-9; see also 6:8-9).[40]

---

[39]Collange, p. 40, Martin, p. 50, and McDonald, p. 43 each indicate their understanding of 2:14-17 as introductory to the next section of the epistle (3:1-7:4). Margaret Thrall, JSNT 16, p. 114, also takes such a position and defends it with a cursory survey of repeated vocabulary and themes, which our own survey here develops.

[40]Many of the words which Paul uses to describe his life in II Cor. 6:1-12 can be found in the curse lists of the Pentateuch (LXX). For example, θλῖψις (6:4), πληγή (6:5), and παιδεύειν (6:9), can be found in Lev. 26:21-29; στενοχωρία (6:4) appears repeatedly in Deut. 28:53, 55, 57; while the verb ἀποθανεῖν (6:9b) and substantive form of λυπεῖν (6:10) are the words which characterize the effect of the curse on both the woman and the man after the "fall" in the garden of Eden (Gen. 3:3, 16-17). It could well be, we would suggest, that Paul's

In response to such an assessment of his life, Paul in no way denies that his appearance is one which at first sight is characterized by a pervasive and deathly tribulation. What he does deny, however, is the interpretaion of that appearance as one which signifies his abandonment by God. Indeed, in 4:10-11 Paul argues that quite the opposite is true. That is, he argues that the "living death" which characterizes his existence takes its place within his salvation as the divinely ordained means through which the very life of Christ can become manifest within him.

This divinely ordained means of accomplishing God's saving work is not, however, equated by Paul merely with discipline -- as if God had determined that "suffering" was "good for one." Rather, if the suffering was in fact good for Paul, and had been ordained as the means of manifesting Christ's life within him, Paul argues that such was the case not only because it would prove that the power inherent in salvation was not human but divine (4:7b), but also because such suffering reflected and was a participation in Christ's suffering, and even in his death. Thus Paul, in refuting any suggestion that his troubled life had somehow strayed out of God's will, describes the physical appearance and true interpretation of his life as

[10] always carrying in the body the death of Jesus so that the life of Jesus
may also be manifested in our bodies
[11] For while we live we are always being given up to death for Jesus' sake,
so that the life of Jesus may be manifested in our mortal flesh. (RSV)

Quite clearly, the link between the intimate association of Christ's sacrificial death with the whole nature of Paul's existence, and Paul's ability to make Christ's salvation manifest (φανερόω; so also 2:14b) is made explicit here in II Cor. 4:10-11; an observation which is crucial to our understanding of the use of ὀσμή and εὐωδία in 2:14-16. Before returning, however, to a consideration of these latter verses in any depth, one further observation can be made to strengthen the case for our assessment of Paul's thought in 4:7-11,

---

opponents used such Scripture references to demonstrate that Paul was a man under God's curse, and thus not an apostle. Paul's rejoinder to such an accusation is not to deny the curse-like appearance of his life, but simply to declare that the day of salvation has dawned (II Cor. 6:2), thus implying that henceforth the curses of the Mosaic covenant have been rendered null and void so that the life which appears to be cursed, such as that of the servant of Isa. 52:13-53:12 -- whose life was filled with ἄτιμος, πληγή, παιδεία and the lack of visible δόξα (see LXX Isa. 52:14, 53:3,4, 5 with II Cor. 6:5,8,9 -- can in fact be regarded as "redeemed from the curse of the law" (Gal. 3:13), and thus as still acceptable to God. In particular, this was precisely the experience of Christ himself, as well as, Paul claims in II Cor. 4:7-11, of those who identify their lives with Christ.

and consequently for the assessment of his usage of ὀσμή and εὐωδία in 2:14-16 as being thoroughly determined by the cult. Our observation stems from II Cor.4:7, in which Paul describes the Christian's body, and thus his own, as an "earthen vessel" (ὀστρακίνοις σκεύεσιν).

There is certainly no good reason to deny the fact observed so frequently that Paul employs the phrase "earthen vessels" to portray the weakness and/or worthlessness of his life in contrast to the power of God which comes through the inestimable value of the work of Christ.[41] However, it would seem to us to be pertinent, in contrast to the opinion of C. K. Barrett,[42] to observe that the specific phrase, "ὀστρακίνοις σκεύεσιν," has an important OT usage in the LXX, referring to the vessel used either to bear the sin offering after its death in sacrifice (Lev. 6:28; LXX, 6:21), or to contain sacrificial birds as they are killed for the cleansing of leprosy (Lev. 14:50).

The former of these two possibilities, that in referring to his body as an earthen vessel Paul is actually portraying his life as one in which the "sin offering" of Christ's death has been placed, seems to us to be more than a mere possibility given his description of Christ as "sin," "ἁμαρτία," in II Cor. 5:21. That is, although the significance of this description of Christ as "sin" remains debated,[43] it is hard for us to ignore the fact that ἁμαρτία is the word used in the LXX throughout the Leviticus discussion of the "sin-offering" (see, e.g., 4:24, 29, 34; 5:6) not just as a reference to "sins," but as the technical term for *the sin-offering itself*. Indeed, this usage of ἁμαρτία is found precisely in the same context as, and in intimate connection with, as the content of, the σκεῦος ὀστράκινον of Lev. 6:25-27 (LXX, 6:18-21), and

---

[41]See, for example, Héring, p. 32; Collange, p. 145; and Rudolf Bultmann, p. 111, who argue that the "earthenness" of the vessel indicates Paul's sense of weakness, while Plummer, p. 127; Barrett, II Corinthians, pp. 137-38; and Bruce, p. 197, stress the relative worthlessness of such vessels in comparison with the treasure which is Christ. Martin, p. 85, (who provides a helpful summary of other scholarship) and Furnish, pp. 253, 278, embrace both positions.

[42]Barrett, p. 137, claims, without support, that "It does not seem relevant that earthenware vessels were in use in the Temple (Lev. 6:28; 11:33; 14:50)." Furnish, p. 253, also indicates this LXX use of the phrase "σκεῦος ὀστράκινον," but makes no use of his observation.

[43]Plummer, p. 187; Barrett, II Corinthians, p. 180; and Furnish, p. 340, each declare themselves against any link between ἁμαρτία and the understanding of Christ as a sin-offering. Their arguments are no stronger than Furnish's subjective assessment that such an understanding "would import an idea foreign to this context." Our position, on the other hand, is that the context of the totality of II Cor. 2:14-7:4 is fundamentally cultic, and thus we find no difficulty in agreeing with scholars such as Héring, p. 47; Bruce, p. 210; and Martin, p. 157, who claim that the LXX background of ἁμαρτία determines its meaning as "sin-offering."

is one of the offerings which when burned on the altar emits an "ὀσμὴν εὐωδίας)," a pleasing odor, to the Lord (as, for example, in Lev. 4:31).

Placed in such a context, then, when Paul in II Cor. 4:7 declares the Christian life to be one that possesses "treasure in earthen vessels," then the "earthen vessel" can be conceived as the container for the sin-offering, the "treasure" can be conceived as the sin-offering itself, and the sin-offering as the death of Christ, treasured for its power to restore fellowship (cf. "righteousness," II Cor. 5:21; 3:9) with God. Moreover, such an interpretation of II Cor. 4:7 would certainly not be out of place within II Cor. 4:7-12 as a whole, for Paul in 4:7 would be saying nothing substantially different from what he says in 4:10: that he is "always carrying in the body the death of Jesus." What difference there is, we would suggest, lies merely in the fact that the depth of Paul's cultic conceptualization of his relationship with Christ is made manifest in 4:7, and can be assumed at least throughout 4:7-12, and applied as a high probability to 2:14-17, which, we have argued, is intimately related, perhaps as a thematic introduction, to the later passage. In particular, of course, what we would want to argue with respect to 2:14-16 is that now it can be seen how Paul quite naturally characterizes his propagation of the gospel as he does, in terms of being an "ὀσμή" and a "εὐωδία": because of the sacrificial association of the words and because of the cultic manner in which he views his life as being integrally connected to Christ's death, which functions as a sin-offering sacrificed on the altar of the tabernacle in the presence of God.

Objections to the Cultic Interpretation of Ὀσμή and Εὐωδία in II Cor. 2:14-16

The sacrificial interpretation of ὀσμή and εὐωδία has not, however, been universally adopted by scholars. The reasons given are generally similar to those which suggest either that the idea of sacrifice "is really alien to this context," or that in II Cor. 2:14-16 the words do not occur connected in the genitival phrase "ὀσμὴν εὐωδίας," as is the case in Phil. 4:18, Eph. 5:2, and in the overwhelming majority of passages in the LXX in which the usage is clearly sacrificial.[44] Victor Furnish, for example, in rejecting the sacrificial connection of the imagery, argues in part that the "purpose" of sacrificial odor is merely to rise to the realm of God, and not to spread itself through the

---

[44] So Furnish, pp. 176-77; also, Plummer, p. 71. For the texts in which the phrase "ὀσμή εὐωδίας" occurs, see above, note 32.

world of humanity, while for Paul in 2:14-16, on the other hand, the aroma of Christ is to be diffused primarily to other human beings, and is thus unlikely, he argues, to refer to the aroma of sacrifice.[45] Furnish's argument here is uncharacteristically weak, for, as, for example, C. K. Barrett suggests,[46] the odor of sacrifice brings life not merely as it arises to God and is found to be pleasing by him, but also as it spreads to human lives and reveals to them "the knowledge of God that is communicated in the cross": that God wants to be known through the death of his Son, and thus in his mercy.

A seemingly stronger argument which Furnish raises against any interpretation of εὐωδία and ὀσμή as having cultic or sacrificial content, derives from the appearance of these words in the same context, yet as in II Cor. 2:14-16 not immediately connected, in such inter-testamental works as Ben Sira, the Apocalypse of Baruch, and I Enoch.[47] The thrust of the passages to which Furnish refers in these books confirms, he claims, that the terms for fragrance or aroma are used by Paul as symbols of the direct presence of God as revealed, for example, through "Wisdom," rather than as symbols linked with matters of cult. Thus, Furnish quotes Ben Sira 24:15, which speaks of Wisdom as follows:

Like cassia or camel-thorn
   I was redolent of spices (ὀσμήν);
I spread my fragrance (εὐωδίαν)
   like choice myrrh. (NEB)

Furnish's quotation, however, although it correctly points to the use of ὀσμή and εὐωδία as symbols for the presence and therefore the knowledge of God, is quite misleading as an argument against the cultic and sacrificial association of the words. For not only does the quoted verse not end after the word "myrrh," but the rest of the verse reads as follows: "like galban, aromatic shell, and gum resin; I was like *the smoke of incense in the sacred tent* (λιβάνου ἀτμὶς ἐν σκηνῇ)." The reference to the "smoke of incense" and to the "tent" or "tabernacle" are clearly cultic, and imply that the ὀσμή and εὐωδία referred to by Ben Sira, despite their slight separation from each other, are not devoid of the cultic association which we have observed elsewhere in relation to the phrase "ὀσμὴν εὐωδίας."

---

[45]Furnish, p. 177.
[46]Barrett, II Corinthians, pp. 99-100.
[47]Furnish, p. 188. See Sir. 24:15, 2 Apoc. Bar. 67:6, and I Enoch 24-25.

Furthermore, what is true of this text is also true of the other two texts to which Furnish refers. That is, the use of the words in 2 Apoc.Bar. 67:6 is also connected with the smoke of sacrifice; and although in I Enoch 24-25 the odor of fragrance arises from the "Tree of Life", the passage makes it clear that the Tree of Life is to be located "upon the holy place," in Jerusalem, "in the direction of the house of the Lord" (I Enoch 25:5).

These objections, then, which are representative of those expressed by others,[48] carry no weight in denying the cultic and sacrificial association of ὀσμή and εὐωδία when used in the same general context as each other, even if, as in II Cor. 2:14-16, the terms are not connected within the genitival phrase, "ὀσμὴν εὐωδίας." Indeed, to the contrary, we understand the terms ὀσμή and εὐωδία in II Cor. 2:14-16 as functioning to express Paul's belief that he proclaims the Gospel not only by his word, but more especially by his life, as it carries, participates in, results from, and resembles Christ's sacrificial death, offered, as it were, like the sacrifices of the cult, on the altar in God's presence.

III. THE INTERPRETATION OF II CORINTHIANS 2:14-17 IN THE LIGHT OF THE CULTIC SIGNIFICANCE OF Ὀσμή AND Εὐωδία

We take it, therefore, that the cultic understanding of οσμή and εὐωδία in II Cor. 2:14-16 is correct, and more than supports the possibility that the word "κατέναντι" in 2:17 should be interpreted literally to convey Paul's intimate interest in establishing that he is a person who lives within the presence of God. Consequently, we are now in a position to see how these conclusions clarify the interpretation of II Cor. 2:14-17 as a whole, and this we shall do by focusing on some of the problematic issues which have been of concern to others (see above, p.76): issues such as understanding the link between 2:14-17 and the passage which precedes it; the use of "θριαμβεύω" in 2:14; and the sense of the question "Who is sufficient for these things?"in 2:16. Furthermore, within this enquiry our interest will turn once again to Paul's use of "κατέναντι" in 2:17, though first of all our concern will be with the relationship of II Cor. 2:14-17 to its preceding context.[49]

---

[48]Such as Bultmann, p. 63; Héring, pp. 18-19; Plummer, pp. 70-71; McDonald, p. 40; Rissi, p. 65.
[49]Concerning the context of 2:14-17 see above, n. 27; concerning θριαμβεύω, see note 28; on the issue of "sufficiency" see note 30; and on κατέναντι see p. 176.

The Preceding Context of II Corinthians 2:14-17

A quick reading of II Corinthians easily establishes that II Cor. 2:14 begins an extensive "interruption" of a travel narrative in which, as it were, Paul leaves Troas for Macedonia in II Cor. 2:13, to arrive in Macedonia in II Cor. 7:5. While some scholars (see above, n.28) have argued that the transition from II Cor. 2:13 to 2:14 is so abrupt that 2:14-7:4 must be regarded as an interpolation, the majority of scholars, while noting the abruptness of the transition, have argued for the integrity of the letter at this point, and yet without satisfactorily explaining the flow of Paul's thought between the two verses.

There certainly seems to be no good reason to reject the majority position on this particular issue. However, what we wish to observe in addition, and in support of the unity of 2:14-7:4 with its context, is that the presence of οσμή and εὐωδία as terms relating to Paul's suffering can in fact be seen to be quite appropriate in the verses immediately following II Cor. 2:13, if one of Paul's major intentions in the "interruption," 2:14-7:4, was to provide an extensive theological explanation of the tribulation which he suffered on his arrival in Macedonia (as described in 7:5) -- such suffering occuring fast on the heels of that which he had previously incurred in Asia (1:8), and which, in fact, always (πάντοτε, 4:10) seemed to be dogging his path (4:8-10).[50]

Indeed, as we have already observed,[51] and as seems quite clear from 6:3-10, for example, one of the major accusations levelled against Paul by his opponents was precisely that his ministry was being invalidated by the afflictions and calamities that seemed to strike him at every turn, as if to indicate that he was an impostor (6:8), forsaken by God (4:9), and thus not a servant of God (6:4) at all. In response to such an accusation (among other accusations which seemed to be surfacing in Corinth)[52] it would have been natural for Paul to demonstrate as convincingly as possible -- theologically,

---

[50]Furnish, p. 117, recognizes the continuity between Paul's description of tribulation in II Cor. 1 and in II Cor. 7. Furthermore, he also observes the importance of the theme in 4:7-15 (see p. 121) as being a fundamental issue with regard to determining the validity of Paul's apostleship (see p. 54). What Furnish (along with others) does not do, however, but what we are attempting to do, is to understand the theme of suffering or tribulation as the critical thread flowing through Paul's whole discussion of the Christian life and the defence of his apostleship, from 2:14 to 7:4.

[51]See above, pp. 47, 81.

[52]See above, n. 40.

christologically, and biblically -- that his suffering was integral to his calling, and that his authority as a proclaimer of God's Word remained valid.

We would suggest, then, that the sacrificial connotation of ὀσμή and εὐωδία, used in II Cor. 2:14-16 to describe Paul's life of suffering, not only opens the door to a satisfactory explanation of Paul's abrupt transition from II Cor. 2:13 to 2:14, but also confirms the fact that the defence of "suffering apostleship" (and, indeed, of "suffering discipleship" in general) -- that his suffering was not an indication that God had cast Paul out of his presence -- is precisely the theme that the Apostle begins to introduce in 2:14-17, verses which many regard as introductory for much of the section 2:14-7:4 as a whole.[53]

The Use of θριαμβεύω

Once such a context is assumed, the use of θριαμβεύω as a term relating in some way to God's ability to use what otherwise would seem to be a life of mere degradation would also be appropriate. Thus, if θριαμβεύω were to be understood in terms of God's leading Paul from place to place (from Asia to Macedonia, for example) as within a Roman triumphal parade, the implication would be that Paul's position in the parade would not be that of a victorious soldier, but rather that of a degraded prisoner who, precisely in his degradation, shame, and even his death, serves his captor and fulfils his will by spreading the knowledge of his captor's victory and salvation.[54]

The Question of Sufficiency

Furthermore, to ask, as Paul does in 2:16b, "Who is sufficient for these things?"is to raise a question which relates well both to Paul's suffering and to the validity of his ministry, and which possibly provides a transitional link between one and the other. In relation to suffering, for example, if Paul's intent in raising the question was to refer the issue of "sufficiency" to his work as the ὀσμή and εὐωδία of a sacrifice, then his purpose might well have been in part to show the ultimate absurdity of the question (raised previously

---

[53] On the introductory nature of 2:14-17, see above, n. 26.

[54] Scott Hafemann's excellent discussion of θριαμβεύειν in Suffering and the Spirit, pp. 18-39, serves both to confirm our general understanding and to further emphasize the triumphal procession as one that led in the end to the death of the captives (see especially, p. 27). See also the general understanding of Furnish, pp. 173-75.

by his opponents against Paul in all seriousness)[55] when directed towards qualifications for apostolic ministry--for who in their right mind (as Paul reminds the Corinthians, 11:23), once ministry is conceived as a sacrificial, death-like experience, would even raise the question of sufficiency, as if to boast in such a degrading existence?[56] Indeed, for Paul to use such irony here would not be out of place, for irony appears again not only implicitly in 3:1-3, where Paul scorns the use of "letters of recommendation" by those who claimed that it was God himself who validated their ministry,[57] but also quite explicitly in Paul's extended *exposé* of his weaknesses and tribulations in 11:1-12:13.[58]

On the other hand, Paul's intent is surely not merely to express irony: like his opponents, he also asks the question in all seriousness (as he himself seems to do in 3:5) in reference to the general validity of his status and ability to be a proclaimer of the word of God, and thus to impart "ζωή" or confirm "θάνατος" (2:16). In either event, whether the question is ironic, or serious, or both, the response provided in 2:17 to the question of sufficiency is given in all seriousness, and can stand as an answer both to the questioning of Paul's authority to proclaim God's word by the character of his life as a servant of the altar (before it as a priest, or on it as a sacrifice, infused with and effusing the sweet odor of Christ) as well as to the questioning of his authority as a divinely ordained proclaimer of God's word in general.

Specifically, the response begins in 2:17 with a denial of the suggestion (probably first made by his opponents) that Paul's ministry is insufficient because he was, in reality, only "hawking" (καπηλεύων) God's word -- "hawking" implying that he was in the business of religion for profit or deceit and thus that his manner of life and his product were separable from each other.[59] That is, in speaking of himself in terms of sacrifice, Paul was effectively claiming that his life and his proclamation of Christ were

---

[55]On the question of Paul's sufficiency being raised by his opponents, see, for example, Bultmann, p. 69; Furnish, p. 184.

[56]On the opponents' own claim to sufficiency, see Barrett, II Corinthians, pp. 102-3; Rissi, p. 65. See also, E. Richard, "Polemics, Old Testament and Theology: A Study of II Cor. 3:1-4:6," RB 88 (July 1981): 365, on the importance of the issue for 3:1-18.

[57]See Rissi, p.67.

[58]E.g., II Cor. 11:1: "I wish you would bear with me in a little foolishness." (RSV); 12:13: ". . .I did not burden you. Forgive me this wrong!"

[59]On the meaning of καπηλεύω as hawking or selling, see Scott J. Hafemann, Suffering and the Spirit, pp. 106-26. That καπηλεύω is thus also linked with the divorce between the life of the messenger and the message, is inferred from Georgi's assessment (p. 234) of the use of the word by Plato.

inseparable -- the pattern of Paul's very existence being controlled by the pattern of Christ's sacrifice.[60] Furthermore, whereas for Paul's opponents, a Paul who provided a gospel that did not emphasise the *glorious* nature of the experience of salvation, free from suffering, *right now* in the present, might be considered a deceitful salesman who provided less than the full product, for Paul, the opposite was true: to run away from the call to suffer by appearing as a glorious "angel of light" (II Cor.11:14) was to provide less than the "full gospel" of the suffering, and only later exalted, Christ.

The Question of Sufficiency and the Interpretation of Κατέναντι

Sufficiency as referring to "Cultic" Proclamation. Whatever the intent of the specific denial in II Cor. 2:17 of "hawking" the Gospel, Paul's more important and positive affirmation of his sufficiency occurs in the second half of the verse where he declares that his proclamation stems from the character of his life as one who is pure (ἐξ εἰλικρινείας), who is from God (ἐκ θεοῦ), and who stands in God's presence (κατέναντι θεοῦ). It is quite possible to interpret these words as intending merely to affirm Paul's veracity in claiming to be an apostle or in denying that he was a hawker; as if to say "God will vouch (κατέναντι θεοῦ ἐν Χριστῷ λαλοῦμεν) that I am a sincere (ἐξ εἰλικρινείας) and religious (ἐκ θεοῦ) person." However, what we have already attempted to demonstrate (above, pp. 63-74) is that εἰλικρίνεια and κατέναντι both have strong cultic associations, and that such an association cannot be ruled out in the present verse. Indeed, if we are correct in our assessment of the preceding verses, 2:14-16, as being fundamentally cultic in orientation, then it would be quite natural for Paul to continue in the same vein in 2:17.

For example, Paul's description of himself in 2:17b can be understood, without forcing the text, as a literal representation of the conditions for approaching the presence of God, either as a sacrifice itself, or as a priest bearing the sacrifice on behalf of others; εἰλικρίνεια being the condition of purity necessary to make such an approach. In this context, "ἐκ θεοῦ" would function as does "ἐκ τοῦ θεοῦ" in 3:5, to indicate that Paul's sufficiency -- possibly referring to both his purity and his authority to speak for God -- is not his own, but comes directly *from* God; and "ἐν Χριστῷ" would function either to describe the means through which God provided the purity that had

---

[60]See Paul J. Achtemeier, Unity, pp. 80-82.

gained Paul's access to God's presence (it is *by* Christ), or to describe the "location" in which God provided his presence (it is *in* Christ, the "holy space" created by the new covenant, rather than, for example, at Sinai or in the "σκηνή" of the old (see, e.g., LXX, Exod.33:8, Num.1:1, 8:22, 26; Deut. 31:14-15).

Indeed, both ideas, both "means" and "location" can stand together. The concept of the temple, for example, incorporates both the definition of the proper *location* or "holy space" (e.g., in Jerusalem, or wherever the tent or tabernacle was carried) as well as the *proper means* for making access to God possible (e.g., through the priesthood, or through the rules of purity and sacrifice).[61] That is, if "ἐν Χριστῷ" is understood as being parallel to being "in the Temple," then Christ can be understood as providing both the means and the location through which access to God is made possible. In either case the literal understanding of κατέναντι makes excellent sense and indicates that Paul is claiming that his proclamation of the Gospel comes from one who has unhindered access to God's presence, and who therefore has the necessary "sufficiency" to speak (λαλεῖν) on God's behalf.

Sufficiency as referring to Mosaic and Authoritative Proclamation in General. The use of the word λαλεῖν in this context (κατέναντι θεοῦ ἐν Χριστῷ λαλοῦμεν), may well be indicative of a new concern of Paul to begin to shift the thrust of his argument towards the question of sufficiency for authoritative proclamation in general; sufficiency not merely to proclaim the gospel by *embodying* or *carrying* it -- as sacrifice or priest, as ὀσμή and εὐωδία -- but to proclaim it authoritatively with words, as did Moses.[62] Indeed, given the fact that much of II Cor. 3 is concerned with a comparison between the ministry of Paul and that of Moses, it would seem quite natural to suggest that 2:17b functions as such a point of transition, introducing the comparison to come.

If such is the case, however, it would be wrong to think of such a transition as implying a radical break from the cultic conception of ministry

---

[61]On the understanding of ἐν Χριστῷ see, for example, F. Neugebauer, In Christus (Göttingen: Vandenhoeck & Ruprecht: 1961). To Neugebauer's understanding of ἐν Χριστῷ as referring to the eschatological salvation made possible by Christ (e.g., see p. 92), we are claiming that such a salvation is also "locative," in the sense that to be "in Christ" is to be in the sphere of God's presence, as represented, for example, by the image of a temple or tabernacle.

[62]See Martin, p. 49, on Paul "embodying" Christ's sentence of death, and on the correlation of the apostolic life and the Gospel message.

which we have attempted to describe: as if to take Moses as the model for ministry (whether Paul's model or his opponents') was to leave the "priestly" and enter the "prophetic" conception of religion. In particular, the story of Moses in Exodus 32-34, the passage which forms the basic background for the discussion in II Cor. 3:7-18,[63] demonstrates quite clearly that Moses' authority itself derived from God's call to enter his presence, either on Sinai or in the tent of witness, there to receive from God the Word that he would deliver, *ex cathedra*, to the people (e.g., as in Exod. 33:9; 34:1-11). Thus, for Paul to declare that he too had been granted access to God's presence, in or through Christ, would be to declare at the same time that he potentially stood where Moses stood, in a position of authority to declare the word of God, not as a "hawker" but as a legitimate heir of Moses, and a "sufficient" minister of Christ.

Indeed, Carol Stockhausen's analysis of II Cor.3:1-6 provides substantial confirmation for our position.[64] Stockhausen argues that Paul's use of the the word "sufficient" (ἱκανός) derives from the only parallel use in the LXX, that in Exod. 4:10. Furthermore, the Exodus passage provides a remarkable parallel to the situation confronted by Paul at Corinth. That is, Exodus 3-4 concerns a conversation between God and Moses on "holy ground" (Exod. 3:5) at the foot of Horeb/Sinai, and the content concerns God's call to Moses to be the leader through whom God would deliver his people from slavery in Egypt. Moses, however, does not accept this call without question, since he fears that no one will accept his authority. Various questions to God are then followed up by Moses' doubt about his own personal ability to fulfil his call. Exod. 4:10 (LXX, with my own translation) reads as follows:

Εἶπεν δὲ Μωυσῆς πρὸς κύριον Δέομαι, κύριε, οὐχ ἱκανός εἰμι πρὸ τῆς ἐχθὲς οὐδὲ πρὸ τῆς τρίτης ἡμέρας οὐδὲ ἀφ' οὗ ἤρξω λαλεῖν τῷ θεράποντί σου· ἰσχνόφωνος καὶ βραδύγλωσσος ἐγώ εἰμι.

And Moses said to the Lord, "I pray, Lord, I have not been sufficient in the past, nor from the third day, nor from the time when you began to speak to your temple servant; I am weak in speech and slow tongued."

---

[63]The commonly held assumption is that Exod. 34:29-35 forms the background for II Cor. 3:7-18. See for example, Barrett, II Corinthians, p. 113; Morna Hooker, "Beyond the Things that are Written: St Paul's Use of Scripture," NTS 27 (April 1981): 297; and others. Concerning our reasons for assuming that Paul's interest in II Cor. 3:7-18 is guided not just by Exodus 34, but by the narrative section, Exod. 32-34, see below, pp. 266-67.

[64]Carol K. Stockhausen, Moses' Veil and the Glory of the New Covenant: The Exegetical Substructure of II Cor.3.1-4.6, Ana.Bib.116 (Rome: Pontifical Institute, 1989), pp. 82-86.

To this self-questioning by Moses of his sufficiency, God responds in Exod. 4:11-12 by assuring Moses that all he needs for the task -- his sufficiency -- will be supplied. Exod. 4:12, LXX is as follows:

καὶ νῦν πορεύου, καὶ ἐγὼ ἀνοίξω τὸ στόμα σου καὶ συμβιβάσω σε ἃ μέλλεις λαλῆσαι.

and now go, and I will open your mouth and I will instruct you as to what you will say.

To Stockhausen, not only the parallel context -- Paul claims in II Cor. 3:5 that (as with Moses) his sufficiency comes from God -- but also important lexical evidence confirms the idea that in thinking of "sufficiency" Paul was implicitly comparing himself with Moses. The lexical evidence simply comprises the presence of a seemingly superfluous "καὶ" in II Cor. 3:6, which refers to nothing explicit in the context; unless, that is, Paul is saying that God has *also* (καί), that is, like Moses, made him competent to be a covenant servant (Paul's covenant, however, being a new one).

Stockhausen's argument is convincing, and in the context of II Cor. 2:16b-17, leads us to see Paul's expression that he is "ἀλλ᾽ ὡς ἐξ εἰλικρινείας, ἀλλ᾽ ὡς ἐκ θεοῦ κατέναντι θεοῦ ἐν Χριστῷ λαλοῦμεν" as paralleling the experience of Moses, whose authority to speak came both through his experience of being called into God's presence at Sinai, and through the promise of God's continuing presence during the task itself ("Ἔσομαι μετὰ σοῦ," Exod. 3:12, LXX).

Furthermore, that Paul broadens his imagery while still continuing in II Corinthians 3 to think in terms by no means devoid of cultic thought, is demonstrated by Stockhausen in her analysis of II Cor. 3:1-6. In a discussion of Paul's unexpected use of "ἐγγράφω" in II Cor. 3:2,[65] Stockhausen argues that Paul's choice of the word derives from his use of Exod. 36:21 (LXX), in which the word is used to describe the *engraving* of the names of the twelve tribes on the stones in the breastplate of Aaron the priest. As Stockhausen observes, this breastplate "Aaron wore when he ministered before the Lord, so that he might bring their names into the presence of God."[66] Consequently, with respect to Paul, Stockhausen writes,

---

[65]Stockhausen, pp. 51-53, 80-81.
[66]Stockhausen, p. 52.

rather than wearing an external stone engraving . . . Paul bears an internal
heart-engraving . . . Paul carries the Corinthians themselves before the Lord
in his heart as his "letter," not just the letters of their names as on a stone
tablet.[67]

Both in II Cor. 2:14-17 as well as in II Cor. 3:1-18, then, it is not
unreasonable to suggest that Paul sees his authoritative role in terms of both
priest and prophet. Clearly, however, the most explicit model in II Cor. 3 is
that of Moses the prophet, and to that extent the "λαλοῦμεν" of II Cor. 2:17
provides a point of transition. In either case, Paul's ability to perform his role
remains dependant on his ongoing access to God himself.

IV. II CORINTHIANS 2:14-17: SUMMARY AND DEVELOPMENT

In each of the issues we have examined in II Cor. 2:14-17, then, the cultic
understanding of ὀσμή and εὐωδία and the literal understanding of
κατέναντι can not merely be read into the context without doing violence
to the flow of thought, but can actually be seen to clarify the logic and
provide a sense of unity both within the passage and between the passage and
its context, preceding and following. Our study can therefore turn to a
detailed investigation of the verses which follow in II Corinthians 3 with the
confidence that Paul proceeds to develop his argument on the basis of the
claims set forth in II Cor. 2:14-17, as we have interpreted them.

Before making this transition to II Corinthians 3, however, one further
observation concerning II Cor. 2:14-17 must be made. That is, within these
verses Paul has claimed much but has provided no proof of any assertion--no
proof that he stands in God's presence, no proof of his purity, no proof of the
effectiveness and sufficiency of his ministry; only assertion, mere claim. In
pursuing the flow of Paul's developing argument, therefore, what we would
expect in II Corinthians 3 is for Paul to provide such proof, either from
experience, or from Scripture, or from both. Indeed, as we shall see, such
proof is precisely what Paul does in fact provide, and does so from both
experience and Scripture.

---

[67]Stockhausen, pp. 80-81.

CHAPTER FIVE

II Corinthians 3:1-11

I. THE DEFENSE OF PAUL'S APOSTOLIC STATUS, PAST AND CONTINUING

II Corinthians 3:1-3

Paul's immediate question in II Cor. 3:1 (RSV), "Are we beginning to commend ourselves again?", and his use in 3:5-6 of the idea of sufficiency, introduced previously in 2:16b, make it clear that the transition from II Cor. 2:17 to 3:1 does not indicate a radical break in the development of his argument. Indeed, whether Paul's mind, as he continued to deal with the issue of sufficiency for apostolic ministry, was focused on the "ministry of the tent" described either in sacrificial terms or in terms of Mosaic proclamation (see, e.g., Exod. 34:34-35 with 33:7-11), the continuation of his defense in II Cor. 3:1 and the verses following was almost inevitable. That is, in II Cor. 2:14-17, his proof-less claim to possess the sufficiency to convey ζωή and confirm θάνατος through his life as ὀσμή and εὐωδία, as one having the necessary εἰλικρίνεια to stand in God's presence, there to receive and speak a word from God ("ἐκ θεοῦ"), could have accomplished nothing to assuage the antagonism of opponents who had cast the shadow of doubt on every aspect of his character. To the contrary, all that such a claim could achieve, as Paul well knew, would be to stir up a renewed charge against him of "self-commendation" (3:1), a charge which the apostle inevitably had to counteract as his argument developed; and this he could do sufficiently only by demonstrating that his ministry "delivered the goods" -- that it actually conveyed life to others.[1]

In this regard, the evidence which Paul presents in II Corinthians 3 is both brief and powerful, constituting the lives of the Corinthians themselves (as in I Cor. 9:2), whose reception of the "Spirit of the living God" (3:3) through the service of Paul and that of none other functions, he argues, as the only commendation, or "letter of recommendation" (3:2), necessary to establish the validity of his claim.[2] However, even assuming that some of the Corinthians would have been convinced in some measure by this seemingly incontrovertible evidence -- that *at one time* in their lives God had used Paul in a mighty way to bring them salvation through the life-giving power of God's Spirit -- nevertheless, to others a further question would have still remained unanswered: whether the sufficiency once possessed by Paul was *still* effective, or whether by some act of disobedience (such as, for example, "hawking" the gospel, 2:17a) Paul had, in the course of time, been abandoned by God (e.g., 4:9) as evidenced, perhaps, by his life of suffering and tribulation.

The Developing Argument

What we wish to suggest now, therefore, is that it is with *this* question -- "Can Paul, admitting that he was *once* an apostle, yet given the extent of the tribulation that *now* characterizes his life, *still* be conceived of as an Apostle, one who stands in the presence of God?" -- that II Corinthians 3-5 is primarily concerned.[3] Indeed, the purpose of our discussion below will be to attempt to establish the validity of this hypothesis within the portion of Paul's argument contained in II Corinthians 3, a chapter in which Paul seems to lay the foundation for his overall answer. However, before proceding to

---

[1]With, for example, Collange, p. 55; Plummer, p. 76; and Hughes, pp. 85-86. Rissi, p. 67, is certainly correct in stressing that self-commendation was characterisitic of Paul's opponents. It is not necessary for our argument to assert that Paul himself had previously been accused of commending himself, though Bultmann, p.70, Barrett, II Corinthians, p. 106, and Martin, p. 50, indicate this possibility. See Paul's continued use of the motif of commendation in 4:2, 5:12, 6:3, and 10:12,18.

[2]We fully agree with Scott Hafemann, Suffering and the Spirit, p.185, who follows many in declaring that "inasmuch as the church in Corinth is a direct result of Paul's ministry, to deny Paul's apostleship would be tantamount to a denial of their own existence as Christians." Our own position, however, does not assume that "apostolicity" is necessarily a permanent gift, and so we suggest the question which now arises is whether or not Paul is still an apostle.

[3]I know of no discussion which approaches the argument of II Corinthians 3 from this perspective.

examine the chapter in any detail two caveats must be provided to steer us clear of possible false expectations concerning the content and direction of Paul's thought.

The first caveat is that to claim that Paul's primary concern is with the defense of his *on-going* apostolic authority is not to imply that the content of his entire argument must focus explicitly on such concepts as apostleship or the limits of apostolic authority, since it could well be that some general premises must be established before the primary concern can be broached. Indeed, this appears to be the case in II Corinthians 3-5 in that Paul's discussion focuses on the status not merely of "apostles," but of *all Christians* in general within the new covenant era established by Christ. Thus, for example, the specific concern of Paul's argument in II Corinthians 3 seems to be to demonstrate that through Christ access to God's presence, the location of every true apostle, has now been granted to *all* Christians, who, without fear of death, are free to gaze upon and to be transformed by the revelation of God's presence.

This conclusion, however, is by no means beside Paul's primary point in that although the issue of "apostolicity" is not explicitly mentioned, yet it provides a basis from which Paul can easily complete his argument (as he does in II Corinthians 4 and 5) by reminding the Corinthians that the revelation of God which has now been given, and which is to transform the lives of Christians, is to be seen in the face of Christ, a face which bears the mark of suffering and even of death. In such a light, suffering and tribulation cannot simply be regarded as evidence of rejection from God's presence, either of Christians in general, or of apostles in particular -- which is the conclusion Paul had to demonstrate.

The second caveat is the observation and reminder that to establish the location of all Christians, even those who suffer, as being within God's presence, is not to provide "proof" of apostleship, but is only to provide good reason for believing that suffering does not necessarily invalidate a claim to apostleship previously acknowledged as valid. Indeed, if the necessary and sufficient criterion for being an apostle lay only in the claim that, like Moses, one was able to stand in such a position, then, assuming our representation of Paul's argument in II Corinthians 3 is correct, Paul would have proven too much -- that *all* Christians were apostles![4] Thus, to re-state the basis from which our understanding of Paul's argument proceeds: while having access to God's presence is a necessary criterion for valid apostleship (and must be demonstrated), it is not a sufficient criterion; the sufficient criterion of apostolicity is the ability to impart "life" (2:16b with I Cor. 9:2). Within II Corinthians 3, therefore, the only real *proof* that Paul provides of his apostleship is that which the Corinthians cannot deny -- that it was through Paul's ministry alone that the Corinthians had found "life" (II Cor. 3:3). To such a "proof," that Paul had at one time exercised divine authority in his proclamation of the Gospel, his argument (which dominates the remainder of the chapter) concerning the location of all Christians, himself included, within God's presence adds nothing, except the *crucial* refutation of any suggestion that his tribulation had rendered his status invalid.

Our hypothesis in specific terms, consequently, is that Paul's immediate concern in II Corinthians 3 is to overturn the suggestion that the Christian experience of God's presence and the consequent evidence of that experience on a human life is not significantly different from that observed in the case of Moses.[5] Indeed, we shall argue that Paul regarded the Mosaic experience of God as one that was fraught with the danger of death,[6] and was thus quite undesirable, while, in contrast, through Christ an entirely new experience of God's presence had been made possible that led not to death but to life, although the immediate and superficial evidence of that experience appeared, paradoxically, to be the opposite. Our hypothesis requires justification, however, and in this regard we need now to demonstrate, having already argued the case for II Cor. 2:14-17, that a deep concern with the theme of God's presence is in fact present within, and perhaps throughout, II Corinthians 3.

In the discussion which follows, then, we shall examine the remainder of II Corinthians 3, dividing the passage into two significant sections, 3:7-11 and

---

[4]Barrett, II Corinthians, p. 126, quotes Lietzmann as making this point: that in 3:18 Paul has proven too much. Hickling, NTS 21, p. 395, correctly observes that in the focus on all Christians in 3:18, "something more than the theology of Christian ministry is at issue." On the other hand, such a claim cannot imply that something less than the theology of Christian ministry is at stake, since II Cor.4:1 continues the argument on ministry without any hint of a break in Paul's concern for this fundamental issue.

[5]That is, the opponents have not grasped the newness of the eschatological situation and its accompanying covenant made possible by Christ, thus they cannot see that the Mosaic representation of δόξα need not be the relevant one in the present, Christian, situation. See, for example, Rissi, p. 71.

[6]With Levenson, p. 15. Morna Hooker, NTS 27, p. 300, speaks of the "terrifying symbol of the presence of God," but carries the idea no further.

3:12-18, and incorporating a brief discussion of aspects of 3:4-6 into the discussion of the latter passage, 3:12-18 (see below, pp. 126, 132). Our investigation must begin, however, by attempting to establish the significance of the most frequently used noun in the chapter: "δόξα."

II. THE KEY WORD IN II CORINTHIANS 3: Δόξα

The Frequency of Paul's Use of Δόξα

Paul uses δόξα nineteen times in II Cor. 1-8, including eleven times in II Cor. 3, and four times in II Cor. 4 -- a concentration in these chapters which would tend to indicate the possibility of the usage of the word by Paul's opponents and its consequent repeated usage in response by Paul himself.[7] True as this may be, however, it by no means implies that the concept of δόξα was of interest to Paul only insofar as it was of interest to those whom he opposed. Indeed the abundant usage of the word by Paul elsewhere -- 58 times outside II Corinthians in the canonical epistles which bear his name -- demands that δόξα be considered as a term of interest to Paul in II Corinthians not merely because of the polemical situation, but much more because of its significance in and of itself.[8]

The Significance of Δόξα in Paul and the LXX

A cursory survey of Paul's use of δόξα outside II Corinthians easily confirms that Paul generally employs the word in the traditional manner established by the LXX and developed through the apocalyptic and inter-testamental literature -- although this foundation has been modified to embrace salvation through Christ.[9] Thus, for example, in line with the

---

[7]Indeed, the primary cause of the use of δόξα here by Paul may well have been that his opponents had wielded the story of Moses' "glorification" (δεδόξασται) against him as evidence of his non-apostolic status. See Collange, p. 74, and Rissi, p. 73.

[8]With John Koenig, SBL Seminar, Atlanta, Ga., Nov. 24, 1986. It is in fact important to note that although Paul's discussion as a whole throughout II Corinthians 3 has a polemical intent, yet, as Furnish, p. 44, and Hickling, "Is the Second Epistle to the Corinthians a Source for Early Christian History?", ZNW 66 (1975): 285, have argued, Paul remains in full control of the material he is handling.

[9]L. H. Brockington, "The Septuagintal Background to the New Testament use of Δόξα," in Studies in the Gospels: Essays in Memory of R. H. Lightfoot, ed. D. E. Nineham (Oxford: Blackwell, 1957) p. 2, makes this observation with regard to the New Testament as a whole, within which Paul's thought clearly lies. See also, G. von Rad and G. Kittel, TDNT 2, pp.

tradition, while Paul can use the word to signify the manifestation of the divine presence (Rom. 9:4), he can also use it to refer to the revelation of God's divine activity or character (Rom. 1:23, 6:4; II Thess. 2:14), made visible sometimes as light (I Cor. 15:40-41).[10] Indeed, in connection with God's revelation of himself, δόξα can frequently be employed to refer to the praise (Gal. 1:5; Rom. 3:7, 16:27; Phil. 1:11) and obedience (I Cor. 6:20; 10:31) from God's creatures that such a revelation ought to have engendered, and which sometimes (Phil. 2:11), though not always (Rom. 1:21), it did.[11]

In addition, Paul can use δόξα to refer to the eschatological realm of God's presence (Rom. 5:2, 8:18, 9:23, 15:7; I Cor. 2:8; I Thess. 2:12) and the type of existence appropriate to it (I Cor. 15:43; Rom. 8:30; Phil. 3:21).[12] Entrance into this realm, and conformity with it, can be seen by Paul as the very goal or essence of salvation itself (Rom. 2:7, 5:2, 8:18, 15:6-9; I Cor. 2:7; I Thess. 2:12), while sin, by way of contrast, is to be regarded as the source of the initial loss of δόξα and thus of the need for salvation -- the restoration of righteousness (Rom. 3:23; cf. also I Cor. 11:7).[13]

232-55; S. Aalen, "Glory, Honour," DNTT 2, pp. 44-49; L. H. Brockington, "The Presence of God: A Study of the Use of the Term 'Glory of Yahweh,'" ExpTim 57 (October 1945): 21-26.

[10]The use of δόξα to describe the revelation of God's presence can be seen for example in Isa.6:1-3; Ezek.1:28; 3:12; 9:3; 10:4,18; Exod.24:16-17; 29:42-43; 33:17-23; I Kings 8:10-11; Zech.4:5. For God's character and activity: Num.14:21-22; LXX Pss.18:1; 56:6; 62:3; 95:3; 144:5,11,12 (MT Pss.19:1; 57:5; 63:2; 96:3; 145:5,11,12); I Enoch 102:3 "the presence of the Great Glory." For the connection with what is visible or audible -- for example, light, fire, storms, cloud, thunder --: Isa.24:23; 60:1; Pss.29:1-11; 97:1-6; Exod.24:17; Ezek.1:4; 10:4; Zech. 2:4; I Kgs.8:10; Exod.16:10; I Enoch 14:20-22. Brockington, "Septuagint," pp. 2, 7-8, also notes the close connection in the LXX (see, e.g., Isa.52:14) and in Paul (e.g., in I Cor.11:7, and Rom.1:23) between the use of δόξα and the concept of image (εἰκών). So also II Cor.3:18. See also Jacob Jervell, Imago Dei: Genesis 1:26f im Spätjudentum, in der Gnosis und in dem paulinischen Briefen (Göttingen: Vandenhoeck & Ruprecht, 1960), pp. 176-80.

[11]For the use of δόξα to describe the appropriate human response (praise and obedience) to divine δόξα, see Sir.51:17; Jer.13:16; LXX Pss.28:1; 95:7. Barrett, II Corinthians, p. 252, writes that for Paul, "Man exists to give glory to God."

[12]For the use of Δόξα in reference to the heavenly realm, see LXX Pss.18:1; 144:11 (MT 145:11); Dan.7:14; I Enoch 45:3; 55:4; T.Lev.18:5; IV Ezra 7:98. Also, see von Rad, TDNT 2, p. 240. As blessing: Lev.9:6, 23. As eschatological blessing in particular: Ezek. 43:2-5; 44:4; Isa.6:3; LXX Ps.71:19 (MT 72:19); Isa.40:5; IV Ezra 7:91; I QH 17:15; Bar. 5:1; Sir.55:26; Wis.Sol.10:14.

[13]The close connection between δόξα and righteousness, for example, can be seen in LXX Ps. 96:6, "The heavens proclaim his righteousness; and all the peoples behold his glory"; while the connection with salvation can be seen in LXX Ps.56:3-6; Isa.40:5; 60:1-7. See Brockington, "Septuagint," p. 6, and Jervell, pp. 180-83. Bultmann, p. 30, argues that "for Paul God's δόξα is the ultimate goal of all happening and striving." Both in the Rabbis and in the inter-testamental literature reference is made to the loss of the glory that belonged to Adam before the "fall": see Kittel, TDNT 2, p. 246; Gen.Rab. 11 on 2:3; and on the need for

Outside II Corinthians, Paul's primary contribution as a Christian to this traditional formulation of the concept seems to have been to explain the tension between the present inheritance of δόξα and the future:[14] a tension created by the reality of suffering in Christian lives. In this regard, while Paul in no way denies that suffering is a Christian possibility in the present earthly existence, he certainly does deny that that suffering negates the association of Christians with δόξα (Rom. 5:2-5). In particular, Paul argues that δόξα as a blessing of salvation must be conceived of primarily as "hope" (Rom. 5:4, 5),[15] and that suffering takes its place within this understanding, as a necessary (Rom. 8:17) process through which Christians must pass before that hope becomes a visible reality.

To call δόξα "hope," however, is not to say that Paul considers it to be mere wishful thinking, for this hope has a guarantee -- the indwelling presence of God's Spirit (Rom. 5:5; cf.Gal. 5:5; Eph. 1:13), without which no one can claim to be a Christian at all (Rom. 8:9). On the other hand, this guarantee or "first-fruits" (Rom. 8:23) is not iron-clad (Phil. 3:20; I Thess. 5:19), for Paul still regards it as the responsibility of the individual Christian to embrace the present path of life (with its suffering and uncertainty) in faith, giving "δόξα" to God (Rom. 4:20; 12:12).[16]

Paul's understanding of δόξα as "blessing" and "realm," as well as his understanding of the tension between the present and future aspects of the concept can be seen well from I Thess. 2:12, in which Paul uses the words "βασιλεία" (kingdom) and "δόξα" in parallel, urging the Thessalonians to "lead a life worthy of the Lord who calls you into his own kingdom and glory" (RSV). The present tense of the verb (καλοῦντος) in I Thess. 2:12, translated literally as "the one who is calling," signifies that the kingdom and

---

restoration of glory, I QH 17:15.

[14]This is not to deny that Paul has a solid Old Testament foundation for using δόξα within an eschatological framework. See, for example, Haggai 2, to which we shall refer in detail later. Also, Isa.40:5, 58:8, 60:1-2; Ezek.43:1-9; Mic.5:5; Hab.2:4.

[15]See also, Rom.8:24, "τῇ γὰρ ἐλπίδι ἐσώθημεν"; Col. 1:27; I Thess.5:8, in which Paul speaks of the "hope of salvation."

[16]Ernst Käsemann's comments on righteousnes in "'The Righteousness of God' in Paul" in his New Testament Questions of Today, trans. W. J. Montague (Philadelphia: Fortress, 1969), p. 170, are quite applicable to Paul's understanding of δόξα:

"Further, this dialectic of having and not quite having is here projected on to the very condition of being a Christian. For λογίζεσθαιεἰς δικαιοσύνην, used as a technical formula in Rom.4 and Gal.3:6, certainly means that righteousness is only to be had on earth as a pledged gift, always subject to attack, always to be authenticated in practice."

the glory are here conceived as future realities.[17] In the case of the word "kingdom," however, Paul clearly shows elsewhere that he believes that in some measure this kingdom is also a present reality for Christians (Rom. 14:17; I Cor. 4:20). One could by inference, aided by the observation that Paul elsewhere clearly acknowledges that God's δόξα is at work in the world in the present, draw a similar conclusion for Paul's general understanding of δόξα. Indeed, to move ahead of ourselves to II Corinthians, on at least one occasion Paul, in speaking of the Christian experience as a transformation from "one degree of glory to another" (ἀπο δόξης εἰς δόξαν, 3:18) clearly conceives of δόξα as a present blessing;[18] though the emphasis here, consistent with the thrust elsewhere (cf. II Cor. 4:17; I Cor. 15:43), seems to be on the greatness of the *future* δόξα in contrast to the preliminary (though by no means unimportant) δόξα revealed in the *present*.

Further Observations on the Significance of the Word "Δόξα" in the LXX

To further clarify the possible significance of Paul's use of "δόξα" in II Corinthians, four further observations about its use in the LXX need to be re-emphasized or made explicit. The first is that in the LXX, although we have not observed this as yet in Paul, the appearance of δόξα seems to function as a legitimizing element for authoritative revelation and proclamation of God's word. This connection with authority has not passed unobserved by scholars such as Jervell, Martin, and Collange,[19] and can be seen, for example, in Num. 14:10b-15; 16:19-21, 42-45; 20:6; Isa. 6:1-9; Ezek. 1:28-2:3; and I Enoch 14:20-15:2. Of these, for instance, Num. 16:42 reads:

> And when the congregation had assembled against Moses and against Aaron, they turned toward the tent of meeting; and behold the cloud covered it, and the glory of the Lord appeared. (RSV)

In context, the cloud and the glory (LXX, δόξα) clearly appear as the ultimate seal of God's approval on the ministry of Moses.

---

[17]For these observations, see also I. H. Marshall, 1 & 2 Thessalonians (Grand Rapids: Eerdmans, 1983), pp. 74-75; and A. L. Moore, I & II Thessalonians (London: Nelson, 1969), pp. 40-42.

[18]With Bultmann, p. 81.

[19]Jervell, pp. 176-77; Martin, p. 59; and Collange, p. 74.

The second observation is that much of the interest in God's δόξα in the Old Testament is concerned with the establishing of the proper location in which that δόξα can be found. Thus, for example, Ezekiel describes visions in which he sees the flight of God's δόξα from the Jerusalem temple (11:22-23) and its relocation to the eschatological temple (Ezek. 43:1-9). Furthermore, concerning the books of Moses, Gerhard von Rad has written of the Hebrew word *cabod*, translated frequently in the LXX by "δόξα,"[20] that

> For P heaven is certainly the sphere of Yahweh, but He constantly descends to all peoples, e.g., to speak with Moses, to execute judgment, etc. The place of supreme encounter is . . . the tent of meeting, or more exactly, the place which shelters the ark. Thus according to P God has chosen a place where he will maintain His connexion with the people and institute encounter without consuming man through his holiness.[21]

The third observation is related to this latter remark of von Rad which implies that if in fact God's δόξα can at times be regarded as blessing, then it can also at times, paradoxically, be regarded as potential threat, with the power to consume and kill those who treat it in an unprescribed manner. Von Rad speaks of the "cloud" which is often associated with the δόξα as a type of "veil" to hide its ultimate fiery nature which can consume sacrifices (as in Lev. 9:24) as well as people -- such as the two sons of Aaron who "died before the Lord" (ἀπέθανον ἔναντι κυρίου) because they offered unholy fire before the Lord (ἔναντι κυρίου). Indeed, through their death, we are told, God was "glorified" (δοξασθήσομαι, Lev. 10:1-3, LXX).

The fourth observation is that the many varied uses of δόξα tend to overlap each other and can only be separated artificially to enable the differing shades of meaning to be seen more clearly. Seen in their unity, however, the one abiding element in each use of δόξα concerns the presence of God.[22]

This association of δόξα with the concept of God's presence would seem at first glance, however, to be of little or no significance when the word is

---

[20]Kittel estimates that cabod is the Hebrew translation for about half the LXX appearances of δόξα. See TDNT 2, p. 242.

[21]Von Rad, "Δόξα," TDNT 2, p. 240.

[22]See, Kittel, TDNT 2, p. 244. Brockington, "Presence," p. 22, writes of God that "Once His work is recognized and acknowledged and He is given the glory who shall say how far He Himself is removed from His work?"

used to describe the characteristics, activities, or blessings of God, or the praise they engender. That is, it would seem to be quite possible to separate the character or activity of a person from the actual presence of the person from whom they originate. On the other hand, such a separation is certainly not always possible, as can be seen when the dominant characteristic of God to which δόξα is applied, *power*,[23] is considered: the characteristic, "power," is meaningless without its activity; and no such activity is possible without God's actual presence, for power does not somehow originate from God like a thunderbolt, and then leave God behind in its wake. Furthermore, the actual necessity of *not* separating character (or activity, or gift) from the presence of the person from whom they derive has been strongly argued by Ernst Käsemann.

While Käsemann's argument for insisting on the inseparability of God's presence from his character or attributes focuses on Paul's understanding of God's *righteousness*, his conclusions affect the manner in which all of God's activities and characteristics must be viewed, including, we would add, God's δόξα, which is closely associated with *righteousness* in both the LXX (e.g., in Ps. 96:6) and in Paul (e.g., in II Cor. 3:9 and Rom. 5:1-2).[24] In this regard, Käsemann concludes that

> the gift which is being bestowed here is never separable from its Giver. . . .
> The widely-held view that God's righteousness is simply a property of the divine nature can now be rejected as misleading. It derives from Greek theology, which speculates about such properties . . . .[25]

"Δόξα": Summary and Development

These remarks of Käsemann's complete our brief survey of the varied use of the word "δόξα" in Paul and his LXX background. We are therefore now in a position to turn again to II Corinthians 3, and to ask how Paul's use of δόξα is informed by the general understanding of the word as portrayed in the above discussion. In particular, we should not be surprised to find either that the assumption of Paul's deep interest in maintaining God's

---

[23]The association of δόξα with "power" has perhaps been over-stated by Bultmann, pp. 81-83. However, the association remains important. See Brockington, "Presence," p. 21, and Kittel, TDNT 2, p. 243-44. Examples in the LXX include Ps.67:34; Isa.45:24; 63:12. In the New Testament, see Matt.6:13; 24:30; Rev.5:12.

[24]See note 13 above.

[25]Käsemann, New Testament Questions, p. 174.

presence is of value in unravelling his argument, or, given the variety of possible nuances, that in the course of the argument, Paul's usage of δόξα varies. Our attention turns first of all to the argument of II Cor. 3:7-11.

III. II CORINTHIANS 3:7-11

In II Cor. 3:7-11 Paul presents an argument in classical rabbinic fashion in which he compares the "δόξα" of the Mosaic covenant with that of the new covenant established by Christ.[26] A number of questions about this comparison need to be asked to ascertain what it is exactly that Paul wishes to accomplish through it. Three questions in particular will concern us here. The first is the basic question as to why Paul wishes to focus his comparison primarily on the concept of δόξα; the second is to establish what conclusions this comparison yields; and the third is to ask on what basis such conclusions are in fact drawn. These questions overlap to a certain degree, and so cannot be considered consistently in sequential order. Nevertheless, the order in which we have just stated them will form the general outline of the discussion below.

The Reason for Paul's Use of Δόξα in II Cor. 3:7-11

Despite much recent debate on the issue, there seems to be no good reason to doubt the possibility that it was in fact Paul's opponents who intially brought the concept of δόξα into the arena of debate, and this in the process of questioning Paul's apostolic authority.[27] Indeed, given the observation (see above, p. 102) that the appearance of God's δόξα could be conceived as a validation for authoritative proclamation, it would have been quite appropriate for such a concept to occupy a central position in the discussion, not only for Paul's opponents, but for Paul himself.

---

[26]On the Jewish nature of the argument in II Cor. 3:7-11 see, for example, Bultmann, p. 79, and Furnish, p. 203.

[27]With Collange, pp. 74-75; Martin, p. 67. Rejection of the extreme view of Georgi, pp. 254-71, that in 3:7-18 Paul takes over and edits a pre-formed Jewish Christian midrash on Exod. 34:29-35, need not lead to the rejection of the possibility that Paul uses the Exod. 34 passage because his opponents first used it. Thus we reject the conclusions in this regard (though not all the insights) of, for example, Earl Richard, pp. 352, 365; and T. E. Provence, p. 54; and agree with Victor Furnish, pp. 244-45. Our reasons for this position are provided in the text below. See also the mediating position of Stockhausen, Moses' Veil, pp. 12-14, p. 16 note 46, and pp. 39-42.

In this regard, the major proof-text used by Paul's opponents seems to have been the passage from Exodus 34:29-35 to which Paul clearly refers in II Cor. 3:7 (and again in 3:13-16). This passage describes the appearance of Moses following his return to the Israelites from being in God's presence on Mt. Sinai where the two stone tablets of the Law had been inscribed. Paul, closely following the LXX of Exod. 34:30, 35, which proclaims that Moses (and in particular his face, πρόσωπον) was "glorified" (δοξάζω), declares that the δόξα on Moses' face (πρόσωπον) was so overwhelming (MT: *qaran*, "shone") on this occasion that the Israelites were not even able to look at it.

By noting in addition that Paul elsewhere in II Corinthians can describe his opponents as those who "boast in (the appearance of) a face, and not in a heart" (τοὺς ἐν προσώπῳ καυχωμένους καὶ μὴ ἐν καρδίᾳ, 5:12), it takes no great leap of imagination to suggest that the fundamental argument raised against Paul through the teaching of this passage was quite simply that his face did not "shine" (presumably with the figurative light of a charismatic and dynamic personality) as it ought to have done were he truly ordained by God to the task of proclamation, as was Moses. To re-state more fully this understanding of Paul's opponents' objection, Paul's apostolicity was to be doubted precisely because God had provided in Moses the paradigmatic example of the appearance of a person who had been where δόξα was, and who thus could be conceived of as authoritative; and Paul's life did not fit the paradigm. Or, to re-formulate the objection yet again, the Mosaic evidence that a person had been in the presence of God was the transformation of the human face (and life as a whole) so that it reflected one of the traditional appearances of δόξα, radiant light;[28] such "radiant light" however, whether understood literally or figuratively, was manifestly absent from the face and life of Paul.

The Expected Conclusions from Paul's Argument in II Cor. 3:7-11

What Paul must accomplish in II Cor. 3:7-11, therefore, in order to nullify his opponents' objections to his apostolic status is to question the validity of applying his opponents' interpretation of Exodus 34 -- the passage which provided Biblical warrant for their position -- to his ministry. Indeed, the

---

[28] On δόξα as visible divine radiance see TDNT 2, p. 247, with, for example, Luke 2:9 ("and the δόξα of the Lord shone around them").

options for challenging their use of the passage are not hard to determine. That is, either Paul *must deny, and prove the denial,* that δόξα has anything to do with validating apostolic authority; or deny that experiencing δόξα necessarily leads to the visible transformation of one's life by it; or that the visible transformation engendered by δόξα is necessarily connected with its manifestation as radiant light; or that such light is the necessary evidence for the experience of δόξα in the present eschatological situation (though it may be necessary later); or he must argue for a combination of these denials. No other options for rejecting the power of Paul's opponents' argument present themselves, assuming that our understanding of Paul's opponents is correct.

With regard to these possible denials, a preliminary assessment of Paul's argument in II Corinthians (not limiting ourselves just now to 3:7-11) leads to the initial observation that Paul in no way defends his apostolic status by denying the importance of δόξα as a necessary sign of the validity of his standing. Indeed, given the traditional understanding of the importance of the concept in this regard, and given that his own interest in it had been expressed to the Corinthians on a prior occasion (e.g., in I Cor. 15: 40-43), such a denial would surely have been counter-productive. Nevertheless, the absence of any denial that δόξα was inevitably connected with any ministry that was valid, along with Paul's argument in 3:7-11 that there was in fact *more* δόξα in the covenant of which he was a servant than in the covenant administered by Moses, could only seem to confirm the apparent appropriateness of Paul's opponents' question as to why such δόξα had made no visible appearance on his life, as was the case with Moses in Exodus 34.[29]

One possible method of dealing with such a question could well have been for Paul to claim that the Mosaic example of Exodus 34 was only partially applicable to Christian ministry in that though the concept of δόξα remained of importance, nevertheless the experience of δόξα need not necessarily be conceived as leading to the transformation of the life of someone who had been in its presence. This claim, however, Paul does not make either. Indeed, he affirms, in complete agreement with his opponents,

---

[29]Morna Hooker, who does not agree that Paul's use of Exod. 34 derives from his opponents, nevertheless correctly notes, NTS 27, pp. 297-98, that Paul's argument about the greatness of the new covenant δόξα would seem to indicate that Paul's face should have been shining more brightly than that of Moses. Hooker accuses Paul of inconsistency at this point. We, however, hope to demonstrate that Paul's logic is perfectly consistent.

that the opposite was true; that the function of δόξα was precisely to transform the lives of those who experienced it (see 3:18).

Only three further options remained likely for Paul to use in thwarting his opponents' attacks against him based on the Mosaic paradigm of Exodus 34. Either Paul had to argue that the traditional form of evidence for the presence of δόξα must be re-evaluated (so that the appearance of δόξα should not be defined by the appearance of Moses in Exod. 34); or that the appearance of δόξα must be re-considered in covenant and eschatological perspective (so that the appearance of Moses need no longer be considered the necessary evidence for the presence of δόξα *in the present covenant, for the time being*);[30] or that a combination of both these alternatives best reflected the truth.

With regard to the first of these possibilities, a fairly convincing argument can certainly be made from the thrust of Paul's remarks in various places throughout II Cor. 3-5 that Paul did in fact want to argue that the traditional evidence for the presence and experience of δόξα, as represented, for example, by Moses, needed to be re-evaluated and altered. Indeed, Paul clearly asserts that the outward appearance of God's glory which is to leave its impression on Christian lives is not to be that of radiant light (literally or figuratively) but rather that of Christ, and him crucified (cf. 3:18 with 4:6 and 5:14-16). It is, however (to take up the next option, eschatological perspective), to press the point too far to argue that in making such a proposal Paul was completely abandoning the association of literal "radiant light" with δόξα, for in both I Corinthians (15:41-43) and in I Thessalonians (5:4-10, with 2:12) the association of the Christian life with "light" and "δόξα" together is maintained, at least as eschatological hope.

In this perspective, therefore, the fifth option suggested above would seem to be the most likely possibility for Paul to have chosen in refuting the criticisms of his opponents. That is, in assessing the argument of 3:7-11, what we would *expect* to find is that Paul lays the groundwork both for a re-definition of the visual manifestation of δόξα (to be conceived in some way other than as "light") and for an assessment of δόξα in eschatological perspective (to argue that, at least in the new covenant for the time being, "light" is not the "form" of the visible manifestation of δόξα). This latter

---

[30]See Carol Stockhausen's emphasis on the covenantal nature of Paul's argument in Moses' Veil, pp. 16-18, 118, note 4.

focus on eschatology would certainly place Paul's argument in II Corinthians 3 squarely within the center of the Jewish tradition (see our survey above, pp. 100-102) and in consistency with Paul's emphases elsewhere (e.g., in Rom. 8:18-25).

With such an expectation of the general direction of Paul's argument in II Cor. 3:7-11, we turn now to an assessment of the conclusions which Paul does in fact explicitly draw.

Preliminary Assessment of the Conclusions Paul explicitly draws in II Cor. 3:7-11

The Prominence of II Cor. 3:10 in the Structure of II Cor. 3:7-11.
The Nestle text of II Cor. 3:7-11, arranged to highlight its inherent structure, is as follows:

⁷ Εἰ δὲ ἡ διακονία τοῦ θανάτου
    ἐν γράμμασιν ἐντετυπωμένη λίθοις
    ἐγενήθη ἐν δόξῃ,
        ὥστε μὴ δύνασθαι ἀτενίσαι τοὺς υἱοὺς Ἰσραὴλ
        εἰς τὸ πρόσωπον Μωϋσέως διὰ τὴν δόξαν τοῦ
        προσώπου αὐτοῦ τὴν καταργουμένην,

⁸ πῶς οὐχὶ μᾶλλον ἡ διακονία τοῦ πνεύματος
    ἔσται ἐν δόξῃ;

⁹ εἰ γὰρ τῇ διακονίᾳ τῆς κατακρίσεως
    δόξα,
    πολλῷ μᾶλλον περισσεύει ἡ διακονία τῆς δικαιοσύνης
    δόξῃ.

¹⁰ καὶ γὰρ οὐ δεδόξασται τὸ δεδοξασμένον ἐν τούτῳ τῷ μέρει
    εἵνεκεν τῆς ὑπερβαλλούσης δόξης.

¹¹ εἰ γὰρ τὸ καταργούμενον
    διὰ δόξης,
    πολλῷ μᾶλλον τὸ μένον
    ἐν δόξῃ.

We have already made the observation that in II Cor. 3:7-11 Paul compares the δόξα of the old Mosaic covenant with that in the new covenant established by Christ: the argument in rabbinic manner (*qal wa-homer* -- "if with the lesser . . . how much more with the greater") being generally that there is more δόξα in the new covenant than in the old one associated with Moses. To be sure, this is not the only comparison to be found in these verses, though it can be seen by glancing at the above arrangement of the text that it dominates the passage. The other comparison, however, is by no means insignificant, and develops the contrast begun in 3:6 between the two covenants. In tabular form the secondary contrast between characteristics of the old covenant and the new in 3:7-11 is as follows:[31]

killing,	ἀποκτέννει, v.6	:the making of life,	ζῳοποιεῖ, v.6
death,	θανάτου, v.7	:the Spirit,	πνεύματος, v.8
judgment,	κατακρίσεως v.9	:righteousness,	δικαιοσύνης, v.9
abolition,	καταργούμενον, v.11	:permanence,	μένον, v.11

We shall question the function of this series of mutually exclusive characteristics later. However, for the present our attention will remain with the one characteristic which Paul does not regard as the exclusive possession of one covenant as over against the other, but which he affirms as belonging, in some measure at least, to both: δόξα.[32] The question that occupies our attention in this regard concerns Paul's primary purpose in making this comparison of "δόξα's."

We have already observed that Paul's first conclusion in comparing the δόξα of one covenant with another is that there is more δόξα in the new covenant than in the old. Such a conclusion by itself, however, certainly does nothing to resolve any issue involved in the validity of Paul's apostolicity. Indeed, since Paul's opponents would probably have actually agreed with Paul on this point, Paul would surely have only made them all the more eager to press their question as to why this greater δόξα was not apparent on his face. Consequently, it seems more than likely that this initial conclusion serves primarily as a foundational premise for one that is more significant (and controversial) -- like that, for example, which can be found in II Cor. 3:10, a verse which clearly stands apart from the surrounding verses.[33]

That II Cor. 3:10 does in fact stand apart from the surrounding verses can best be seen by observing the structure of the passage in which Paul's major comparison between covenantal "δόξα's" is made through three parallel statements in 3:7-8, 3:9, and 3:11: each beginning with "εἰ," with the

---

[31]With, for example, Plummer, p. 89; C. J. A. Hickling, NTS 21, p. 386; Martin, p. 59.

[32]With, for example, Hickling, NTS 21, pp. 390-91.

[33]It is hard to see how II Cor. 3:10 functions as an explanation of (so, Bultmann, p. 83) or support for (so, Furnish, p. 204) the argument of 3:7-9. The interpretation of "γάρ" as indicating the addition of another remark (a further conclusion), which Furnish suggests as a possibility, is to be preferred.

contrast being indicated by πῶς or πολλῷ μᾶλλον.[34] The first contrast, 3:7-8, is certainly longer than the other two, though this additional length by no means destroys the parallel structure of all three comparisons -- the expanded text in 3:7-8 serves only to draw attention to some of the narrative elements that establish the text of Exodus 34 as the Scriptural background from which Paul's argument proceeds.

The difference in structure of II Cor. 3:10 from the parallel comparisons of 3:9 and 3:11, cannot, however, be dismissed so easily as that of 3:7-8; for in no way at all can the verse be seen to fit the *qal wa-homer* pattern. Rather, the verse, 3:10, serves as a further conclusion drawn from the three (or the previous two) parallel comparisons. That is, Paul argues that the δόξα of the new covenant is in fact so great (the conclusion of the *qal-wahomer* argument which now serves as the new premise) that it renders the δόξα of the old covenant to be of no consequence (the new conclusion) -- "what has had splendor has not had splendor" (Furnish's translation of καὶ γὰρ οὐ δεδόξασται τὸ δεδοξασμένον, 3:10).[35]

The Need for a Scriptural Basis and Reason for Paul's Conclusion in II Cor. 3:10. We have no reason to doubt this general interpretation of II Cor. 3:10 which understands Paul to conclude that the δόξα of the old covenant is rendered of no account by the δόξα of the new, although we shall attempt shortly to add a further nuance to it. There are, however, at least two questions which the conclusion begs. The second question concerns Paul's objective in drawing this conclusion (what exactly did he hope to achieve by it?), while the first concerns the basis for the conclusion (on what authority does the conclusion rest?).[36]

---

[34]See the format of the Greek text of the passage, above, p. 110. Also, Martin, p. 59. With Furnish, p. 205, we find to be unconvincing the argument of E. Hill, "The Construction of Three Passages from St. Paul," CBQ 23 (July 1961): 299-301, that τὸ δεδοξασμένον in II Cor. 3:10 refers to the δόξα of the new covenant rather than the old. Hill's concern with the logic of the text within its context, however, is notable.

[35]Furnish, p. 201.

[36]The question of the authority behind Paul's claims is raised by Brevard Childs, The Book of Exodus: A Critical, Theological Commentary (Philadelphia: Westminster, 1974), pp. 620-21, in connection mainly with the argument of II Cor. 3:7 (that the δόξα of the old covenant was fading). Childs writes:

"But what Paul simply assumes from his readers is their agreement with his description of the first splendor as 'about to fade away'. Paul does not establish this point even though it has no obvious basis in the Old Testament text. He takes it for granted even though, if it were to be denied, the force of his argument would have

Concerning the first question, what needs to be observed is that Paul provides no good reason, but needed to, if his opponents were to accept his conclusion that the super-abundance of δόξα in the new covenant makes the δόξα of the old redundant. That is, the conclusion is merely stated without rationale -- unless some known tradition or text was recognized both to lie behind the argument and to be regarded as authoritative by the opponents.

To illustrate the point, if Paul were to have argued that the δόξα of the new covenant was so bright (premise) that it could not be seen by human eye (conclusion), then his conclusion might well have been regarded by his opponents as patently reasonable (given that the opponents knew that the Israelites shielded their eyes from the Mosaic δόξα, and that the new δόξα was even brighter). Even with such a reasonable argument, however, given the seriousness of the situation it would still have been conceivable for Paul to have taken the precautionary measure of providing an example from Scripture to demonstrate further his argument's ultimate validity. To argue, on the other hand, as Paul actually does in 3:10, that the new covenant δόξα was so great (premise) that it made the old covenant δόξα to be of no consequence (conclusion) -- given that the old covenant δόξα (or an extension of it in the Mosaic tradition) was the opponents' prize possession, and given that Paul still had to prove that his invisible δόξα was not a pure figment of his imagination -- was by no means to make a "reasonable argument" which could be easily accepted by his opponents, but was to launch an offensive against the emotional heart of the opponents' position which "demanded" proof. That is, such an an argument could scarcely have led to any other response than that of laughter or anger, for Paul was either not serious or blasphemous, *unless* he could provide authoritative proof for his assertion.

To repeat ourselves, therefore, the following two questions must now be addressed. First of all, can a Scriptural basis be found for Paul's conclusion that the Old Covenant δόξα had been "de-δόξαfied" by the exceeding δόξα of the New Covenant, invisible though this new δόξα appears to be? Second,

---

been lost."
While we do not agree with Childs's understanding of the Pauline argument in general, his observation here is absolutely crucial to the understanding of the thrust of II Cor. 3:7-11 and to our exegesis which follows. That is, to us it is inconceivable that Paul would make an argument with no authoritative base, and which therefore could be overthrown with a simple "I disagree" from his opponents. Our assumption, therefore, is that such an authoritative base must exist, and must be sought if the text is to be understood.

what *exactly* is Paul trying to argue and why? That is, how does Paul's conclusion function as a defense of his apostolicity?[37]

The Prophecy of Haggai as the Scriptural Basis for Arguing in II Cor. 3:10 that the Mosaic Δόξα was of No Value

The Implicit Use of Haggai 2. Although it has been commonly argued that other passages than Exodus 34 dominate the early verses of II Corinthians 3,[38] discussion of the Scriptural background for II Cor. 3:7-18 has focused almost exclusively on the Exodus 34 passage.[39] What, however, we wish to argue here is that behind Paul's argument in II Cor. 3:7-11 lies not only the Exodus passage, referred to explicitly, but the argument of the prophet Haggai in his second chapter, referred to implicitly. This implicit reference to Haggai, we would suggest, serves not only to provide a sufficient and authoritative answer to any Corinthian questioning of Paul's conclusion in 3:10, that the old covenant δόξα was rendered of no consequence by the δόξα of the new covenant, but also serves to clarify the central thrust of the section 3:7-11 as a whole, which, we shall argue, focuses not so much on the *present* manifestation of δόξα in the new covenant as on its *future* eschatological manifestation.

The Initial Rationale for Suggesting Paul's Interest in Haggai. As far as we can ascertain, Paul nowhere else makes use of the prophecy of Haggai, and thus our suggestion that he does so in the course of II Corinthians 3 naturally raises the question as to why, in the first place, we would even suggest the connection, and why, in the second place, we believe it to be reasonable. With regard to the first question, our intial interest in the Book of Haggai stems directly from the hypothesis that matters of cult,

---

[37]We might note that Windisch, Der Zweite Korintherbrief (Göttingen: Vandenhoeck & Ruprecht, 1970), p. 112, with, for example, Jan Lambrecht, "Structure and Line of thought in 2 Cor. 2:14-4:6," Biblica 64 (1983): 344-46, argues that II Cor. 3:7-18 is a (Pauline) literary insertion into the argument and has nothing to do with the defense of apostleship. Thomas Provence, p. 69, also argues that 3:7-11 provides no direct support for his qualification for the ministry. As explained already (above, p. 97), although we do not regard these verses as directly defending apostleship, we certainly would argue that they are integral to Paul's argument that his apostleship has not been invalidated by the seeming absence of δόξα in his life.

[38]E.g., Martin, p. 52 points to Exod. 31:18; Jer. 31:33; Ezek. 11:19, 32:26.

[39]E.g., Provence, pp. 68-73; Richard, p. 352; Hooker, NTS 27, p. 297; Furnish, pp. 226-29; Bruce, p. 191.

temple, and the presence of God were of great interest to Paul. That is, along with other books of the Old Testament such as Exodus, Leviticus and Ezekiel,[40] for example, Haggai, although brief, explicitly possesses this general interest. In particular, the book centers on events which surrounded the building of the second temple at the end of the sixth century BCE.[41]

With regard to the second question, the word δόξα, the critical word in II Corinthians 3, appears within Haggai (LXX) on three occasions: each time in Chapter two (2:3, 7, 9), and each in connection with the temple.[42] Indeed, in pursuing this observation it becomes clear that the second of these references to δόξα possesses an emphasis that is extremely similar to that in the *qal-wahomer* argument of II Corinthians 3:7-11.[43] That is, the specific context of Haggai's use of δόξα in LXX 2:9 is as follows: "διότι μεγάλη ἔσται ἡ δόξα τοῦ οἴκου τούτου ἡ ἐσχάτη ὑπὲρ τὴν πρώτην, λέγει κύριος παντοκράτωρ." The assertion made here, in the name of God, is that while the δόξα of the post-exilic temple presently under construction seems to be absent, nevertheless it *will be* greater than the δόξα of the former, but now destroyed, pre-exilic temple. The similarity with Paul's thought in II Cor. 3:7-11 is striking -- the only difference is that Paul is comparing the δόξα of covenants, and Haggai, the δόξα of temples.

Confirmation that Paul in II Corinthians 3:7-11 is specifically using the argument of Haggai 2 derives from further parallels with II Cor. 4:16-5:10, to which we will turn shortly (see p. 116). First of all, however, the broader context of the situation in Haggai needs to be discussed to see if Haggai can indeed cast further light on the situation in II Corinthians 3.

---

[40]See, for example, Exod. 25:1-31:18; Lev. 1:1-16:34; Ezek. 40:1-46:24.

[41]On the theme of Haggai see David L. Petersen, Haggai and Zechariah 1-8 (Philadelphia: Westminster, 1984), p. 19; Rex Mason, The Books of Haggai, Zechariah and Malachi (Cambridge: Cambridge University Press, 1977), pp. 9-10; D. R. Jones, Haggai, Zechariah and Malachi (London: SCM, 1962), p. 27.

[42]See also the use of "ἐνδοξάζομαι" in Hag. 1:8. Carol Stockhausen's argument (throughout her monograph, Moses' Veil) concerning Paul's use of the interpretative technique of gezera shava, catchword bonding, would also lend significant weight to our position.

[43]It does not matter for Paul's purposes here whether he correctly understands how Haggai used the word "δόξα." Petersen, pp. 50, 64, 68, believes that the word is used in the general sense of splendor or wealth rather than in any connection with God's presence. Jones, pp. 41, 45, and Mason, p. 21 argue that no mutually exclusive choice need be made, for the splendor of the temple can be understood as deriving from God's presence. What can be said with certainty is that God's presence is definitely an issue for Haggai in this context (see, for example, Hag. 2:5).

The Importance of the Future in Haggai 2. One question in particular arising directly from Hag. 2:9 LXX (as quoted above) is vital to pursue. The question concerns the future tense of the verb "ἔσται" (which is also present in II Cor. 3:8), and asks how significant the temporal element of the tense is. That is, what we wish to ask is *when exactly* the δόξα of the new temple will be greater than that of the former temple. The answer can be established through reading the passage in context.

The problem with which the prophet is dealing in Haggai 2 originated among the older Israelites who were involved in the building of the second temple and who were able to remember the greatness of the Solomonic temple destroyed before the exile. Their memories, rather than inspiring them to work, however, were in fact discouraging them, since it was obvious to them that the new structure simply could not compare in grandeur with that of the old. Why, then, they asked themselves, should they put their heart and soul into what was visibly second-rate at best? To these dismayed Israelites, therefore, whose discouragement was also affecting the zeal of others for the temple project,[44] the prophet asks the following poignant questions (LXX 2:3):

Τίς ἐξ ὑμῶν ὃς εἶδεν τὸν οἶκον τοῦτον ἐν τῇ δόξῃ αὐτοῦ τῇ ἔμπροσθεν;
καὶ πῶς ὑμεῖς βλέπετε αὐτὸν νῦν;
καθὼς οὐχ ὑπάρχοντα ἐνώπιον ὑμῶν.

Who is there among you who saw this house in its former δόξα?
And how do you see it now?
Like something which has no existence before you.

Having asked these questions which presumably reflect the attitudes of the older Israelites, Haggai attempts to renew their strength by giving them the promise of God's presence and of his Spirit (Hag. 2:4-5; cf. II Cor. 3:3),[45] and the further admonition to take courage (Hag. 2:4b-5a):

διότι μεθ᾽ ὑμῶν ἐγώ εἰμι, λέγει κύριος παντοκράτωρ,
καὶ τὸ πνεῦμά μου ἐφέστηκεν ἐν μέσῳ ὑμῶν· θαρσεῖτε.

For I am with you, says the Lord Almighty
and my Spirit is present in your midst: Be of good courage!

---

[44]With Petersen, p. 63.

[45]Rissi, p. 84, and Martin, p. 71 point to the Spirit as the means of access to the presence of God. It seems more than possible that Haggai indicates this same intimate relationship between the Spirit and access to God's presence in presenting God's presence and His Spirit in parallel in 2:4-5.

This latter admonition to take courage (θαρσεῖτε), however, although dependent on the promise of the present presence of the Spirit of God, was not merely dependent on such a promise, but rather on the future which it assured. Thus we find Haggai developing his argument of encouragement further by speaking of a day to come *in the future* when God would shake the whole creation (σείσω τὸν οὐρανὸν καὶ τὴν γῆν καὶ τὴν θάλασσαν καὶ τὴν ξηράν, v.6) at which time he would bring into the temple such treasures (ἐκλεκτὰ) from the nations that it would be visibly and inescapably true that the latter δόξα of the house (or temple) would be greater than the first (Hag. 2:9).

The strong temporal emphasis in the future tense of ἔσται in Hag. 2:9 is, then, clear. However, some ambiguity remains in the verse as a whole for the comparison at issue can be construed either as a reference to the δόξα of the first temple in contrast with that of the second temple, or as a comparison between the initial δόξα of the second temple as opposed to its latter δόξα. It seems to me that the ambiguity is quite intentional. That is, Haggai's resolution to the fundamental problematic, the memory of the δόξα of the former temple disheartening the older builders of the new temple, is both to compare the old temple with the new temple, as well as to compare the δόξα both of the old temple and the new temple as it now appears, with the future eschatological δόξα of the new temple -- a future guaranteed by the promise of God's presence and Spirit. Thus, Haggai's practical conclusion on the basis of this "doxological" hope is that the Israelites need to put the former temple's δόξα out of their minds entirely (they are to reckon it as "οὐ δεδόξασται" we might say with Paul, II Cor. 3:10) even though no δόξα can at present be seen within the new temple in the process of construction; for such visible δόξα in the new temple is nevertheless on its way, to be made perfectly visible in the future to one and all.[46]

Confirmatory Evidence from II Cor. 4:16-5:10 that Haggai provided Scriptural authority for Paul's Argument in II Cor. 3:7-11. Confirmatory evidence of Paul's use of Haggai 2 in II Corinthians 3 is difficult to summarize briefly, except to note that there is a remarkable parallel of thought between the two passages *once* Paul's argument is seen in eschatological perspective. The most explicit evidence, however, confirming that Paul certainly had the Haggai passage in mind in writing II Corinthians

---

[46]God's activity in Hag. 2:6-9 is all future: v.6, σείσω; v.7, συσσείσω, πλήσω; v.9, δώσω.

in general comes from his argument in II Cor. 4:16-5:10, which focuses on the contrast between the nature of the human body in the present and in the future (the eschaton) not only in terms of the body being a building (οἰκητήριον ἐξ οὐρανοῦ, 5:2) but also in explicit cultic terms as a tabernacle (σκηνή, 5:4). That is, the general contrast in II Cor. 4:16-5:10 is precisely the same as in Haggai 2, in that it concerns the present and future form of a certain kind of temple.

Moreover, this connection between the passages also extends to specific vocabulary in that some of the key terms in II Cor. 4:16-5:10 are also to be found in Haggai. For example, the words δόξα, βλέπω and θαρρέω (θαρρέω being a synonym for θαρσέω which increasingly replaced it in common usage by Paul's day)[47] each occurs in Haggai (see 2:3, 5, 9), and in a sense consistent with their use in II Corinthians (see 4:17, 18; 5:6, 8). That is, in a manner which precisely parallels the logic of Hag. 2, Paul argues in II Cor. 4:16-5:10 that while any δόξα at work in the human body is at present invisible, inevitably engulfed by tribulation and not by apparent δόξα, nevertheless there is no reason to doubt that such δόξα exists and will one day become manifest. Indeed, what the Corinthians must do, Paul urges, is to take their eyes off the visible things, the βλεπόμενα, and look to the things which as yet are not visible, μὴ βλεπόμενα, the "hope" (3:12) which one day in the future will become visible. This Paul himself has done, and in so doing found the courage (5:6), which others too can find (see 1:6), to pursue the Christian life to its end.

To use the metaphorical terms employed by Paul (though the terms are more than merely metaphorical), Paul conceives of the progress of the Christian life, from tribulation to manifest δόξα (cf. I Cor. 15:43), as a cultic building project, involving the building, or, more correctly, the waiting for God's building of the house or tabernacle (οἰκία τοῦ σκήνους, 5:1) which constitutes the human body. Such a project Paul has no intention of giving up. Rather, as Haggai admonished the Israelites to be in their own "cultic building project," he was always of good courage -- θαρροῦντες, 5:6; θαρροῦμεν, 5:8.

The consistency of thought with Haggai, then, both here in II Cor. 4:16-5:10, and in II Cor. 3:7-11, provides the justification we shall depend upon in assuming that the argument of Haggai 2 does in fact lie in Paul's

---

[47]So BAG4, p. 352.

thought, and provides the authoritative and logical rationale for his exposition of Exodus 34 in the terms in which he proceeds to use the passage in II Cor. 3:7-11. We have already provided some indication in the paragraphs above that, on the basis of Haggai 2, II Cor. 3:7-11 should be understood as eschatologically oriented. We must now press our case explicitly by reference to two important words in the passage, ἔσται in 3:8, and ὑπερβαλλούσης in 3:10.

The Influence of Haggai's Eschatology on Paul's Argument in II Cor. 3:7-11

That Paul's thought in II Cor.3:7-11 can in fact be read in eschatological perspective -- that Paul is not arguing primarily that the present δόξα of the new covenant is greater than that of the old, but mainly that the future δόξα of the new covenant will one day be visibly greater than that of the old -- can be confirmed both by Paul's use of ἔσται in 3:8, and by his use of ὑπερβαλλούσης in 3:10.

The Use of ἔσται in II Cor. 3:8. We have already noted above that Haggai (LXX 2:9) uses the word ἔσται, and does so to convey the fact that the *future* δόξα of the second temple would be greater than that of the present or the past. The same future tense of the same verb (ἔσται) is used by Paul in his first *qal wa-homer* argument in II Cor. 3:8: "πῶς μᾶλλον . . . . ἔσται ἐν δόξῃ." While some scholars have argued that the function of the future tense in Paul's argument is merely logical,[48] others have argued that it is both logical and temporal.[49] Confirmation for this temporal usage -- as implying that Paul saw the future δόξα of the new covenant as being the focus of his comparison with that of the old (at least in the first *qal wa homer* argument) -- can be found from further observations on the Pauline text.

For example, it is clear even from II Corinthians 3 itself that Paul did not always find it necessary to use a "logical future" tense to make a logical argument. In II Cor. 3:9, for example, in the second *qal wa-homer* argument,

---

[48]The "logical" sense of ἔσται is asserted, for example, by Bultmann, p. 81, and Barrett, II Corinthians, p. 116.

[49]Furnish, pp. 227-28 and Martin, pp. 62-63, follow Collange, pp. 77-78 in seeing both a logical and temporal aspect to ἔσται in II Cor. 3:8. All three are in agreement, furthermore, that in this context the temporal, eschatological sense is dominant.

parallel to that in 3:7-8 in which ἔσται is used, the future tense is not used at all, but the present. Indeed, the verb used in the present tense in 3:9, περισσεύω, carries with it the open-ended sense of process or development ("is abounding" -- and will certainly continue to abound)[50] which the temporal future of II Cor. 3:8 can also have.

The Use of ὑπερβάλλω and ὑπερβολή in II Cor. 3:10 and 4:17. A more important observation, however, in confirming that the thrust of Paul's argument in II Cor. 3:7-11 concerns the future manifestation of new covenant δόξα rather than its present manifestation, derives from a comparison of II Cor. 3:10 with 4:16-5:10, the passage referred to above (p. 116) as also being influenced by Haggai 2. Two related words occur in these passages in II Corinthians: in the former, "ὑπερβαλλούσης"; and in the latter, "ὑπερβολή." In the former, in II Cor. 3:10, Paul's rationale for regarding the δόξα of the old covenant as of no account stems from his understanding of the new covenant δόξα as "ὑπερβαλλούσης" -- which seemingly, though not necessarily, describes the present state of the δόξα.[51] On the other hand, in the latter passage (in 4:17) the use of the related noun, ὑπερβολή, in relation to δόξα is made in reference not to its present manifestation, which cannot be seen, but quite specifically in reference to its eschatological manifestation to be revealed to human sight only in the *future*, and as a result of the present work of tribulation (τὸ γὰρ παραυτίκα ἐλαφρὸν τῆς θλίψεως ... καταργάζεται ...). Consequently, interpreting II Cor. 3:7-11 in the light of the unmistakable emphasis of II Cor. 4:16-5:10, we would argue that Paul's concern in the passage is oriented to the future and to the implications of that future for the present.

To sum up, while it is only within the first of the three *qal-wahomer* comparisons of 3:7-8, 9, and 11 that the future orientation of the comparisons is explicit, nevertheless, our argument is that it is implicit in the use of the verb περισσεύω in the second comparison (3:9), and in the use of ὑπερβαλλούσης" in 3:10. Moreover, we would suggest now, with

---

[50]To press the case more strongly, we might suggest that in 3:9 the present tense of περισσεύω is a "futuristic present," referring to "an event which has not yet occurred, but which is so certain that in thought it may be contemplated as already coming to pass." So, H. E. Dana and Julius R. Mantey, A Manual Grammar of the Greek New Testament (New York: Macmillan, 1955), p. 185.

[51]Dana and Mantey, p. 230, indicate, however, the importance of context for determining the sense of tense in participles.

Furnish,[52] that the emphasis on the future is left as an open possibility in the third comparison (3:11), which has no main verb. Indeed, a supplied main verb in this third comparison *must* have an orientation directed to the future,[53] functioning in connection with the explicit definition of the new covenant as one that remains (μένον), remaining, presumably, for ever, throughout the future.

Furthermore, we would suggest that one reason why Paul did not press this future emphasis consistently throughout 3:7-11 might lie precisely in the fact that he did not wish to argue that there was *no* δόξα in the present, as if the first-fruits of the δόξα had *not* been given to Christians.[54] The eschatological tension, as in Haggai 2, and as is clear elsewhere in Paul's writings,[55] had to be maintained. Nevertheless, as in Haggai 2, when Paul draws his major conclusion in II Cor. 3:7-11, it is, we would argue, the future aspect of the eschatological tension which is unmistakably on his mind -- for the super-abundance of δόξα in the New Covenant, like that of the second temple to Haggai, is only a future, although guaranteed (II Cor. 1:22, 5:5), reality.

Paul's Conclusions in II Corinthians 3:7-11

Paul's conclusion in II Corinthians 3:7-11 can now be described clearly, and can be seen both as pertinent to the issue of his apostleship and as bearing the stamp of authority for his opponents. In his *qal wa-homer* argument, for example, Paul concludes not so much that the present δόξα of the new covenant is (visibly) greater than that of the old, but that the future δόξα of the new covenant *will be* (visibly) greater than that of the old. Thus he explains why there is not more visible δόξα (at least as defined in traditional terms as some sort of radiance) on his face than there was on Moses' face.[56] Furthermore, for such an eschatological argument satisfactory biblical warrant can be found in Hag. 2:9. This conclusion by

---

[52]Furnish, p. 227.

[53]Barrett, II Corinthians, p. 118, translates II Cor. 3:11b as "much more shall that which abides continue in glory" — our underlining indicates the future orientation of the main verb supplied by Barrett. See also the comments of Bultmann, pp. 83-84.

[54]Furnish, p. 228, argues that since Paul regards the Spirit (referred to in II Cor 3:3-6) as the "down-payment" of the future, that the future orientation of II Cor. 3:7-11 is further established.

[55]E.g., in Rom. 6:1-11; Phil. 1:6, 3:7-12.

[56]See Morna Hooker, NTS 27, p. 298, who sees in Paul's thought in II Cor. 3:7-11 a glaring inconsistency.

itself, however, does not explicitly explain why *no* δόξα can be seen on Paul in the present. An appropriate explanation, however, can certainly be found when it is assumed that the background of Paul's argument lies in Haggai 2, which is further drawn to the Corinthians attention by the polemical conclusion of II Cor. 3:10 -- that the former δόξα, or form of δόξα, was of no consequence in the light of what was to come.

Indeed, to draw the Haggai and Corinthian texts together, Paul's implicit argument, we believe, can be expressed as follows: As in the days of Haggai, so the emphasis on visible δόξα was now actually proving a hindrance to God's eschatological work, and had to be cast out of the mind of God's people if they were to obey him in the present. This abandonment of interest in visible δόξα Paul himself has made, so that for him "οὐ δεδόξασται τὸ δεδοξασμένον" (3:10). Now, however, the Corinthians (and Paul's opponents in general) needed to do the same -- if they, like Paul, were to take their place within, and as God's fellow laborers in the construction of, the eschatological covenant or "temple" of God.

IV. II CORINTHIANS 3:7-11: SUMMARY AND DEVELOPMENT

Our study of II Cor. 3:7-11 began with the proposal of several conclusions which Paul might have drawn in rebutting the opposition to his apostolicity (see above pp. 106-109). In terms of these proposals what we have found is that in II Cor. 3:7-11, with Scriptural warrant, Paul has both laid the groundwork for re-defining the present expression of δόξα (by annulling the value of the present appearance of the traditional manifestation of δόξα) and has placed in the future, in the eschaton, the ultimate appearance of δόξα (in its traditional manifestation). What now, we must ask again, might Paul be expected to say as he develops his case in 3:12-18?

Two possibilities suggest themselves, each functioning as part of Paul's defense of the absence of apparent δόξα from his life: either that Paul will begin to re-define the present appearance of δόξα, or that he will expand on the conclusion drawn from 3:7-11 (and especially from 3:10), that the old manifestation of δόξα is not worth possessing. What we wish to argue is that it is in fact this latter option that Paul pursues initially, and this he does by developing and demonstrating the validity of the second comparison within II Cor. 3:7-11 -- the comparison between the Mosaic covenant as one of death, judgment and abolition, and the new covenant as one of the Spirit, righteousness, and permanence.

CHAPTER SIX

II Corinthians 3:12-18

I. INTRODUCTION

In II Cor. 3:7-11 Paul placed before the Corinthians two sets of comparisons. The primary comparison, focusing on the nature of δόξα, led to Paul's conclusion that the δόξα of the old covenant was of no significance at all in comparison to the greatness of the new covenant δόξα to be revealed in the future. The secondary comparison, focusing on the ministry of the two covenants, concluded that the old ministry resulted in death (θάνατος), condemnation (κατάκριμα) and abolition (καταργέω), while the new, established by Christ, led to the Holy Spirit (πνεῦμα), righteousness (δικαιοσύνη) and permanence (μένω).[1] What we wish to argue now is that in II Cor. 3:12-18 Paul proceeds with the defense of his apostleship and the exposition of the type of ministry which it entails, justifying the absence of apparent δόξα from his face by building on the foundation of the comparisons he has drawn in 3:7-11.[2] In particular, we intend to demonstrate

---

[1]Furnish, p. 206, follows van Unnik, NovT 6: 158, in noting that the "οὖν" of II Cor. 3:12 indicates a close connection with the preceding verses so that in 3:12 "Paul moves on to apply the point made in 7-11 to the topic of ministry." Neither Furnish, however, nor anyone else to my knowledge, indicates that it is not only the primary contrast focusing on δόξα, but also the secondary contrast of 3:7-11 which occupies Paul's attention in 3:12-18.

[2]With Plummer, p. 89, Collange, p. 72, Furnish, p. 202, and Bultmann, p. 87, we understand the word "διακονία" (ministry: 3:7-9) to be intimately related to the word "διαθήκη" (covenant: 3:6), so that in speaking of a certain kind of ministry Paul is always thinking of the covenant in which it functions and which determines its character. This interchangeability is most clearly seen in 3:7 where Paul speaks of the "διακονία" of death as one that is engraved in letters on stone. Such a declaration makes no sense when διακονία is translated simply as "ministry," but makes excellent sense when διακονία is interpreted as "covenant." See further the use of "γράμμα" (3:7) in connection with the word "διαθήκη" in 3:6.

that by use of the secondary comparison in 3:7-11 Paul argues in 3:12-18 that the Mosaic δόξα with its radiant appearance is not only insignificant and unnecessary, but that it is in fact quite undesirable, since it contains not only the power to bless, but the power to bring death and condemnation (θάνατος and κατάκριμα), even to those who claim to be Christians.

The immediate question that needs to be asked if this argument is to be entertained is whether the critical terms of II Cor. 3:7-11 occur explicitly in 3:12-18. A cursory observation of the passage reveals that from the first comparison, δόξα occurs in 3:18; while only two of the terms of the second comparison occur: καταργέω, to abolish, twice, in 3:13 and 14; and πνεῦμα, spirit, three times, in 3:17 and 18. What we wish to establish now, however, is that the remaining terms were not absent from Paul's mind when he wrote this passage despite their "literal" absence from the text -- especially those referring to the ministry of the old covenant as leading to death and condemnation. First of all, for example, we will argue that in II Cor. 3:12, the hope to which Paul refers is based both on the permanence of the new covenant from which it springs, as well as on the absence of death and condemantion as the determining realities of that covenant.

II. II CORINTHIANS 3:12

The Antecedent of τοιαύτη in II Cor. 3:12:
Freedom from Death and Judgment

II Cor. 3:12, the first verse of the section 3:12-18, seems to lend clear support to the argument that Paul's thrust in II Cor. 3:7-11 is primarily eschatological (see pp. 113-20), for the verse acts in part as a summary in which Paul, on the basis of the preceding discussion ("Ἔχοντες οὖν"), claims to have established that the Christian experience is one of "hope"-- hope, in particular, that leads to boldness: "Ἔχοντες οὖν τοιαύτην ἐλπίδα πολλῇ παρρησίᾳ χρώμεθα, . . ."[3] While it seems clear that the hope to which Paul

---

In our discussion below, therefore, we shall sometimes simply omit the use of the word "ministry" and speak directly of the "covenant" which determines its character. That is, we shall speak not just of the "ministry of death," for example, but of the "covenant of death." On the other hand, we shall also keep in mind that the issue at stake throughout Paul's comparison of covenants is the validity of his "διακονία," his apostleship.

[3]That the eschatological interpretation of 3:7-11 is reinforced by Paul's reference to "hope" in 3:12 is a point made also by Furnish, p. 228, and Collange, p. 78.

refers here is focused on the nature of the δόξα that he has just described in 3:7-11 -- so that, as in Rom. 5:2, the hope concerns the future sharing of the δόξα of God -- nevertheless it is not entirely clear as to what characteristic of this hope (or of its δόξα) Paul intends to refer in describing it as "τοιαύτην" (of such a kind). Thus, for example, to make some suggestions based on II Cor. 3:7-11 to which the "οὖν" of 3:12 draws attention,[4] "τοιαύτην ἐλπίδα" may refer to the primary contrast in those verses which would emphasize the exceeding greatness of the new covenant δόξα and the future (hoped for) manifestation of that δόξα despite its present apparent absence; or to the secondary contrast which would emphasize the fact that the δόξα belongs to a covenant characterized by the Spirit, righteousness and permanence, rather than by death, condemnation and abolition; or perhaps to a combination of these.[5]

The Rationale for Choosing the Secondary Comparison of II Cor. 3:7-11 as the Basis of Paul's Thought in II Cor. 3:12. Our preference in this regard is to choose the second option as the fundamental one in Paul's thought (while not excluding the other as being contributory), and this for three reasons. The first and most subjective reason would be that in 3:7-11 Paul in no way develops or explains the comparison between these mutually exclusive characteristics of the old and new covenants depicted in the passage, and to which we have referred above in passing (see p. 110). It would seem reasonable, then, for his attention to turn now to such a discussion.

Less subjectively, in the second place, we may point to Rom. 4:23-5:21 (especially 5:1-2) as an interpretive key for II Cor. 3:12. That is, in

---

[4]With Furnish, p. 206 and Van Unnik, NovT 6, p. 158.

[5]Most commentators simply regard "such a hope" as referring to the permanence (τὸ μένον, v. 11) of the new covenant δόξα: so, Bruce, p. 192; Barrett, II Corinthians, p. 118; Collange, pp. 85-86; and Furnish, p. 206. Van Unnik, NovT 6, p. 159, and Provence, p. 74, indicate that the hope of 3:12 is connected more with the covenant in which the δόξα operates than with the δόξα: for them hope is based on the fact that the new covenant is one that is permanent.

Bultmann, p. 84, on the other hand, in speaking of 3:12, declares that the hope is "grounded in the knowledge of the μένον (v.11), or it is knowledge of the πνεῦμα (v.8) and δικαιοσύνη (v.9)." That is, Bultmann sees the hope of 3:12 as related to the positive features of the secondary contrast of 3:7-11 -- to which observation we shall add the further observation that the lack of negative features (death and condemnation) also provide hope. Furthermore, Bultmann also recognizes that in 3:12 "hope" (ἐλπίς) functions as a synonym for "διακονία," which we have already argued (in note 2 above) is virtually synonymous with the word "covenant." Consequently, with Bultmann's help, we might suggest that Paul could equally have used the phrase "therefore, having such a covenant" in 3:12 -- though of course the word "hope" retains an inherent future emphasis not explicit in the word "covenant."

Romans 4-5 Paul provides a theological basis for his "hope of sharing the δόξα of God" (5:2b). This basis, however, is not dependent on the surpassing greatness of that hope, or on the assurance of its future manifestation (though these thoughts are intimately related; see Rom. 5:3; 8:21-25). Rather, the stated basis of hope lies in the fact that a change in covenants has taken place so that now (νυνὶ, Rom. 3:21),[6] (a) *righteousness* has been made possible through faith (5:1), (b) the *Holy Spirit* has been given (5:5), and (c) the *death and judgment* that reigned over mankind from the time of Adam has been made of no effect (5:16-17). Our argument, then, would be that if such is the basis for Paul's hope in Romans, then in II Corinthians it would not be surprising to find the basis of hope to be similar or the same.

Our third reason for choosing this explanation of τοιαύτη, emphasizing the characteristics of the new covenant which contrast with those of the old, is that such an emphasis in II Cor. 3:12 would seem to be in agreement with a similar possible emphasis of τοιαύτη elsewhere within II Corinthians 3 -- in 3:4, to be precise, which reads: "Πεποίθησιν δὲ τοιαύτην ἔχομεν διὰ τοῦ Χριστοῦ πρὸς τὸν θεόν." That is, in II Cor. 3:4, while τοιαύτη is used to describe the nature of Paul's boldness or confidence (πεποίθησις) and not directly the nature of his hope, yet the mutual theme of boldness or confidence can be found in both verses (represented in 3:12 by παρρησία, a word of similar meaning to πεποίθησις in 3:4)[7] and the close connection between hope and boldness in 3:12 ("since we have such a *hope* we act with great *boldness*") makes it possible to suggest that the verses are somewhat similar in thought. Consequently, we would observe that in II Cor. 3:4, although the antecedent of τοιαύτην is itself not unambiguously apparent within the verse or the preceding verses, nevertheless, it is certainly reasonable to argue on the basis of the immediately preceding verse, 3:3 (ἐγγεγραμμένη οὐ μέλανι ἀλλὰ πνεύματι θεοῦ ζῶντος, etc.) that it is precisely in the fact that there is now a new covenant in place which is one

---

[6]The actual term "covenant" (διαθήκη) does not appear in Romans except in 9:4 and 11:27. Indeed, in the Pauline literature the word is used only nine times in all. However, in Gal. 3:15 Paul clearly understands the "law" (νόμος) as a covenant, and given the use of νόμος in 3:21, a verse which clearly refers to a change in eschatological situation (so Käsemann, Romans, p. 92), we feel our use of "covenant" here to be justified.

[7]The connection between πεποίθησις in 3:4 and παρρησία in 3:12 has been noted by Bultmann, p. 85, and Martin, p. 67. Hering, p. 22, notes the close connection between the meaning of the two words.

of the Spirit, as foretold by Ezekiel and Jeremiah,[8] that Paul has found a boldness "of such a kind" as the one he claims to have in 3:4[9] -- the "Spirit" being one of the fundamental characteristics of the old/new covenant contrast in 3:7-11 (see, for example, 3:8).

From such a perspective, then, assuming that τοιαύτη in II Cor. 3:12 refers essentially to the hope that is derived not just from the nature of the new covenant view of δόξα as greater, or as becoming visibly greater in the future, but from the fact that the hope derives from a covenant that is free of death, condemnation and abolition, the following paraphrase of II Cor. 3:12a, "Ἔχοντες οὖν τοιαύτην ἐλπίδα," is possible: "we have a hope that is based on the fact that we need fear neither death nor condemnation because the old covenant is being abolished, and because we have been given the Holy Spirit and have been made righteous through the new covenant which will last for ever."

The Interpretation of the Secondary Comparison of II Cor. 3:7-11: A New Obedience or New Rules? Before proceeding to a discussion of implications of this understanding of the first half of II Cor. 3:12 for the rest of the verse -- which conveys the information that such a hope leads Paul to express great boldness -- our understanding of why exactly death and condemnation are no longer to be feared must be explicated, for most scholars discussing the question (usually in reference to the announcement of the old covenant as a covenant of death in 3:6-7) answer it in different terms from the ones we believe Paul to be emphasizing. That is, the tenedency has been to emphasize that the lack of fear from condemnation and death in the new covenant springs from the *new activity and power* to overcome sin that has been made available to individuals through the Holy Spirit. Thus, as is often pointed out, whereas in the old covenant the demands of God were mere demands with no power provided by God to fulfil them, and consequently to escape the condemnation of death, the new covenant in contrast, at least as expounded by Paul, was one in which, through the Holy

---

[8]The connection with Paul's wording and the eschatological texts of Ezek. 11:19 and Jer. 31:33 (the latter referring explicitly to a "new covenant," has been commonly observed. See, for example, Barrett, II Corinthians, p. 107.

[9]Provence, pp. 60-61, notes the possibility that τοιαύτη in 3:4 refers back both to 3:1-3 and to 2:17. We do not agree completely with him, yet would certainly argue that 2:17 and 3.4 are intimately connected in that a major issue in both verses concerns Paul's boldness to approach God.

Spirit, God had provided the necessary power to fulfil his demands, and so to escape from such condemnation, and consequently from the fear of it.[10]

For our part, we would certainly not wish to deny that Paul considered the Holy Spirit to be a new source of moral power to be experienced freely within the new covenant. However, what we certainly wish to deny is that that new moral power is the basis upon which Paul argues that the new covenant brings with it freedom from death and condemnation. That is, what we wish to stress is that even in the face of moral lapses which plagued the Christian Community at Corinth (and no doubt everywhere) from time to time (see, e.g., II Cor. 2:5-11), freedom from the fear of death and condemnation, though not to be accepted with presumption (see Rom. 6:1-2; 1 Cor. 10:1-13), could nevertheless be presumed -- for the covenantal change instituted by Christ was not first of all a moral one (leading to a change in behavior) but a legal one (leading to a change in covenantal rules).

Thus, in terms of II Corinthians 3, what we are suggesting is that the counterpart to death and condemnation in II Cor. 3:7-11 is not first of all "πνεῦμα," the Holy Spirit, but "καταργέω" -- the fact that death and condemnation, and, indeed, the whole "γράμμα" which kills (3:6), have been, or are being (τὸ καταργούμενον, 3:11) abolished. Or, to be more precise, if πνεῦμα is to be seen in any sense as the counterpart to θάνατος in 3:7-11, which seems to be the implication of 3:7-8, then we are suggesting that πνεῦμα must be understood not first of all as moral power, but as covenant guarantee (see II Cor. 1:22; 5:5: ἀρραβών), guaranteeing (among other things) that the old "rule" that sin inevitably leads to death, so that death has the final word for human existence, is no more.[11]

To use Pauline expressions from Romans to expand upon this point, what is at issue is the old covenant link between sin and death as the automatic punishment for sin. Paul calls this "link" the "law of sin and death" (Rom.

---

[10]See for example, Thrall, Corinthians, p. 132; Bultmann, p. 78; Furnish, p. 201; Plummer, p. 88; Martin, p. 61; Rissi, pp. 72-73; and Bruce, p. 190.

[11]Rissi, p. 71, in speaking of γράμμα and πνεῦμα in 3:6 argues that "they do not represent abstract principles, but the concrete historical realization of the two covenants within the framework of the history of salvation." Although Rissi proceeds, p. 72, to discuss γράμμα in terms of its powerlessness, yet his observation that the terms πνεῦμα and γράμμα are first of all covenantal in orientation is crucial for our own discussion.

See also Bruce, p. 190, who writes that "the written code kills" in that "it pronounces the death-sentence on the law-breaker." It is this "death-sentence," we are arguing, which Paul sees as being removed by Christ, as the initial blessing of the new covenant in that the door is now open for people to enter the realm of the Spirit and righteousness, and to remain in it for ever.

8:2), and at its heart lay the decree that the wages of sin was death (Rom. 6:23), a decree (κρίμα) that had been in effect from the time of Adam (Gen. 2:17) and which declared that if a person commits a single trespass the result would be condemnation (κατάκριμα) and death (θάνατος; see Rom. 5:16-17). It is this *decree,*[12] we are suggesting, whose abolition or annullment (καταργέω) functions as the crucial difference in the old covenant as compared with the new, and which is, furthermore, the basis not only of Paul's hope, but of his boldness and confidence (both in Rom. 5:1-2 and II Cor. 3:4, 12).

The importance of, and the clarification of, the context yielded by this interpretation of the secondary contrast of II Cor. 3:7-11 will be seen shortly in the discussion of Paul's use of τέλος in II Cor. 3:13. First of all, however, our examination of II Cor. 3:12 needs to be completed, for in 3:12 Paul not only speaks of "hope" but also of "boldness." Indeed, Paul claims that he is a man who acts with "great boldness" (πολλῇ παρρησίᾳ) precisely because of the hope which he holds. Our concern, in particular, in the face of Paul's silence, will be to ascertain the object of his boldness: who is it, exactly, before whom Paul knows great boldness?

The Object of Παρρησία in 3:12: Boldness
Towards God, and then Towards People

To argue as we have done, that the primary basis both of Paul's hope and of his boldness lies in the fact that death and condemnation are being abolished through Christ, is to come to the inescapable conclusion that this boldness must be seen as referring to Paul's relationship to God, the one who no longer administers death and condemnation. More specifically, Paul's boldness can be regarded as referring to the same unhindered right of access (προσαγωγή) into the very presence of God of which Paul speaks in Rom. 5:2, and which is the precursor of sharing God's δόξα (Rom. 5:3).

Support for such an interpretation of παρρησία is not lacking from the rest of the New Testament. Indeed, both in Eph. 3:12, and in Heb. 4:16 and 10:19 identical use is made. Eph. 3:12 is quite succinct in this regard and reads as follows: "ἐν ᾧ ἔχομεν τὴν παρρησίαν καὶ προσαγωγὴν ἐν πεποιθήσει . . . ." Furthermore, it is worth noting that the word παρρησία

---

[12]Paul refers to death as a judicial decree in II Cor. 1:9, in the phrase "τὸ ἀπόκριμα τοῦ θανάτου." See the note by Furnish, pp. 113-14.

in this verse is not only connected with the concept of access to God, but so also is the word πεποίθησις -- which is exactly how we understand its function in II Cor. 3:4 as well (see below, p. 132).

This understanding of παρρησία in II Cor. 3:12, as directed towards God, has, however, not passed unchallenged.[13] Indeed, a major objection can be raised on the basis of the very next verse, 3:13, which reads as follows:

καὶ οὐ καθάπερ Μωϋσῆς ἐτίθει κάλυμμα ἐπὶ τὸ πρόσωπον αὐτοῦ πρὸς τὸ μὴ ἀτενίσαι τοὺς υἱοὺς Ἰσραὴλ εἰς τὸ τέλος τοῦ καταργουμένου.

This verse functions (as indicated by the use of καθάπερ) as an illustration of 3:12, and portrays the lack of παρρησία shown by Moses in contrast to that which Paul claims to exercise (and perhaps which all Christians can claim: χρώμεθα, 3:12, is plural). In particular, it seems clear that Moses' *lack* of boldness, and therefore Paul's *possession* of boldness, was directed toward the Israelites and not toward God.

The human orientation of παρρησία in II Cor. 3:12 based upon the counter-illustration of that παρρησία in 3:13 cannot, then, be doubted. However, what needs to be pointed out by way of contrast is that the presence of such an emphasis by no means precludes our claim that Paul's *primary* interest in declaring his παρρησία in 3:12 lies in its power to describe the nature of his access to God. That is, if, as we have argued, the defense of apostolicity (the right to speak with boldness to others) stems ultimately from the right to enter the presence of God (to approach God with boldness), then the two directions of παρρησία, horizontal and vertical, can be seen to be necessarily related -- boldness or authority directed towards people being necessarily based upon boldness to approach God, with the latter being primary.

Furthermore, to suggest a "double" emphasis of παρρησία in II Cor. 3:12, to insist that Paul's boldness is directed both to God and to people, but primarily to God, fits well with the context of II Cor. 3:12-18 as a whole. For

---

[13]Though Bruce, p. 192, Rissi, pp. 76-77, and Windisch, p. 119, indicate the association of the word παρρησία with the concept of access to God, most other commentators argue that Paul's primary concern in using παρρησία in II Cor. 3:12 is to describe his relationship to other people. So, for example, Barrett, II Corinthians, p. 118; Martin, p. 67; Bultmann, p. 85; Thrall, Corinthians, p. 135; and Furnish, pp. 206-7.

example, it cannot be doubted that in 3:18 attention is drawn to the remarkable access *to God* that Paul believes all Christians have -- an access that permits them to gaze freely at the very δόξα of the Lord, and to be changed by it, as was Moses both on Mt. Sinai and in the tent of witness (Exod. 34:29-35), in the presence of God. Indeed, it seems pertinent to suggest that the theme of access to God is not merely a theme of 3:12 or 3:18, but of every verse in 3:12-18, including 3:13b, for Paul changes the subject of his attention from Moses in 3:13a to the Israelites in 3:13b, and in particular to their inability to see God's δόξα, and thus to have unhindered access to it, because of a "veil" (κάλυμμα) which, he argues, shielded the Israelites from the δόξα that radiated from Moses -- a veil which, Paul insists (3:13b-15), remains effective to his own day on those who read the old covenant (as if it were their source of salvation).[14]

Despite the emphasis of 3:13a, then, which necessarily forces us to interpret Paul's παρρησία in 3:12 as referring at least in part to his "horizontal" relationship with people, there seems to be no good reason to doubt, and enough sound evidence to claim, that Paul's primary interest in proclaiming this παρρησία was to describe the nature of his "vertical" relationship with God, a relationship which was crucial to speak about since it was intimately related to the validity of his claim to be an apostle. Paul's argument in II Cor. 3:12, then, to paraphrase the verse again, and to sum up our discussion so far, runs as follows: Therefore, because our hope of receiving God's δόξα is based on the fact that we need fear neither death nor condemnation since the old covenant is being abolished, and because we have been given the Holy Spirit and have been made righteous through the new covenant which will last for ever, we can approach the presence of God with boldness not fear, and so proclaim God's word to others with a boldness that derives from divine authority.

The Application of our Interpretation of II Corinthians 3:12 to its General Context

Before proceeding to ask how such an understanding of II Cor. 3:12 affects the logic of Paul's argument as it develops in 3:13, its immediate context, some indication of its possible impact and appropriateness to the general context of II Corinthians 3 can be made by briefly looking back to II Cor. 3:4-6 and then forward to 3:13-18.

---

[14]See Rissi, pp. 71, 82.

II Cor. 3:4-6 and Paul's Claim to Sufficiency. In II Cor. 3:4, for example, Paul makes the following claim to have boldness: "πεποίθησιν δὲ τοιαύτην ἔχομεν διὰ τοῦ Χριστοῦ πρὸς τὸν θεόν"; and immediately follows this claim with the denial of his self-sufficiency: "οὐχ ὅτι ἀφ' ἑαυτῶν ἱκανοί ἐσμεν λογίσασθαί τι ὡς ἐξ ἑαυτῶν, . ." On the basis of our discussion above it can be seen that Paul's denial of self‑sufficiency here is not mere pious talk, but gospel truth; not mere subjective claim, but objective fact. That is, if Paul's boldness is understood as being directed primarily towards God, so that in 3:4 his declaration is that through Christ he has boldness to approach God himself (πρὸς τὸν θεόν);[15] and if the basis of the boldness is understood not as the possession of the new moral power provided by the Spirit, but as the possession of the new eschatological age guaranteed by the Spirit -- an age in which the decrees of death and condemnation have been abolished -- then quite literally Paul's apostolic authority, based on his ability to enter God's presence, rests on nothing that he himself has done, or could do. Only a change in covenant, something that could be initiated by God alone, could provide Paul safe passage into God's presence, from which point he speaks with authority -- κατέναντι θεοῦ ἐν Χριστῷ λαλοῦμεν (2:17b). The old covenant framework, espoused by Paul's opponents, could provide no such safe passage, for the γράμμα kills (3:6).[16]

Indeed, with Paul's argument understood from this point of view, the connection between 3:5-6 and 2:17 which various scholars have observed through Paul's repeated use of the word "sufficient" (ἱκανός) is further

---

[15]Collange, p. 58, points out that πρός is nowhere else used with πεποίθησις, Elsewhere, for example, to indicate trust "in" someone, Paul uses the preposition "ἐν" (so, Phil. 3:4; II Thess. 3:4) or "εἰς" (so II Cor. 8:22). Barrett, II Corinthians, p. 110, regards the use of πρός here to amount to virtually the same sense, though Collange, p. 58, n. 4, specifically rejects this understanding. Collange, along with other commentators (so Bultmann, p. 74; Furnish, p. 183) understand πρός here as referring to Paul's confidence which derives from God. In this case, as Collange indicates, the prepositions in the phrases "διὰ τοῦ Χριστοῦ" and "πρὸς τὸν θεόν" have identical meaning.

Martin, pp. 52-53, and Héring, p. 22, however, indicate that Paul's concern in 3:4 is to speak of Paul's boldness as exercised in the divine presence. In TDNT 6, p. 8, n. 2, Bultmann indicates, as does Martin, p. 52, the close association of "πρὸς τὸν θεόν" in 3:4 with "κατέναντι θεοῦ" in 2:17b. This observation is foundational to our own understanding.

[16]While the understanding of γράμμα remains debated, we agree with Rissi, p. 71, that Paul's use is eschatological, referring to the old aeon with its old covenant conveyed through the Mosaic Scripture.

strengthened.[17] That is, the claim to stand in God's presence, κατέναντι θεοῦ, in 2:17b can now be seen to be a claim made (and in the process of being defended) in 3:4-6 as well.

Our interpretation of II Cor 3:12 would certainly seem, then, to clarify the flow of Paul's thought in II Cor. 3:4-6. What we must now ask is whether such clarification is also made possible in II Cor. 3:13-18.

II Cor. 3:13-18 and the Change in the Sense of δόξα. Our agreement that Paul, in speaking of his boldness in 3:12, is at least in part referring to his attitude towards people and not just towards God, points us to the possibility that a fundamental shift in his use of δόξα occurs in the passage that follows.[18] That is, in contrasting his boldness with the lack of it in Moses, who "veiled" from the gaze of others the δόξα which his ministry conveyed, Paul's implicit claim is that his boldness towards others is one in which he (or at least the covenant which he represents) can freely and without hindrance from any veil impart δόξα to others. Indeed, such is the explicit meaning of 3:18: "we with unveiled face, beholding the δόξα of the Lord . . ." It is not hard to observe that to speak of δόξα in this manner is to assume a change in its function within the discussion, for it clearly functions now no longer (or, at least, not only) as a symbol of authority *to be received* before proclaiming God's Word, but as a religious benefit or blessing *to be imparted*, and which is therefore desirable not only for apostles, but for every Christian.[19]

Furthermore, this observation necessarily raises the question of the nature of Paul's on-going defense of his apostolicity. That is, if the possesion of δόξα is no longer being viewed by Paul as the confirmation of apostolic authority, then it would also seem that some sort of shift in Paul's argument in defense of his apostolicity is taking place in 3:12-18 in contrast to the

---

[17]For example, see Martin, p. 53; Bultmann, p. 69; Provence, p. 56.

[18]Morna Hooker, NTS 27, p. 298, also notes this transition, while Michel Carrez, ResSciRel 63, p. 328, indicates that Paul has the ability to exploit every nuance, usage and connotation of the word δόξα. Both Hooker and Carrez see no logical unity in Paul's approach, while we, for our part, do.

[19]See our discussion on the various uses of δόξα in the LXX. Above, pp. 99-104.

argument made in 3:7-11.[20] How then, it must be asked, does the defense of his apostolicity proceed in 3:13-18?

What we now wish to argue in response to this question is that the change in the understanding of δόξα evident in 3:12-18 is very much related to the connection which we have suggested that Paul is making between these verses and the secondary comparison of 3:7-11 (involving the contrasting characteristics of the covenant: death/Spirit, etc.). In particular, our understanding is that the change in the use of δόξα, conceived now as religious blessing (at least in 3:13), becomes the basis for Paul's scriptural defense of his radical claim (for, as yet it is only claim) that the old covenant (and thus its ministry) is one that leads to death and condemnation, and therefore ought to be (and is being) abolished.[21]

Moreover, in the second place we would suggest that once Paul has established that the old covenant ought to be and is being abolished by Christ (because it leads to death), he sets himself free to argue as well that the right to approach God with boldness belongs not only to apostles such as himself, but to all Christians, even to those who suffer tribulation -- or at least to all those who, whatever their circumstances, fully embrace the new covenant, and who therefore stand "in Christ."[22] Among such as these are the Corinthians, if, and only if, they hold fast to the gospel as declared not by Paul's opponents, "super-apostles" as they may seem to be (II Cor. 11:5), but by Paul.

---

[20]Hickling, NTS 21, p. 395, makes this observation with regard, specifically, to Paul's thrust in 3:18:

> There is a very far-reaching question underlying the shift from expounding the glory of an apostle to asserting the glory of every Christian. Something more than the theology of the Christian ministry is at issue here.

With Hickling's last comment we agree, but would also observe that this "something more" is not unrelated to the issue of apostolicity. That is, while the ability to "stand in God's presence" is not a sufficient criterion for apostolicity (not everyone who stands in God's presence is an apostle), it is nevertheless a necessary one (all apostles do stand in God's presence), which Paul has to demonstrate as being true at least for himself -- and for as many others as he so chooses -- if his apostolic defense is to stand.

[21]Joseph Fitzmyer, TS 42, p. 636, accurately senses the emotional power of Paul's description of the old covenant ministry in claiming that "With pejorative and unflattering terms he refers to the promulgation of the Mosaic Law as a 'dispensation of death',..."

[22]Bultmann, p. 70, writes of 2:17, that the "ἐν Χριστῷ" is used in the locative sense and denotes a new creature belonging to the new world of Christ." The new world to which Bultmann refers, we interpret not only as the new eschatological age inaugurated by Christ, but to the covenant introduced in the new age by Christ, and which determines the character of the "world" in which Christians are to live.

II Corinthians 3:12: Summary and Development

In our study of II Cor. 3:12, then, we have argued that the "hope" of which Paul speaks is based on the change in covenant characteristics -- from the old covenant characterized by condemnation and death, and in the process of being abolished, to the new, characterized by the life-giving Spirit, righteousness and permanence. Furthermore, on this basis we have understood Paul's "boldness" to refer primarily to his relationship with God, and have seen that this interpretation fits well with the flow of thought from 2:17 to 3:6. On the other hand, we have not denied that Paul's boldness towards God was intimately associated with his boldness towards others (the latter deriving from the former), and that this human orientation to Paul's boldness is clearly reflected in a change in the significance of the word "δόξα" in 3:12-18, to be conceived now not as the symbol of apostolic authority (as in 3:7-11) but as a religious "blessing" given to God's people in general.

Given the importance of Paul's claim in II Cor. 3:12, as we have interpreted it, that the old covenant is one which leads to death and condemnation, and is being superseded in a radical manner by the new covenant established by Christ, we might well expect Paul to provide some evidence from Scripture for his position. Indeed, what we now want to argue is that this is precisely what he begins to do in II Cor. 3:13, and that he does so both by relying on Exodus 34, the passage used against him by his opponents, and by employing the word "τέλος," the interpretation of which has been greatly debated.

III. II CORINTHIANS 3:13

II Cor. 3:13 reads as follows: "καὶ οὐ καθάπερ Μωϋσῆς ἐτίθει κάλυμμα ἐπὶ τὸ πρόσωπον αὐτοῦ πρὸς τὸ μὴ ἀτενίσαι τοὺς υἱοὺς Ἰσραὴλ εἰς τὸ τέλος τοῦ καταργουμένου." The crucial question to answer both in interpreting II Cor. 3:13 itself and in unravelling the development of Paul's argument as he moves from 3:12 to 3:13, concerns the meaning of the word "τέλος." Two directions for interpreting the word are possible.[23] The first is that τέλος should be understood in the temporal sense, as indicating the termination of an object, while the second understands τέλος to signify the object's goal or purpose. In the context of II Cor. 3:13

---

[23]According to BAG4, pp. 818-19.

the object has generally been assumed to be the δόξα on Moses' face, described in Exodus 34, and over which, as Paul reminds his readers in II Cor. 3:13, Moses placed a veil. What should be observed, however, is that although the reference to δόξα may be implicit in II Cor. 3:13, it is certainly *not* explcit: the word does not occur in the verse. We must therefore now look at the two lexical possibilities for interpreting τέλος, while also seeking to understand the object to which τέλος refers. To date, it must be added, no solution to Paul's use of the word in II Cor. 3:13 has proven satisfactory.

The Interpretation of Τέλος in
II Cor. 3:13: Terminus or Goal?

Τέλος as Termination. The general assumption in adopting the understanding of τέλος as "termination" in 3:13[24] has been that Paul's reference is to the fact that when Moses used a veil to cover his face in Exod. 34:35, he was, for some reason, trying to conceal the truth that his contact with God's δόξα failed to leave a permanent effect on his life -- that the effect of God's δόξα upon him came to an end (τέλος). Such a view, however, is not without its difficulties, not the least of which is that there appears to be no evidence from Judaism (indeed, the opposite is true),[25] let alone from Exodus 34, the passage from which Paul draws his basic text, to support the idea that the δόξα on Moses' face was in any way temporary. For Paul to make the suggestion without Biblical or traditional warrant that Moses' δόξα faded from his face would be, as we also argued concerning Paul's assertions in 3:7-11 (see above, p. 112), to achieve nothing other than to stir up the opposition against him, either in the form of laughter or of accusations of heresy.

To be sure, it may be that some warrant unknown to us did in fact exist for what Paul was trying to declare: thus the use of the evidence from silence must certainly be made with caution. However, even if some external evidence were to be found to suggest that the δόξα on Moses face was

---

[24]Τέλος is understood as termination or cessation by Bruce, p. 192; Plummer, pp. 97-98; Hooker, NTS 27, pp. 297-300, Thrall, Corinthians, p. 135; Bultmann, p. 85; Martin, p. 68; Barrett, II Corinthians, pp. 119-20; Collange, p. 96; van Unnik, NovT 6, p. 161; Hickling, NTS 21, pp. 390-91; Furnish, p. 207; and Lambrecht, p. 359 (including nn. 37 and 38).
[25]On the lack of contemporary Jewish evidence on the cessation of Moses' δόξα see for example, van Unnik, NovT 6, p. 161; Hooker, NTS 27, p. 300, n. 10 draws attention to Targum Onkelos, Deut. 34:7 to show a tradition indicating the permanence of Moses' δόξα.

temporary, and thus came to an end (τέλος), it must still be asked whether in II Cor. 3:13 Paul is in fact using τέλος to describe δόξα, since there is neither mention of δόξα in the text nor agreement in gender between δόξα (feminine) and the participle which seems to qualify it, καταργουμένου (neuter).[26] Such agreement in gender between δόξα and the participle of καταργεῖν Paul does in fact make in 3:7, in speaking for the first time about the δόξα on Moses' face -- "τὴν δόξαν τοῦ προσώπου αὐτοῦ τὴν καταργουμένην." Why, then, it must be asked, if the τέλος of 3:13 was intended by Paul to describe the nature of the Mosaic δόξα at all, does he alter the established syntax of 3:7, to refer implicitly to δόξα through the awkward construction of 3:13?

One common explanation for this difficulty, expressed, for example, by C. K. Barrett,[27] is simply that in using the neuter form of the participle, Paul is placing the τέλος of the δόξα within the greater framework of the old covenant to which it belongs. That is, the neuter participle καταργουμένου therefore refers not just to the δόξα but to the whole Mosaic dispensation as represented, for example, by the neuter word γράμμα.[28]

We would note that this understanding of the text is certainly possible, but would also note that if it is correct that καταργουμένου in 3:13 refers to γράμμα in 3:6 (which we believe it does), and if τέλος refers to the termination or cessation of the Mosaic δόξα (which we believe it does not) then Paul has assumed that a conceptual leap will be taken by his readers to associate the idea that the δόξα on Moses' face was fading with the fact that the covenant to which it belonged was also "fading" -- in the process, in fact, of being abolished. To expect that his readers would take such a hermeneutical leap to confirm a conclusion that they presumably did not initially agree with -- that the old covenant was not merely improved upon by the new covenant,[29] but that it was being completely annulled by it -- is, we would suggest, though by no means impossible, at best to assume of the Corinthians a rational objectivity and grammatical sophistication that would have been foolish for Paul to presume; and is at worst to imply that

---

[26]A point observed, for example, by Barrett, II Corinthians, p. 119; Furnish, p. 207; and Hooker, NTS 27, pp. 209, 304.

[27]Barrett, II Corinthians, p. 119.

[28]See II Cor. 3:6; and Morna Hooker, NTS 27, p. 209.

[29]Koenig, p. 126, quotes Georgi as claiming that Paul's opponents stressed such continuity between the two covenants.

Moses, the opponents' hero and role model, was being deceitful,[30] hiding the fact that his authority and/or his covenant was merely temporary. These objections to this understanding of τέλος are, we admit, fairly subjective. Nevertheless they are sufficiently strong to make it sensible to search for another alternative to the understanding of the word τέλος.

Τέλος **as Goal.** The other alternative for interpreting τέλος is that which regards it as teleological. In this case scholars generally understand the goal to which Paul refers by the word "τέλος" as "δόξα," or, more precisely, as the covenant to which the δόξα belongs.[31] Indeed, the arguments in favor of this interpretation are fairly cogent. First, Paul elsewhere frequently uses τέλος in the sense of goal or outcome (e.g. in II Cor. 11:15, Phil. 3:19, and Rom. 6:21-22).[32] Second, such an interpretation would be in line with Jewish tradition as we know it which suggests that the δόξα on Moses' face never faded or came to an end.[33] And third, this interpretation would provide a satisfactory explanation as to why the participle καταργουμένου is neuter, not feminine, and therefore not in agreement with δόξα -- the reason being the one mentioned above, that the neuter refers to all that is involved in the old covenant (including the covenant's "δόξα"), all represented by the neuter noun, τὸ γράμμα (3:6). In this case Paul would be declaring that the (unfading?) δόξα on Moses' face somehow expressed, conveyed or resulted in the goal of the Mosaic covenant which was being abolished.

If, however, τέλος is to be understood in this latter manner, as the goal of the old covenant, then the question must now be asked as to what exactly the goal of the old covenant and its δόξα represents.

---

[30]So, Georgi, p. 265; Windisch, p. 120; van Unnik, NovT 6, p. 162. Barrett, p. 119, writes: "Certainly this proceeding was less than perfect frankness," though Hickling, NTS 21, p. 390, suggests that Moses veiled his face from reverential motives; Lambrecht, however, p. 359, n. 38, finds Hickling "quite unconvincing"! With Barrett, II Corinthians, p. 120, Furnish, p. 207, regards II Cor. 3:14a as an attempt by Paul to diffuse the possible misunderstanding of Moses' motives as deceitful.

[31]Τέλος is understood as "goal" by Rissi, p. 80; Provence, p. 75; Hanson, pp. 15-17; Héring, p. 25; Georgi, p. 261.

[32]That τέλος signifies "goal" in Rom. 10:4 remains highly debated, and so is not suggested in our text.

[33]See above, note 25.

The Object of Τέλος Interpreted
as Goal in II Cor. 3:13

Τέλος as Goal: The Goal of the Old Covenant as Christ. The most common understanding of τέλος interpreted as "goal" is that it refers to Christ himself and the new covenant for which he stands.[34] Indeed, such an understanding would seem initially to find excellent confirmation in Rom. 10:4, in which Paul explicitly calls Christ "the τέλος of the law." However, despite various arguments attempting to confirm the association of "Christ" with the use of τέλος in II Cor. 3:13, Victor Furnish is correct in observing that no persuasive reason has yet been provided to explain *why* Paul thought Moses would have wanted to hide the goal of the old covenant, conceived of as Christ, from Israel.[35]

Clearly, then, we need to search for an alternative to this proposal, that the τέλος, understood as the goal of the old covenant, refers to Christ. In what other terms, we must ask, can Paul conceive the goal of that which is being abolished, the "καταργουμένου," the old covenant (with its δόξα), to be?

Τέλος as Goal: The Goal of the Old Covenant as Death and Condemnation. In seeking an alternative understanding of τέλος as goal we would certainly agree with those who argue that the τέλος which we need to understand is the goal or the outcome of the old covenant as exemplified by γράμμα. Indeed, once such an assumption is made and attention is turned to the use of the word "γράμμα" in II Cor. 3:6, at least one alternative goal can be suggested from Paul's declaration that the γράμμα *kills* (τὸ γὰρ γράμμα ἀποκτέννει): that is, that the τέλος in 3:13 refers to condemnation and death.

---

[34]Rissi, p. 81; Hanson, p. 17; Provence, p. 76; and Héring, p. 25, each understand τέλος in II Cor. 3:13b as referring to Christ, and each look to Rom. 10:4 as supporting evidence for their view.

[35]Bruce, p. 190, writes that Paul's interpretation of the ministry of the old covenant as leading to death "differs radically from the rabbinical statement that . . . 'God sat on high engraving tablets which would give (the Israelites) life' (Exod. Rab. 41.1 on Exod. 31:18)."

The Case for Interpreting Τέλος as the Death and Condemnation Associated with the Old Covenant

The Context of II Cor. 3:13. The theme of death and condemnation is certainly not far from Paul's mind as he writes II Cor. 3:13, for, in II Cor. 3:7-11, as Paul compares the δόξα of the old covenant with that of the new in his primary comparison, in his secondary comparison he explicitly uses the words "θάνατος" and "κατάκριμα." Furthermore, we have already suggested above that Paul brings this secondary comparison to the forefront of his thought in moving to 3:12, and what we would argue now is that this transition in emphasis is maintained at least through 3:13 as well. It remains quite plausible then, to suggest that the τέλος to which Paul refers in 3:13 is not the termination of δόξα, nor Christ himself, conceived as the goal of the old covenant, but *death* and *condemnation* -- or, more precisely, the Mosaic experience of God (as represented by the δόξα on Moses' face) which leads to death and condemnation.

To my knowledge, this proposal has been made on only one other occasion, by Scott J. Hafemann.[36] In general, however, while a scholar such as Dieter Georgi can declare that the veil of Moses to which Paul refers functioned to conceal "the Mosaic experience of God,"[37] yet the intimate connection of τέλος with the death and condemnation which the Mosaic (old covenant) experience of God engendered has simply not been drawn. Before attempting to strengthen the case for this connection, therefore, a slight reformulation of the proposal needs to be made to make our position clear.

To follow the commonly held assumption that καταργουμένου in 3:13 refers to the old covenant as a whole, what we are proposing is that Paul's intent in drawing his readers' attention back to this covenant through the use of καταργέω is not merely to draw them back to an abstract concept, but to a concept which he has already described in graphic, and certainly controversial,[38] terms in 3:6-11. One of those terms is the very same as that which Paul uses in 3:13, καταργέω, used in 3:11 as a participle, τὸ καταργουμένον; the other two terms, linked in the structure of Paul's

---

[36]Scott J. Hafemann, in a recent paper entitled "The Glory and the Veil of Moses in 2 Cor. 3:7-14: An Example of Paul's Contextual Exegesis," delivered at the 1990 meeting of the Society of Biblical Literature. Our similar conclusions were reached quite independently of each other.

[37]Furnish, p. 207.

[38]Georgi, p. 261.

argument in 3:7-11 to τὸ καταργουμένον, are the words θάνατος and κατάκριμα.

Each of these descriptions of the old covenant can satisfactorily be described as some sort of τέλος, goal or outcome, of the covenant, although it can be observed that, of the three descriptions, the latter two (death and condemnation) are of a different kind from the former (what is being abolished). That is, whereas the participle καταργουμένον, "what is being abolished" refers to the outcome or the τέλος of the covenant itself (*it* will be abolished), the two nouns, θάνατος and κατάκριμα refer to the outcome or the τέλος of the covenant members (*they* will receive "death" and "condemnation") -- and thus fit appropriately in the interpretation of τέλος in 3:13 which refers to the effect on the covenant members of gazing at the δόξα on Moses' face -- to continue to gaze at Moses would kill them.

This, then, is our position -- one which needs now to be strengthened by reference to Paul's use of τέλος elsewhere.

Paul's Use of τέλος in Phil. 3:19 and Rom.6:21-22. Support for our understanding of Paul's use of τέλος in II Cor. 3:13 can certainly be derived from the fact that this use of the word by Paul would certainly not be unique. For example, a similar understanding is represented in Phil. 3:19, in which Paul refers to those who are "enemies of the cross of Christ" as those for whom "τὸ τέλος ἀπώλεια" ("the end is destruction"). Furthermore, the same understanding of τέλος can be found in another Pauline text, Rom. 6:21-22, in which the vocabulary bears some remarkable similarities to that of II Cor. 3:6-4:2. Specifically, the contrast in the Romans passage is between the old covenant and the sinful activity appropriate to it (Rom. 6:21) which produces shame (ἐπαισχύνεσθε; see II Cor. 4:2) and death (θάνατος; see II Cor. 3:7), and the new covenant, which produces freedom (ἐλευθερωθέντες; see II Cor. 3:17b) and eternal life (ζωὴν αἰώνιον; see ζῳοποιεῖ, II Cor.3:6). Furthermore, in Rom. 6:21 these fundamental goals or outcomes (the word "outcome" being more natural than "goal" in this case), death and eternal life, Paul explicitly calls the "τέλος" of each respective covenant and of its appropriate behavior.

The Paradoxical Nature of "Δόξα" when Τελος is understood as Death and Condemnation. To return to our text with τέλος now understood as "death" (or "condemnation"), II Cor. 3:13 can be paraphrased as declaring that Moses put a veil over his face so that the Israelites might not gaze at the δόξα on his face with the intensity that it seemed to demand, because this δόξα would ultimately reach its old covenant "goal" by killing those who set their gaze upon it. For Paul to speak of this τέλος of the old covenant as a τέλος του καταργουμένου (as he does in 3:13), would consequently be quite natural: for the most appropriate and beneficial action that could possibly be taken with a covenant which provides a genuine experience of God, yet one that ultimately only leads to death, is that it should be abolished.

Clearly, if such an interpretation of τέλος, and consequently of δόξα is to be adopted, then it must be admitted that Paul's understanding of δόξα is paradoxical. That is, although there is no question that his use of the word in II Cor. 3:13 has little to do with validating apostolic authority, but refers instead to δόξα as religious benefit, yet in the present verse, as interpreted above, the δόξα appears to be of no benefit at all, but rather to be a substance of the utmost danger.

In understanding δόξα in such a manner, however, Paul can certainly not be accused of straying outside the bounds of tradition, for, as noted above (p. 103), the Scriptural evidence for this paradoxical nature of δόξα, as not only blessing but as dangerous, is abundant. Moreover, this evidence is not only of a general kind, but can be found in the contextual background of Exodus 34 (comprising Exodus 32-34) which forms a single narrative section in Exodus,[39] and which, as Walter Brueggeman has observed,[40] plays a critical role in informing Paul's thought in II Corinthians 3-5. Indeed, what we want to suggest now is that whereas other interpretations of τέλος imply that Paul is in some way misrepresenting the text of Exod. 34 from which his illustration of Moses and the veil derives,[41] the present interpretation does no injustice whatsoever to the text, but quite the opposite, it represents it fairly and in context.

---

[39]So Childs, Exodus, pp. 557-58, 610.

[40]Brueggeman, Horizons in Biblical Thology 1, pp. 64-66, with n. 55. Morna Hooker, "The Johannine Prologue and the Messianic Secret," NTS 21 (October 1974):56-58, draws attention to the importance of Exod. 33-34 in understanding the Johannine prologue, which in turn she connects with Paul's theology in II Cor. 3:1-4:6. Hooker's observations are both pertinent and worth pursuing. See also the related comments of Hanson, pp. 22-23, and Brueggeman, p. 84, n. 57.

[41]For example, see Barrett, II Corinthians, p. 119; J. D. G. Dunn, "2 Corinthians 3:7: 'The Lord is the Spirit,'" JTS 21 (October 1970): 311.

Exodus 32-34 as the Scriptural Proof that the Τέλος of Old Covenant Δόξα can be Understood as Condemnation and Death. We shall not attempt to re-establish the case already made by Brueggemann to show that in II Corinthians Paul has the whole episode of Exod. 32-34 in mind, but will only make three observations on the passage which are at least suggestive of this thesis. The first is that the section in Exodus concerns covenant renewal -- the re-writing on the second set of stone tablets (34:1, LXX: πλάκας λιθίνας; cf.II Cor. 3:3, ἐν πλαξὶν λιθίναις) of the commandments of the law.[42] The second is that the covenant renewal takes place after Moses has interceded for the people in God's presence, κατέναντι κυρίου τοῦ θεοῦ (LXX, Alexandrian text, Exod. 32:11; cf.II Cor. 2:17), and returns to that presence on Sinai, from which he descends with his face having been transformed by the δόξα experienced there (Exod. 33:22, 34:1-9, 29-35). The third is that the major issue in Exod. 33:1-17 is the difficulty for God to dwell in the midst of sinful people without consuming them (Exod. 33:3) -- a major problem given Moses' insistence that such a presence was vital for Israel as the distinguishing mark and blessing of God on his people.[43]

With regard to this last problem the narrative relates that there was, nevertheless, one location in which God could be found: just outside the Israelite camp, in the tent of witness (σκηνὴ μαρτυρίου; see 33:7-11 with 34:29-35, and II Cor. 5:1-5), into which Moses alone was allowed to enter.[44] There Moses would speak with God, in the midst of the "cloud" (33:9; 34:5). This cloud may well have symbolized the fact that even Moses did not have the right to see God's face directly, despite God's positive response to Moses' request to see God's δόξα (33:18); for, as the narrator tells us, no one was able to see God's face and live ("οὐ γὰρ μὴ ἴδῃ ἄνθρωπος τὸ πρόσωπόν μου καὶ ζήσεται," LXX, 33:20; though see II Cor. 4:6, which speaks of the possibility of seeing the "δόξης τοῦ θεοῦ ἐν προσώπῳ Χριστοῦ.[45]

---

[42]Georgi, p. 259, seems to argue that Paul, with his opponents, completely ignores the context of Exod. 34, which, Georgi observes with us, focuses on covenant renewal. Paul's emphasis on covenant language in II Cor. 3:1-6 surely suggest the opposite of Georgi's argument -- that Paul is fully aware of the covenant context of Exod. 34.

[43]See, for example, the comments of Childs, pp. 588-93.

[44]With Noth, Exodus: A Commentary, trans. J. S. Bowden (Philadelphia: Westminster, 1959), p. 256.

[45]Josephus, Ant. III.76-83, relates in graphic fashion the Biblical story of Moses' ascent of Sinai. His clear emphasis is on the fact that on the mountain Moses was entering God's presence, and that such a presence was to be feared in that it might lead to death:

"... the rumor current concerning this mountain, that here was the very resort of God, deeply disturbed their minds. They kept to their tents, dispirited, imagining that

We would argue, then, that the context of Exodus from which Paul draws the story of Exod. 34:29-35 on which he depends in II Corinthians 3, and with which his opponents would have been familiar, can be seen to function as the scriptural basis for Paul's claim in II Cor. 3:13 that Moses placed the veil upon his face in order that the Israelites would not look at the radiant impression of δόξα left on it, so that its τέλος would not take effect -- its τέλος being understood as the Mosaic experience of God with its intimate association with death.

II Corinthians 3:13: Summary and Development

We may sum up what we believe Paul's argument to have achieved so far: Paul has argued in 3:7-11 that δόξα need not be visible in the present in order to remain an assured reality for the future; consequently the Corinthians need not be bothered by the desire for a present Mosaic appearance of δόξα. Now, however, in 3:13, he is arguing that such an appearance of δόξα is not merely not necessary in the present, but that it is in fact quite undesirable -- because this δόξα, at least as made manifest in the old covenant and as represented by the Exodus 34 story of Moses, will literally *kill you* if you fix your gaze upon it (ἀτενίζω, 3:13): if you allow yourselves to desire it intensely, as if, for example, salvation depended upon it.

Indeed, assuming that our understanding of Paul's use of τέλος is correct and that the Exodus narrative with its warning about the possibly deadly nature of δόξα was being brought to the minds of the Corinthians with sobering effect, it is not too far-fetched to suggest that another of Paul's goals would have been accomplished simultaneously: to convince his opponents of his controversial declaration -- stated and re-stated without defense in 3:7, 11, 13, and 14 -- that the old covenant is one that is to be abolished (καταργέω); not merely to be improved upon, but to be annulled. For, acknowledging such a τέλος and thus the impossibility of finding δόξα within the old covenant framework, one would either have to give up the religious quest altogether, or to cry to God to provide a radically new means of obtaining δόξα: through a new covenant, perhaps, quite distinct from the old, in which the life-giving Spirit would reign in righteousness for ever, so that δόξα, the ultimate religious "benefit," could now be embraced safely. Such

---

Moses had perished beneath the wrath of God and expecting a like fate for themselves." (Loeb edition)

a covenant, of course, Paul claimed to participate in, and to do so with boldness (3:12) -- boldness both to approach God's new covenant revelation of δόξα and to proclaim it authoritatively; proclaiming it authoritatively knowing that it would not kill those who embraced it, but would give them life, transforming them from δόξα into δόξα (3:18).

Such, then, is our understanding of II Cor. 3:13, its relationship to the previous context (3:6-12), and to the general outline of the developing argument (3:12-18). Not only, we suggest, does it involve Paul in no twisting of Scripture (from which he must, by all means be seen to distance himself; see 4:2), and not only is the logic easily comprehensible to his readers (assuming they are familiar with Exodus 32-34), but, furthermore, it provides authoritative confirmation for his secondary contrast in 3:7-11 (by its dependence on the well-known Exodus narrative) as well as continuity in developing his apostolic defense (who would even want to look on any "apostle" emanating Mosaic δόξα given such a τέλος?), even though, as we have observed, his use of δόξα in 3:13-18 is based more on the function of the concept as blessing than as validation of authoritative proclamation.

What remains for us to do now is to discuss briefly the development of this argument in 3:14-16 and 3:17-18.

II CORINTHIANS 3:14-16

If in II Cor. 3:13 Paul's argument is that Moses' lack of boldness in displaying the δόξα that had transformed his face came as the result of his knowledge that to fix one's gaze upon it would result in death, then in developing his argument in 3:14-16 he turns his attention to the continuing implications of Moses' action for those Israelites -- those who were at Sinai, and those who were contemporaries of Paul -- who clung to the old covenant and to the radiant δόξα which it seemed to offer. Of these Israelites Paul writes in II Cor. 3:14 that their minds (τὰ νοήματα) were hardened, for up to the present day the same veil (τὸ αὐτὸ κάλυμμα) remains on the reading of the old covenant -- it has not been lifted up -- because only in Christ is it being abolished (καταργεῖται).[46]

---

[46]Linda Belleville, Society of Biblical Literature Annual Meeting, November 17, 1990, has rightly questioned the significance of the present tense of the verb καταργέω in II Cor. 3:14c (see also 3:7, 11, 13). Our response to this observation is to turn again to Paul's eschatological perspective. That is, just as Paul understood that new covenant salvation was a present reality, yet one which would not reach its fulfillment until the resurrection (see Romans 8:18-25 with

Concerning the "veil" mentioned in this verse, Paul asserts in 3:15 that it is to be regarded as lying not merely over the old covenant as an object (hindering the impartation of δόξα,[47] but over the hearts (καρδία) of any people who read Moses — "Moses" understood, with Georgi,[48] as referring to the scripture as understood within the Mosaic covenantal framework, that is, the γράμμα (see 3:6); and "hearts" being the human organ through which δόξα, or at least its first fruits, the Spirit, is received (see 3:3; 4:6).[49] The full text of 3:14-16, with the introductory verse, 13, is as follows:

13 καὶ οὐ καθάπερ Μωϋσῆς ἐτίθει κάλυμμα ἐπὶ τὸ πρόσωπον αὐτοῦ
   πρὸς τὸ μὴ ἀτενίσαι τοὺς υἱοὺς Ἰσραὴλ εἰς τὸ τέλος τοῦ καταργουμένου.

14 (a) ἀλλὰ ἐπωρώθη τὰ νοήματα αὐτῶν,
   (b) ἄχρι γὰρ τῆς σήμερον ἡμέρας
   τὸ αὐτὸ κάλυμμα ἐπὶ τῇ ἀναγνώσει τῆς παλαιᾶς διαθήκης μένει
   (c) μὴ ἀνακαλυπτόμενον, ὅτι ἐν Χριστῷ καταργεῖται·

15 ἀλλ᾽ ἕως σήμερον ἡνίκα ἂν ἀναγινώσκηται Μωϋσῆς,
   κάλυμμα ἐπὶ τὴν καρδίαν αὐτῶν κεῖται·

16 ἡνίκα δὲ ἐὰν ἐπιστρέψῃ πρὸς κύριον,
   περιαιρεῖται τὸ κάλυμμα.

II Cor. 3:14a: The Israelite Hardness of Heart

In attempting to understand the development of Paul's thought in II Cor. 3:14-15, scholars have focused their attention on the difficulties of the syntax in 3:14c; on the fact that the veil of 3:13 is transferred by Paul to the reading of the old covenant in 3:14, and from the covenant to the hearts of the Israelites themselves in 3:15; and on explaining the abruptness of the transition from 3:13 to 3:14a: from the covering of Moses' face to the declaration that the minds of the Israelites were hardened.[50] With regard

---

our future understanding of ἔσται in II Cor. 3:8), so he understood the power of the Old Covenant still to be operative outside of Christ. To this extent the abolition of the Old Covenant was also not yet complete, leading to the posssibility that some would, in futility, attempt to return to it. This, of course, was precisely what was happening.

[47]With, for example, Provence, p. 77.

[48]Georgi, p. 250.

[49]Eduard Schweizer, TDNT 6, p. 417, correctly understands the Spirit as understood by Paul and others to refer at times to "the sphere of divine glory." Schweizer regards this spatial manner of thought as Hellenistic; we, on the other hand, understand it to be just as much at home in the thought world of temple-oriented Judaism, with its emphasis on "holy space."

[50]On the difficulties in interpreting the phrase "μὴ ἀνακαλυπτόμενον, ὅτι . . ." see for example, Barrett, II Corinthians, pp. 120-21 and Collange, p. 98. On Paul's moving of the veil, see, for example, Bultmann, p. 86, Bruce, pp. 192-93 and Lambrecht, p. 368; and on the abrupt

to this latter issue, Furnish follows Calvin in suggesting that the declaration of 3:14a about Israelite hardness of mind was intended by Paul to serve as a defense of Moses.[51] That is, if Moses' action in 3:13 of veiling the τέλος of "that which is being abolished" could be conceived as deceitful, then in 3:14a Paul could be seen as implicitly declaring that any "blame" for the veil would lie not with Moses, but with the Israelites -- "hardened people that they were"!

Clearly, however, since our own understanding of Moses' action with the veil does not regard Paul as behaving in any way that was less than "above-board" -- to the contrary in fact, from our point of view his desire was to save his people from death -- this interpretation must necessarily be considered redundant. Nevertheless, agreement can still be found with others in suggesting that the transition of thought from the "τέλος καταργουμένου" of 3:13 to the hardness of the Israelites' minds of 3:14 occurred naturally as a description of the Israelites' inability to grasp the nature of the ultimate τέλος of the old covenant[52] -- τέλος in our interpretation understood neither as "termination" nor as "Christ," but as "death." In this case, then, Paul's transitional statement in 3:14a can be paraphrased as declaring quite simply that the Israelites never grasped the significance of Moses' action with the veil: they never saw that the veil was intended to shield them from *death*; they never realized that death and condemnation were the ultimate consequences of the covenant of which Moses was a servant, and of the δόξα which it promised.

II Cor. 3:14b-15: The Function of the Veil

Furthermore, we would suggest that the references to the veil (κάλυμμα) that follow in 3:14b-15 must also be understood from this perspective since Paul expressly states that the veil about which he is talking in 3:14 as placed over the old covenant is precisely the *same* veil (τὸ αὐτό κάλυμμα) as, and none other than, the one of which he was speaking in 3:13 as placed over Moses' face. That is, the κάλυμμα referred to in 3:14b-15 must be regarded not merely as a symbol of the hardness of the Israelites' hearts, but, more fundamentally, still as a symbol of the protection

---

connection between 3:13 and 3:14a, see Hickling, NTS 21, p. 391 and Provence, p. 76.

[51]Furnish, p. 233; Calvin, The Second Epistle of Paul the Apostle to the Corinthians and the Epistles to Timothy, Titus and Philemon, trans. A. T. Smail (Grand Rapids: Eerdmans, 1964), p. 47.

[52]So, for example, Bultmann, p. 86; Rissi, p. 81; Thrall, Corinthians, pp. 135-36.

needed against the penetration of δόξα into the Israelites' lives because of the power of such δόξα, at least in its Mosaic context, to bring not life, but death.[53]

Consequently, the function of the veil throughout 3:14-15 must be viewed, as in the case of Moses in 3:13, as initially positive not negative, one of mercy given to those who foolishly persist in seeking for that which would kill them if they were to find it. On the other hand, it must also be observed that if the covenant should change so that the τέλος of the old covenant were to be abolished, this same veil that functioned as a merciful protector from death would, paradoxically, now function as a hindrance to blessing -- preventing δόξα (or at least the guarantee of δόξα, the Spirit, see II Cor. 5:5), now no longer life-threatening, from penetrating to the human heart (καρδίαν, 3:15) there to transform it, as the prophets had promised, from the death-like hardness of stone to the life-pulsating warmth of flesh (see II Cor. 3:3 with Jer. 31:33 and Ezek. 11:19).

Such an understanding of the dual function of the veil, as positive or negative depending on the nature of the covenant in effect, is, we believe, crucial to bear in mind in following the flow of Paul's argument in II Cor. 3:14b-15. That is, for example, when Paul says in 3:14b that the "same veil" remains to this very day over the reading of the old covenant, the implication is that to trust in the old covenant and the scriptures which pertain to it (which constitute the subject of "the reading" -- τῇ ἀναγνώσει) to impart Mosaic δόξα as a religious benefit or blessing is futile, for the stipulation of death associated with the covenant and its δόξα, and represented by the word "veil" (κάλυμμα), is still in effect for those who cling to that covenant. Indeed, declares Paul, "it" is only abolished in Christ -- "it" referring explicitly to the veil, and implicitly, we are arguing, to the old covenant and its decree of death which the veil mercifully prevented from having immediate effect;[54] and "in Christ" referring to the new covenantal sphere within

---

[53]Morna Hooker, NTS 27, p. 300, comes close to our position in regarding the veil in 3:13 as "concealing from them the terrifying symbol of God's presence," and by declaring that in 3:14 "the veil . . . goes hand-in-hand with a refusal to see the truth." What Hooker does not say, and what we do, is that the truth in 3:14 is precisely that the δόξα hidden in 3:13 is terrifying -- in fact, deadly.

[54]Furnish, p. 210, provides a good discussion of scholarly opinion which divides fairly equally in interpreting the subject of "καταργεῖται" either as κάλυμμα, veil, or as the παλαιᾶς διαθήκης, the old covenant. We have attempted to hold both opinions together, but would ultimately acknowledge with Hanson, pp. 14, 18, that καταργεῖν, understood as to abolish or annul, is a verb which can more easily be associated with covenants than veils.

which, and only within which, the death penalty (integrally related to the *curse* of Gal. 3:13) is being abolished (καταργέω).[55]

Furthermore, with the introduction in 3:14c of the idea that through Christ the old covenant is being abolished and the new covenant instituted (see 3:4), the function of the veil as a positive blessing for the Israelites must necessarily be seen to change in the verses that follow. For, with death from δόξα no longer a threat, any veil between God's δόξα and humanity must now be seen as functioning negatively, effectively hindering the positive, life-producing effects of δόξα.[56] Indeed, what we wish to argue now is that Paul's continuing discussion of the veil in 3:15 (and 3:16) must be understood from this perspective, addressing the situation in which the veil can be removed without fear because the δόξα is no longer a threat. If our argument is correct, the explicit question that Paul will almost inevitably be addressing in 3:15-16 will concern the conditions for receiving the "blessing" of δόξα in the new covenant context. It is to these verses, then, that we need now to turn.

II Cor. 3:15-16: The Location of the New Covenant Δόξα

It is in fact clear that in II Cor. 3:16 Paul's discussion has turned to the question of the conditions which must be met for the new δόξα to be received, for the verse ("whenever a person turns to the Lord the veil is lifted up") explains how exactly the veil which prevents δόξα from entering the human life can be removed: by turning to the Lord. Indeed, what we wish to suggest now is that in II Cor. 3:15 ("but to this day, whenever Moses is read a veil is placed on their heart") Paul informs the Corinthians quite specifically

---

[55]Neugebauer's comments, pp. 81-82, on the significance of the phrase "in Christ" in II Cor. 3:14b, as unrelated to covenant change, are to the point. Furthermore, when read with Neugebauer's comments immediately following on Gal. 3:13-14, in which Paul speaks of the curse of the law (which we regard as death, Gen. 2:17; 3:19b) having been removed "in Christ Jesus," our own position is reached.

[56]Morna Hooker, NTS 27, p. 298, speaks of "the basic inconsistency in Paul's picture. For he has told us that Israel could not gaze on Moses' glory: how then, does it come about that Christians can now gaze on the overwhelming glory which belongs to Christ?" Professor Hooker's question is to the point, reflecting accurately, we believe, the kind of question that Paul's opponents would have raised. Her comment on the "inconsistency in Paul's picture" is, on the other hand, quite unfounded, for the understanding of Paul's argument suggested here provides an adequate solution to the problem: Paul's freedom to gaze on the "overwhelming glory that belongs to Christ" arises because the death and condemnation associated with Mosaic δόξα are being abolished.

of both the manner and location in which δόξα is to be received (in the presence of the Lord himself), and that he does so in response to a possible mis-application of his declaration of 3:14b that in Christ the veil is abolished.

The Possible Mis-Application of Paul's Argument: Contentment with a Second-Hand Experience of God. Just as Paul was well aware in writing to the Romans (Rom. 6:1) that his understanding of the Gospel could be mis-applied, so we would suggest, he was well aware of the same possibility in writing to the Christians in Corinth. Specifically, if we have been correct in arguing that the abolition of the veil is a declaration that the "death penalty" of the old covenant has been removed, then it could easily be suggested by Paul's opponents that the implication for believers was not that Mosaic δόξα was now not worth pursuing at all, but rather that the Mosaic δόξα with its attractive outward appearance was in fact worth pursuing all the more, and with impunity, for it would now (according to Paul himself) no longer kill you.[57] Furthermore, the claim could easily be made that with the danger of "death" gone, Christians could now stand where the children of Israel stood of old, at the foot of Sinai in front of Moses, the only and crucial difference being that the Christians were now free to fix their gaze on "Moses" with no veil at all between their faces and his (as in 3:18). Moses, of course, could not be literally present with these Christians, although he could certainly be represented in effect by the books that bore his name and by those who claimed to be his interpreters. Paul's opponents could claim, therefore, that it was by turning towards these books and these people that new covenant δόξα with its life-transforming power was to be found.

It is as a response to such a mis-application of Paul's argument that we wish to understand the function of 3:15. That is, Paul's answer to the implicit question as to how and where new covenant δόξα can be found is first of all negative, as if to say in 3:15, "you cannot receive it by stepping back to the model set forth in the old covenant, despite the absence of the fear of death." Or, to paraphrase 3:15 more closely, we would suggest that Paul is saying that if you want new covenant δόξα to enter your hearts (καρδία) then reading "Moses" -- as if the Moses story of Exod. 34 were your model -- will do you no good, δόξα will still not be able to penetrate your hearts beneficially, even though you have arrived at the very day (σήμερον ἡμέρας; the day of

---

[57]Such an argument by Paul's opponents would be somewhat akin to that of Romans 6: Why not sin that grace might abound?

covenant renewal? Deut. 29:1-14) when Christ's work of abolishing the τέλος of the old covenant has been accomplished.

On what basis, then, it must be asked, does Paul make his assertion that the Israelites cannot go back to Moses as a model, or more precisely, to the model of the Israelites who gazed upon Moses, in order to share in the δόξα which God had given to him? Or, on what basis does Paul make his claim that the veil still lies over the heart of those who read Moses, even though he has just argued in 3:14b that the veil (and its basis, death) has been abolished in Christ? The basis suggested by 3:16 would be that Paul believed that although the time was right (the new covenant had been inaugurated) for the veil to be lifted and for δόξα to be received as blessing, the place (which for Paul's opponents amounted to the Scripture as they interpreted it) was wrong -- for, as far as Paul was concerned there was only one place indicated by Scripture in which the Mosaic veil could be removed:[58] in the tent of witness, in the presence of God (Exod. 34:34). It was there, in God's presence that the Scripture portrayed the veil to be lifted, and it was consequently there, with Moses, not looking at Moses (or his books), but looking directly at God (as represented by his "δόξα") as Moses himself did, that Christians were to stand. Boldness to make such a claim, Paul's opponents never had!

Paul's Use of ἐπιστρέφω: The Call to a First-Hand Experience of God. This understanding of Paul's argument as it touches on II Cor. 3:16 needs to be defended, however, and this we shall now do by examining the choice and significance of Paul's wording in the verse. II Cor. 3:16 reads as follows: "ἡνίκα δὲ ἐὰν ἐπιστρέψῃ πρὸς κύριον, περιαιρεῖται τὸ κάλυμμα." Commentators are generally agreed that the basis for Paul's declaration here that "whenever a person turns to the Lord the veil is removed" lies in the activity of Moses in entering the tent of meeting in which place alone, as described in Exod. 34:34, the removal of the veil took place.[59] Indeed, we would suggest that Paul's intent in II Cor. 3:16 is to call Christians to become like Moses, so that Moses' action of entering the tent has been generalized to everyone -- teaching, we might suggest, the simple

---

[58]J. D. G. Dunn, "2 Corinthians 3:17: The Lord is the Spirit," JTS 21 (Oct. 1970): 312, observes correctly that in II Cor. 3:14-16 the veil on the Israelites is the "same" veil (τὸ αὐτὸ κάλυμμα) as on Moses: "This being so, the action which will remove the veil is the same action as that which resulted in Moses' veil being removed." We would add that Moses' action was to go to a certain place, where alone the removal was possible.

[59]For example, Plummer, p. 101; Furnish, p. 210; Collange, p. 101; Barrett, II Corinthians, p. 122; Martin, p. 70.

lesson that if one wants δόξα, and, furthermore if one wants to be faithful
to the Mosaic pattern, then one does not just *look* at Moses, but one must
actually *act* like him, and meet with God directly without an intermediary
such as the old covenant Scripture; for it is only in this place of immediate
communion that this Scripture itself affirms that the veil hindering the
reception of δόξα can be removed.

Although the observation has been made by others[60] that in II Cor.
3:18 Paul is generalizing the Mosaic experience of God to all Christians, the
importance of this observation in the development of Paul's thought in
3:16-18 has, we believe, been dealt with insufficiently.[61] One reason for this
insufficiency seems simply to be that priority in scholarly discussion of 3:16
has been given to another issue to which we ourselves must now turn our
attention. The issue concerns Paul's alteration in II Cor. 3:16 of the text of
Exod. 34:34 -- the original text from which, it is agreed by common
consensus, the text of II Cor. 3:16 derives.

The original text in Exod. 34:34 (LXX) reads "ἡνίκα δ' ἂν
εἰσεπορεύετο Μωϋσῆς ἔναντι κυρίου λαλεῖν αὐτῷ, περιηρεῖτο τὸ
κάλυμμα . . . " The alteration in II Cor. 3:16 involves the omission of
"εἰσεπορεύετο Μωϋσῆς ἔναντι" and its replacement by "ἐπιστρέψῃ πρὸς
κύριον." The general explanation of this change is that elsewhere the verb
ἐπιστρέφω can describe the act of Christian conversion, and, indeed, Pauline
evidence for such a usage can be provided from I Thess. 1:9 which refers to
the Thessalonian experience of conversion, their "turning to God from idols"
(ἐπεστρέψατε πρὸς τὸν θεὸν ἀπὸ τῶν εἰδώλων).[62]

Our initial difficulty with this interpretation of ἐπιστρέφω lies in the fact
that it simply does not seem to fit the context. That is, it would seem to be
beside the point for Paul to speak about conversion to those who would
presumably claim that they were already converted (or had "turned to the
Lord"), but who *still* believed that as Christians they could view the δόξα of
the Lord through the mirror of the Mosaic scripture, or even through the
faces of Moses' contemporary interpreters, Paul's opponents, with no veil to

---

[60]See Héring, p. 27, n. 21, for example.
[61]Though van Unnik, NovT 6, pp. 166-67, also argues that the extension of Mosaic practice
to all those in the New Covenant is part of Paul's thrust from II Cor. 3:16 to 3:18.
[62]For the understanding of "ἐπιστρέφω" as connected with conversion, see for example,
Bultmann, p. 89; Furnish, p. 211; Collange, p. 103; Martin, p. 70.

hinder them.[63] To be sure, such a subjective objection to the "conversion" hypothesis for the use of ἐπιστρέφω in 3:16 does not render it impossible: our logic and Paul's may not coincide! However, what it does force us to do is to search for an alternative reason for Paul's choice of the word ἐπιστρέφω before adopting the one offered.

In this regard, we would argue that such an alternative lies within the narrative context to which Exod. 34:34 belongs, Exodus 32-34, and with which, as we have observed above (p. 142) Paul was familiar. In particular, the words which Paul inserts into the Exod. 34:34 quotation, "ἐπιστρέψῃ πρὸς κύριον" can be found in the Alexandrian text of LXX Exod. 32:31, which reads "ἐπέστρεψεν δὲ Μωϋσῆς πρὸς κύριον." It seems to us to be beyond doubt that Paul is here joining the two texts of Exod. 32:31 and 34:34 together. But to what end it must be asked? -- for the reason could still be the commonly held one, that the word ἐπιστρέφω functioned as a catch-word for conversion, thus making it appropriate to join the two texts from Exodus together in II Cor. 3:17. If, on the other hand, Paul had some other reason for joining these two verses together, it would seem reasonable to suggest that the rationale would lie within the context of Exod. 32:31, which, consequently, we need briefly to assess.

In this regard, the immediate context of Exod. 32:31 is one which speaks of Moses descending (καταβαίνω, LXX Exod. 32:15) from Sinai with the first pair of stone tablets of the law only to find the Israelites involved in idolatry. Moses' first reaction to this sin is one of wrath, in which the sons of Levi are commissioned to destroy the idolaters (Exod. 32:25-29). However, by the next day Moses appears to be much more conciliatory, and declares his intention of re-ascending (ἀναβαίνω, LXX Exod. 32:30) the mountain to make atonement (ἐξιλάσωμαι) for the people -- willing even to give his life that the lives of others might not be blotted out from God's book (Exod. 32:32). Indeed, it is to this return to Mount Sinai, conceived as the place at which Moses meets God and at which atonement can be made, that the words "ἐπέστρεψεν δὲ Μωϋσῆς πρὸς κύριον" in LXX Exod. 32:31 refer.

What seems to us to be possible to claim from the Exodus context, then, is that in using the words of Exod. 32:31 Paul was simply attempting to

---

[63]See Furnish, p. 211, on the various interpretations of the subject of ἐπιστρέφω: "anyone"; the Jews; or "their hearts." Our difficulty with understanding the "conversion" hypothesis in this context remains no matter which option is adopted (though we prefer the first option with Furnish).

emphasize the basic understanding of II Cor. 3:16 which we have already suggested was of primary importance: the generalization of the experience of Moses himself to apply as the example for *every* Christian to follow. That is, Paul's point in referring to Exod. 32:31 in conjunction with Exod. 34:34 would have been to stress the location in which the veil of the Mosaic covenant could be legitimately removed. In Moses' case, this location was to be found in God's immediate presence, not only in the tent of witness, as Exod. 34:34 might indicate, but on Mount Sinai itself, to which he returned (ἐπέστρεψεν), as Exod. 32:31 indicated.

The implications of such an interpretation for the understanding of Paul's argument in 3:15-16 would therefore be as follows. Paul would be arguing that the Christian life made possible "in Christ" through the annulment of the old covenant and the inauguration of the new, and to which all were now called by the authoritative example of Scripture was not merely one in which the individual could gaze "from afar" upon the δόξα which the new covenant offered; gazing second-hand as it were on God's δόξα through the mirror of Scripture, just as the Israelites had gazed second-hand at God's δόξα mirrored on the face of Moses *after he had left* the most intimate presence of God, whether on Mount Sinai or in the tent of witness. Rather, to Paul, the Christian life was one in which the experience of God was to be first-hand, and thus infinitely more "Mosaic" than that made possible by reading the Mosaic Scripture -- the manner and "location" for obtaining δόξα suggested by Paul's opponents.

That is, like Moses, any and every Christian was called -- as the Israelites never were (see Exod. 19:12, 21) -- to a relationship of intimate communion with God, with no veil needed, not only as in the tent of God's presence but even as on Mount Sinai itself, the dwelling place of God in his awesome holiness, and yet in his mercy -- for in such a place, Moses believed, atonement was to be found (Exod. 32:30). Only a man of great boldness, who knew what true "παρρησία" was, would dare to proclaim such a presumptuous Gospel!

To impose the "conversion" explanation of "ἐπιστρέφω" on the text, is therefore, we would suggest, not only to complicate Paul's intention in 3:16 unnecessarily, but is, in fact, to cause the impact of the first half of the verse to be lost, which summons Christians to climb ("to return" to) Mount Sinai with Moses, just as the second half of the verse calls them to join Moses in the tent of witness.

V. II CORINTHIANS 3:17-18

The thought of II Cor. 3:15-16, and indeed the thought of 3:12-16, is completed in 3:17-18. That is, if Paul has in 3:16 called the Corinthians to take their place with him in God's immediate presence, the question naturally arises as to where that immediate presence is to be experienced: where, for those who live in Corinth, can "Sinai" or the "tent" now be found? II Cor. 3:17 ("Now the Lord is the Spirit; and where the Spirit of the Lord is, there is freedom" RSV), functions as the reply to such a question,[64] pointing to the immediate experience of God made available by his Spirit to those who embrace the new covenant of Christ:[65] the Spirit manifesting the same Lord whom Moses encountered on Sinai,[66] and in the presence of whom for Moses (though not for the Israelites as a whole) there was perfect freedom from death and condemnation.[67]

The practical effects of this freedom to experience God's presence by his Spirit are portrayed in 3:18, which sums up, we believe the ultimate significance of the secondary comparison which Paul entertained in 3:7-11. II Cor. 3:18 (RSV) reads as follows: "And we all with unveiled face, beholding the glory of the Lord, are being changed into his likeness, from one

---

[64]Furnish, p. 212, for example, points to the use of "δὲ" in 3:17 as functioning to introduce a comment on what precedes. Dunn, JTS 21, p. 313, calls 3:17 an "exegetical note," and points to other Pauline instances in Gal. 4:25 and I Cor. 10:4.

[65]On the connection of the Spirit with "δόξα," see E. Schweizer, "Πνεῦμα," TDNT 6, p. 417. Walther Eichrodt, Theology of the Old Testament, Vol. 2, trans. J. A. Baker (Philadelphia: Westminster, 1967), p. 61, says of the prophetic understanding of the Spirit, "it is the spirit . . . . in which the transcendent God, dwelling in light inapproachable, in very truth draws near to his people." And, of Isa. 63:11-14, Eichrodt also writes: "Here, as in other passages, the spirit is the medium through which God's presence in the midst of his people becomes a reality . . ." Martin, p. 71 writes, "When we seek 'the Lord' by the Spirit, it is the Spirit of the Lord that grants us access to God, Paul concluded." Martin understands "freedom" in 3:17 to mean "access" to God. Finally, Stockhausen, Moses' Veil, p. 132, writes that "the Spirit is the gift and sign of the New Covenant, just as the presence of the Lord in the tent of meeting was the gift and sign of God's covenant through Moses."

[66]With, for example, Barrett, II Corinthians, pp. 122-23; Martin, pp. 70-71, Bultmann, p. 88. See also Dunn, JTS 21: 313. With Furnish, p. 212, we agree that the verb "to be" in the clause "the Lord is the Spirit" has no metaphysical connotation. Furthermore, this understanding of 3:17 as explaining the Old Testament reference in 3:16 rules out as irrelevant the question, asked by among many others, Hanson, pp. 18-19, as to whether the "Lord" refers to Christ or to God.

[67]Dunn, JTS 21: 313, argues cogently that in 3:16 Paul is arguing that "It is when (a person) turns his attention and devotion from the γράμμα to the πνεῦμα that he will be freed from the bondage and condemnation of the law which kills . . . ."

degree of glory into another; for this comes from the Lord who is the Spirit."[68] To re-phrase 3:18 in terms of Paul's comparison of covenants in 3:7-11, the declaration of 3:18 is to claim that the freedom from death and condemnation which have been made possible through the abolition of the old covenant by Christ, have provided the necessary righteousness for those in Christ not only to approach God himself (as made manifest by his Spirit) with boldness and freedom, but to be transformed by that presence for ever: "ἀπὸ δόξης εἰς δόξαν."

VI. II CORINTHIANS 3:12-18: SUMMARY

With such a conclusion Paul's argument in II Cor. 3:12-18 has been made. He has explained why Mosaic δόξα is not merely *not necessary* (the argument of 3:7-11), but *not even desirable* (it kills you; 3:12-13); and he has explained why such δόξα must not be sought through an understanding of the old covenant Scripture, γράμμα, untransformed by Christ -- for such reading of Scripture cannot bring the permanent and intimate experience of God's presence (the hope and the boldness, 3:12) that is made possible "in Christ" through the Spirit (3:14-18), and which, through Paul's Spirit-imparting ministry, the Corinthians have already received (3:3).

---

[68]The textual evidence for the presence of the word "all" (πάντες) is missing from P46. However, the great majority of manuscripts include the word, and along with the context suggest to us that Paul's reference in this verse is indeed to all Christians, and not just to himself.

CHAPTER SEVEN

Conclusion

The people of ancient Israel, along with many others of their age, simply did not assume that God's presence was *a given*. God's dwelling places had to be discovered, and once discovered, maintained. Indeed, other blessings from God depended upon it. God's presence was understood as primary; other blessings secondary. Without God's presence no other blessing of any substance was either possible or meaningful.[1]

Our argument in this study has been that the quest for the presence of God was consequently a pervasive one in ancient Judaism. Furthermore, this was true in particular of the pre-70 CE Pharisees, and provides the key to understanding their passionate interest in keeping the precepts of the Law. Through the Law, understood as a gracious gift from God, their intent was to re-create the atmosphere of the Temple outside the Temple, and thus to re-create the God-given Biblical conditions within which God delighted to be present.

Paul was a Pharisee, and we have therefore argued that his interpretation of the significance of Jesus Christ must be understood precisely in terms of his fundamental Pharisaic quest. That is, Paul's quest as a Pharisee was for the presence of God, and this he found, not in or through the Law or its covenant, but through Christ and within the sphere of the new covenant established by Christ.

---

[1]For example, in the case of a "blessing" such as justification, the related concept of "forgiveness" must not be understood in abstraction, but rather as the necessary means to the greater end of a restored, righteous, relationship with God; a relationship that clearly can only exist if God is present. This intimate connection between presence and blessing also holds true in the case of seemingly physical desires such as a good harvest, or victory over enemies: no victory or abundant reaping is possible unless God is present to bring it to pass.

To begin to defend this proposal (and our study is no more than a beginning) we have not attempted a thoroughgoing analysis of the Pauline literature as a whole, but rather our focus has been on a single passage, renowned for its complexity, II Corinthians 2:14-3:18. The question at stake has simply been whether *the assumption* of this fundamental interest in finding and maintaining God's presence bears fruit in the attempt to unravel the sense and logic of the passage. This we have demonstrated to be the case. That is, in II Corinthians 2:14-3:18 we have demonstrated that Paul has defended the validity of his apostleship, not merely by describing the nature of apostleship but also by describing the nature of the Christian life as a whole, and each in terms of God's presence.

This latter emphasis in Paul's argument, concerning the nature of the Christian life as a whole, seems at first glance both to weaken and confuse the main argument. It raises the question as to whether Paul has argued too much: that is, if, as Paul argues, access to God's presence is available to all Christians (3:18), does Paul thereby nullify the argument of access to God's presence as a *sine qua non* of apostleship? No! -- for Paul's argument is that while the absence of access would certainly render apostleship invalid, nevertheless access by itself is not the sufficient proof of apostleship. Rather, the sufficient proof of apostleship lies in the ability to impart the Spirit of God to others. This Paul had beyond question done with the Corinthians (3:3).

If, then, Paul had at one time been an apostle (a position that was irrefutable) the question still remains: had Paul at some stage been disqualified from such a ministry, cast out of God's presence, as evidenced by his seeming lack of the visible sign of God's presence, δόξα? Once again, No! -- the specific manifestation of δόξα that Paul's opponents required, and which Paul lacked, was, Paul argues, not only not necessary, but was actually undesirable and unwarranted by Scripture properly understood. That is, the Mosaic pattern of δόξα as some kind of radiance (as in Exodus 34) -- literal or figurative -- was demonstrated by Paul to be no longer necessary, desirable, or authoritative for Christian experience in the present age (II Cor. 3:7-16).

How then, it might be asked, was the present expression of δόξα to be conceived if not in terms of such radiance? In II Corinthians 3 Paul does not answer this question directly, though in the sacrificial imagery of II Cor. 2:14-17, and in the covenantal argument of II Corinthians 3, he lays the essential groundwork for the redefinition of δόξα which he makes explicit in II Corinthians 4. In this latter chapter (especially 4:1-11) it becomes clear that the glowing face of Moses (translating into the "charismatic life" of an apostle) was no longer to be regarded as the image and pattern of the manifestation of δόξα in the present age. Rather the appropriate image was that of the face of Christ -- Christ crucified. This image, and this alone was the image which held life-transforming power, and after which not only apostles but all Christians were to pattern their lives.

Consequently, it could not be argued that Paul's suffering in any way disqualified him from apostleship. Indeed, because of the new covenant of Christ, even in his suffering, or, rather, especially in his suffering, Paul remained, as he had claimed to be in II Cor. 2:17b, a man accepted by God as *pure* enough to approach God (ὡς ἐξ εἰλικρινείας), as one who, like Moses descending the mount or coming out of the tent of witness, came *from God* (ὡς ἐκ θεοῦ) and who spoke authoritatively with both words and life combining to reflect his ongoing status as one who lived on the altar of God, as a sacrifice, or as a priest caring for the altar of God, *in the presence of God*, κατέναντι θεοῦ ἐν Χριστῷ.

With the defense of his apostolic status thus confirmed, Paul was quite free to broaden the discussion beyond the realm of apostolicity to the life of every person who fully embraced the new covenant as represented by Paul's ministry. Consequently, without weakening or confusing his argument, Paul could claim that every Christian was now free to stand where Moses stood, "κατέναντι θεοῦ": a proximity and relationship to God he had sought as a Pharisee, and which was only now made broadly possible, and this through the Spirit given *by* Christ and *in* Christ (κατέναντι θεοῦ ἐν Χριστῷ, 2:17). Furthermore, this experience of God was not death-dealing, but life-transforming, transforming the member of the new covenant from "δόξα into δόξα" (3:18), from one experience and effect of God's presence to another.

By way of summary, finally, the critical phrase "in Christ," so frequently used by Paul throughout his epistles to describe the fundamental nature of Christian existence, was for Paul, we would suggest, not merely a description of the new covenant reality construed abstractly, though that it was. More than that, however, it was a description of a new location: holy space, a sphere or area in which God was present. Indeed, this sphere is one which can be conceived best when the words "Christ" and "Temple" are used inter-changeably. Thus, to be "in Christ" was to be in the Temple, or, more precisely, to stand upon the foundation of the eschatological temple which

God himself was building without human hands (II Cor. 5:2).[2] This was the location in which Paul the Apostle of the new covenant saw himself as standing, despite his suffering and despite the various objections to his ministry. Here Paul stood, and not alone, but with many others *in Christ* -- indeed, with all, including the Corinthians, who through the ministry of the new covenant proclaimed by Paul were now able to live their lives freely, with boldness, in the *glorious*, life-giving, life-transforming, presence of God.

---

[2]II Cor. 6:14-7:1 has often been counted as a non-Pauline interpolation. See the detailed discussion in Furnish, pp. 371-383. While not attempting to resolve the issue, it is worth pointing out that the use of cultic terminology along with the claim in 6:16 that "we are the temple of the living God" is by no means out of place in the context of II Cor. 2:14-7:4 as we have begun to interpret it in 2:14-3:18.

BIBLIOGRAPHY

I. Part One: General

Baumgarten, J. "The Essenes and the Temple -- A Re-appraisal." In *Studies in Qumran Law*, pp. 57-74. Leiden: E. J. Brill, 1977.

Brandenburger, Egon. *Die Verborgenheit Gottes im Weltgeschehen: Das literarische und theologische Problem des 4. Esrabuches*. Abhandlungen zur Theologie des Alten und Neuen Testaments, bd. 68. Zurich: Theologische Verlag, 1981.

Breech, Earl. "These fragments I Have Shored Against My Ruins: The Form and Function of 4 Ezra." *Journal of Biblical Literature* 92 (September 1973): 267-74.

Büchler, A. *Types of Palestinian Piety From 70 BCE to 70 CE: The Ancient Pious Men*. (First published, 1922). New York: Ktav, 1966.

Charlesworth, James H. "The Society for New Testament Studies Pseudepigrapha Seminars at Tübingen and Paris on the Books of Enoch." *New Testament Studies* 25 (April 1979): 315-23.

_____., ed. *The Old Testament Pseudepigrapha*. Vol. 1: *Apocalyptic Literature and Testaments*. Garden City, N.Y.: Doubleday, 1983.

Clements, Ronald E. *God and Temple*. Oxford: Basil Blackwell, 1965.

Crenshaw, James L. Review of *Weisheit in Wandel* by J. Marbock. *Journal of Biblical Literature* 91 (December 1972): 543-44.

_____. "In Search of Divine Presence: Some Remarks Preliminary to a Theology of Wisdom." *Review and Expositor* 74 (July 1977): 353-69.

_____. *Old Testament Wisdom: An Introduction*. Atlanta: John Knox, 1981.

Davenport, Gene L. *The Eschatology of the Book of Jubilees*. Studia Post-Biblica, vol. 20. Leiden: E. J. Brill, 1971.

Denis, A. M. *Introduction aux Pseudepigraphen Grecs D'Ancien Testament*. Leiden: E. J. Brill, 1970.

Dictionnaire Biblique. S.v. "Psaumes de Salomon," by M. S. Delcor. Supplementary Volume 9, (1979): 214-45.

Dupont-Sommer, A. *The Essene Writings from Qumran*. Translated by G. Vermes. Cleveland: World, 1962.

Eissfeldt, Otto. *The Old Testament: An Introduction including the Apocrypha and also works of Similar Type from Qumran.* Translated by Peter R. Ackroyd. New York: Harper & Row, 1965.

Encyclopedia Judaica. S.v. "Solomon, Psalms of," by Uriel Rappaport. 15:115-16.

Fournier-Bidoz, Alain.   "L'arbre et la Demeure: Siracide XXIV: 10-17." *Vetus Testamentum* 34 (January 1984): 1-10.

Frizzell, L. E., ed. *God and His Temple -- Reflections on Professor Terrien's "The Elusive Presence: Toward a New Biblical Theology."* Institute of Judaeo-Christian Studies. S. Orange, N.J.: Seton Hall University, 1980.

Gärtner, Bertil. *The Temple and the Community in Qumran and the New Testament: A Comparitive Study in the Temple Symbolism of the Qumran Texts and the New Testament.* Cambridge: University Press, 1965.

Gilbert, M. "L'éloge de la Sagesse." *Révue Théologique de Louvain* 5 (3, 1974): 326-48.

Haran, Menachem. *Temples and Temple Service in Ancient Israel: An Enquiry into the Character of Cult Phenomena and the Historical Setting of the Priestly School.* Oxford: Clarendon, 1978.

Hengel, Martin. *Judaism and Hellenism: Studies in their Encounter in Palestine during the Early Hellenistic Period.* Vols. I & II. Translated by John Bowden. Philadelphia: Fortress, 1974.

Jaubert, Annie. *La Notion d'Alliance dans le Judaisme Aux Abords de l'Ère Chrétienne.* Paris: Éditions du Seuil, 1963.

Kee, Howard C. "'The Man' in Fourth Ezra: Growth of a Tradition." In *Society of Biblical Literature 1981 Seminar Papers,* pp. 199-208. Edited by K. H. Richards. Chico, Cal.: Scholars Press, 1981.

Klijn, A. F. J., ed. *Der Lateinische Text der Apokalypse des Esra.* Berlin: Akademie-Verlag, 1983.

Klinzing, Georg. *Die Umdeutung des Kultus in der Qumrangemeinde und im Neuen Testament.* Göttingen: Vandenhoeck & Ruprecht, 1971.

Knibb, Michael A., in consultation with Edward Ullendorf. *The Ethiopic Book of Enoch. A New Edition in the Light of the Aramaic Dead Sea Fragments.* Vol.2 *Introduction, Translation, and Commentary.* Oxford: Clarendon, 1978.

Knibb, Michael A. *The First and Second Books of Esdras.* Cambridge: Cambridge University, 1982.

Levine, Baruch. "On the Presence of God in Biblical Religion." In *Religions in Antiquity,* pp. 71-86. Edited by Jacob Neusner. Leiden: E. J. Brill, 1968.

Levine, Baruch. *In the Presence of the Lord.* Leiden: E. J. Brill, 1974.

MacKenzie, R. A. F. *Sirach.* Wilmington, Del.: Glazier, 1983.

Maier, J. *The Temple Scroll: An Introduction, Translation, & Commentary.* Journal for the Study of the Old Testament Supplements, no. 34. Sheffield: JSOT Press, 1985.

Marbock, Johann. *Weisheit im Wandel: Untersuchungen zur Weisheitstheologie bei Ben Sira.* Bonn: Peter Hanstein Verlag GMBH, 1971.

Meeks, Wayne. A. *The First Urban Christians: The Social World of the Apostle Paul.* New Haven: Yale, 1983.

Milgrom, Jacob. "Israel's Sanctuary: The Priestly Picture of Dorian Gray." *Révue Biblique* 83 (1976): 390-99.

Neusner, Jacob. *The Idea of Purity in Ancient Judaism*. Leiden: E. J. Brill, 1973.

Newsom, Carol. *Songs of the Sabbath Sacrifice: A Critical Edition*. Harvard Semitic Studies, no. 27. Atlanta: Scholars Press, 1985).

Newton, Michael. *The Concept of Purity at Qumran and in the Letters of Paul*. Cambridge: University Press, 1985.

Nickelsburg, G. W. E. "The Apocalyptic Message of I Enoch 92-105." *Catholic Biblical Quarterly* 39 (July 1977): 309-28.

_____. *Jewish Literature between the Bible and the Mishnah: A Historical and Literary Introduction*. Philadelphia: Fortress, 1981.

_____. "The Books of Enoch in Recent Research." *Religious Studies Review* 7 (July 1981): 210-17.

_____. "Enoch, Levi, and Peter: Recipients of Revelation in Upper Galilee." *Journal of Biblical Literature* 100 (December 1981): 575-600.

O'Dell, Jerry. "The Religious Background of the Psalms of Solomon (Re-evaluated in the Light of the Qumran Texts)." *Révue Qumran* (May 1961): 241-47.

Perdue, Leo G. *Wisdom and Cult: A Critical Analysis of the Views of the Cult in the Wisdom Literatures of Israel And the Ancient Near East*. Society of Biblical Literature Dissertation Series, no. 30. Missoula, Montana: Scholars Press, 1977.

von Rad, G. "The Wisdom of Ben Sira." In *Wisdom in Israel*, pp. 240-62. Translated by James D. Martin. London: SCM, 1972.

Rost, Leonhard. *Judaism Outside the Hebrew Canon: An Introduction to the Documents*. Translated by D. E. Green. Nashville: Abingdon, 1976.

Roth, Wolfgang. "On the Gnomic-Discursive Wisdom of Jesus Ben Sirach." *Semeia* 17 (August 1980): 59-77.

Ryle, H. E., and James, M. R. *Psalmoi Solomontos: Psalms of the Pharisees Commonly called the Psalms of Solomon. The Text newly Revised from all the manuscripts. Edited with Introduction, English Translation, Notes, Appendix and Indices*. Cambridge: University Press, 1891.

Sanders, E. P. *Paul and Palestinian Judaism: A Comparison of Patterns of Religion*. Philadelphia: Fortress, 1977.

Schupphaus, J. *Die Psalmen Salomos: Ein Zeugnis Jerusalems Theologie und Frömigkeit in der Mitte de vorchristlichen Jahrhunderts*. Leiden: E. J. Brill 1977.

Snaith, John G. "Ben Sira's Supposed Love of Liturgy." *Vetus Testamentum* 25 (April 1975): 167-74.

Stone, M. E. "Reactions to Destructions of the Second Temple: Theology, Perception and Conversion." *Journal for the Study of Judaism in the Persian, Hellenistic and Roman Period* 12 (December 1981): 195-204.

Suter, David W. "Fallen Angel, Fallen Priest: The Problem of Family Purity in I Enoch 6-16." *Hebrew Union College Annual* 50 (1979): 115-36.

_____. "*Masal* in the Similitudes of Enoch." *Journal of Biblical Literature* 100 (June 1981): 193-212.

_____. "Weighed in the Balance: The Similitudes of Enoch in Recent Discussion." *Religious Studies Review* 7 (July 1981): 217-21.

Terrien, Samuel. *The Elusive Presence: The Heart of Biblical Theology*. San Francisco: Harper & Row, 1978.

Testuz, Michel. *Les Idées Réligieuses du Livre des Jubilées*. Paris: Libraire Minard: 1960.

Thompson, Alden Lloyd. *Responsibility for Evil in the Theodicy of IV Ezra: A Study Illustrating the Significance of Form and Structure for the Meaning of the Book*. Society of Biblical Literature Dissertation Series, no. 29. Missoula, Montana: Scholars Press for Society of Biblical Literature, 1977.

Vermes, Geza. *The Dead Sea Scrolls in English*. New York: Penguin, 1962.

Westerholm, Stephen. *Israel's Law and the Church's Faith: Paul and His Recent Interpreters*. Grand Rapids: Eerdmans, 1988.

Wintermute, O. S. "Jubilees: A New Translation and Introduction." In *The Old Testament Pseudepigrapha*, vol. II: *Expansions of the "Old Testament" and Legends, Wisdom and Philosophical Literature, Prayers, Psalms, and Odes, Fragments of Lost Judeo-Hellenistic Works*, pp. 35-142. Edited by James H. Charlesworth. Garden City, N.Y.: Doubleday, 1985.

Wright, Robert B. "Psalms of Solomon: A New Translation and Introduction." In *The Old Testament Pseudepigrapha*, vol. 2: *Expansions of the "Old Testament" and Legends, Wisdom and Philosophical Literature, Prayers, Psalms, and Odes, Fragments of Lost Judeo-Hellenisitc Works*, pp. 639-70. Edited by James H. Charlesworth. Garden City, N.Y.: Doubleday, 1985.

II. Part One: The Pharisees

Bowker, J. *Jesus and the Pharisees*. Cambridge: Cambridge University Press, 1973.

Cook, Michael, J. *Mark's Treatment of the Jewish Leaders*. Leiden: E. J. Brill, 1978.

_____. "Jesus and the Pharisees: The Problem as it Stands Today." *Journal of Ecumenical Studies* 15 (1978): 441-60.

Danby, H. *The Mishnah: Translated from the Hebrew with Introduction and Brief Explanatory Notes*. Oxford: Clarendon, 1933.

Interpreter's Dictionary of the Bible. S.v. "Pharisees," by Matthew Black. III: 774-81.

_____. S.v. "Pharisees," by Ellis Rivkin. Supplementary Volume: 657-63.

Jeremias, J. *Jerusalem in the Time of Jesus*, Philadelphia: Fortress, 1969.

Lane, W. L. "Paul's Legacy from Pharisaism: Light from the Psalms of Solomon." *Concordia Journal* 8 (July 1982): 130-38.

Lauterbach, J. Z. "The Pharisees and their Teachings." *Hebrew Union College Annual* 6 (1929): 69-140.

Lightstone, Jack. "Sadducees versus Pharisees: The Tannaitic Sources." In *Christianity, Judaism and other Greco-Roman Cults: Studies for Morton Smith at Sixty*, part 3, pp. 206-17. Studies in Judaism in Late Antiquity, vol. XII. Edited by J. Neusner. Leiden: E. J. Brill, 1975.

Marcus, R. "The Pharisees in the Light of Modern Scholarship." *Journal of Religion* 32 (1952): 153-64.

Neusner, J. *Rabbinic Traditions about the Pharisees before 70.* Part III: *Conclusions.* Leiden: E. J. Brill, 1971.

_____. *Contemporary Judaic Fellowship in Theory and in Practice.* New York: Ktav, 1972.

_____. "Rabbinic Traditions about the Pharisees before 70 A.D.: The Problem of Oral Tradition." *Kairos* 14 (1, 1972): 57-70. (Reprinted in *Early Rabbinic Judaism,* pp. 73-89, Leiden: E. J. Brill, 1975.)

_____. *From Politics to Piety: The Emergence of Pharisaic Judaism.* Englewood Cliffs, N.J.: Prentice-Hall, 1973.

_____. *The Idea of Purity in Ancient Judaism.* Leiden: E. J. Brill, 1973.

_____. *Early Rabbinic Judaism.* Leiden: E. J. Brill, 1975.

_____. "The History of Earlier Rabbinic Judaism: Some New Approaches. *Historical Review* 16 (1977): 216-36.

_____. "The Formation of Rabbinic Judaism: Yavneh from A.D. 70-100," pp. 3-42 in *Aufstieg und Niedergang der romischen Welt.* Principat II. 19. 2. Edited by H. Temporini and W. Haase. Berlin: W. de Gruyter, 1979.

_____. Review of *A Hidden Revolution: The Pharisees' Search for the Kingdom Within,* by Ellis Rivkin. *American Historical Review* 85 (October 1980): 863-64.

_____. "History and Purity." In *Method and Meaning in Ancient Judaism, Second Series,* pp. 45-51. Chico,Cal.: Scholars Press, 1981.

_____. "The Pharisees in the Light of the Historical Sources of Judaism." In *Formative Judaism: Religious, Historical and Literary Studies,* pp. 71-83. Chico, Cal.: Scholars Press for Brown University, 1982.

_____. "Two Pictures of the Pharisees: Philosophical Circle or Eating Club." *Anglican Theological Review* 64 (October 1982): 525-38.

_____. *From Mishnah to Scripture: The Problem of the Unattributed Saying With Special Reference to the Division of Purities.* Chico, Cal.: Scholars Press for Brown University, 1984.

Rivkin, Ellis. "Internal City: Judaism and Urbanization." *Journal for the Scientific Study of Religion* 5 (Spring 1966): 225-40.

_____. "Defining the Pharisees: The Tannaitic Sources." *Hebrew Union College Annual* 40-41 (1969-70): 205-50.

_____. "Pharisaism and the Crisis of the Individual in the Greco-Roman World." *Jewish Quarterly Review* 61 (July 1970): 27-53.

_____. *A Hidden Revolution.* Nashville: Abingdon, 1978.

_____. "Scribes, Pharisees, Lawyers, Hypocrites: A Study in Synonimity." *Hebrew Union College Annual* 49 (1978): 135-42.

Sanders, E. P. *Paul and Palestinian Judaism: A Comparison of Patterns of Religion.* Philadelphia: Fortress, 1977.

Schürer, Emil. *A History of the Jewish People in the Time of Jesus Christ.* Vol. II:2: *The Internal Condition of Palestine and of the Jewish People in the time of Christ.* Translated by S. Taylor and P. Christie. New York: Scribner's, 1891.

166   PAUL THE TEMPLE, AND THE PRESENCE OF GOD

_____. *The History of the Jewish People in the Age of Jesus Christ.* Vol. II. Revised and edited by G. Vermes, F. Millar, and M. Black. Edinburgh: T. & T. Clark, 1979.

Schwartz, D. R. "Josephus and Nicolaus on the Pharisees." *Journal for the Study of Judaism in the Persian, Hellenistic, and Roman Period)* 14 (December 1983): 157-71.

Simon, Marcel. *Jewish Sects at the Time of Jesus.* Translated by J. H. Farley. Philadelphia: Fortress, 1967.

III. Part Two -- Pauline Literature

Achtemeier, Paul. J. *The Quest for Unity in the New Testament Church.* Philadelphia: Fortress, 1987.

Baird, Wm. "Letters of Recommendation: A Study of II Corinthians 3:1-3." *Journal of Biblical Literature* 80 (June 1961): 166-72.

Barclay, Wm. *The Letter to the Hebrews.* Philadelphia: Westminster, 1955.

Barrett, C. K. *The Epistle to the Romans.* New York: Harper & Bros., 1957.

_____. "Paul's Opponents in II Corinthians." *New Testament Studies* 17 (April 1971): 233-54.

_____. *The Second Epistle to the Corinthians.* London: A & C. Black, 1973.

Bauer, W. *A Greek-English Lexicon of the New Testament and Other Early Christian Literature.* 4th ed. Translated and edited by W. F. Arndt and F. W. Gingrich. Chicago: Chicago University, 1952.

Black, Matthew. *Romans.* New Century Bible. Greenwood, S.C.: Attic Press, 1973.

Brockington, L. H. "The Presence of God: A Study of the Use of the Term 'Glory of Yahweh'." *Expository Times* 57 (October 1945): 21-25.

Brockington, L. H. "The Septuagintal Background to the New Testament use of DOXA." In *Studies in the Gospels: Essays in Memory of R. H. Lightfoot,* pp. 1-8. Edited by D. E. Nineham. Oxford: Blackwell, 1957.

Bruce, F. F. *1 and 2 Corinthians.* New Century Bible. London: Oliphants, 1971.

Brueggemann, W. "The Crisis of Promise and Presence in Israel." *Horizons in Biblical Theology* 1 (1980):47-86.

Bultmann, Rudolf. *The Second Letter to the Corinthians.* Translated by R. Harrisville. Minneapolis: Augsburg,1985.

Calvin, J. *The Epistles of Paul the Apostle to the Romans and to the Thessalonians.* Translated by Ross Mackenzie. Grand Rapids: Eerdmans, 1979.

_____. *The Second Epistle of Paul the Apostle to the Corinthians and the Epistles of Timothy, Titus and Philemon.* Translated by T. A. Smail. Grand Rapids: Eerdmans, 1964.

Carrez, Maurice. "Présence et Fonctionnement de L'ancien Testament dans L'annonce de l'évangile." *Réscherches de Science Réligieuse* 63 (July-September 1975): 325-41.

Childs, B. S. *The Book of Exodus: A Critical, Theological Commentary.* Philadelphia: Westminster, 1974.

Collange, J. -F. *Énigmes de la Deuxième Épitre de Paul aux Corinthiens: Étude Exégètique de 2 Cor. 2:14-7:4.* Cambridge: University Press, 1972.

Conzelmann, H. *An Outline of the Theology of the New Testament.* Translated by John Bowden. New York: Harper & Row, 1968.

Cranfield, C. E. B. *A Critical and Exegetical Commentary on the Epistle to the Romans.* Vol. 1. Edinburgh: T. & T. Clark, 1975.

Crenshaw, James L. "In Search of Divine Presence: Some Remarks Preliminary to a Theology of Wisdom." *Review and Expositor* 74 (July 1977): 353-69.

Dana, H. E., and Mantey, Julius R. *A Manual Grammar of the Greek New Testament.* New York: Macmillan, 1955.

Dictionary of New Testament Theology. S.v. "Glory, Honour," by S. Aalen, 2:44-49.

Dodd, C. H. *The Epistle to the Romans.* London: Hodder & Stoughton, 1932.

Dunn, J. D. G. "2 Corinthians 3:7: 'The Lord is the Spirit'". *Journal of Theological Studies* 21 (October 1970): 309-20.

Egan, Rory B. "Lexical Evidence on two Pauline Passages (2 Cor. 2:14; Col 2:15)." *Novum Testamentum* 19 (January 1977): 34-62.

Eichrodt, W. *Theology of the Old Testament.* Vol. 2. Translated by J. A. Baker. Philadelphia: Westminster, 1967.

Fitzmyer, J. A. "Glory Reflected on the Face of Christ (2Cor. 3:7-4:6) and a Palestinian Motif." *Theological Studies* 42 (December 1981): 630-44.

Furnish, V. P. *II Corinthians: Translated with Introduction Notes, and Commentary. The Anchor Bible,* vol. 32. Garden City, N. Y.: Doubleday, 1984.

Georgi, D. *The Opponents of Paul in Second Corinthians.* Philadelphia: Fortress, 1986.

Gordon, T. David. "Paul's Understanding of the Law: A Tri-Polar Analysis." Ph.D. Dissertation, Union Theological Seminary in Virginia, 1984.

Greenwood, David. "The Lord is the Spirit: Some Considerations of II Cor. 3:17." *Catholic Biblical Quarterly* 34 (October 1972): 467-72.

Hafemann, Scott J. *Suffering and the Spirit: An Exegetical Study of II Cor. 2:14-3:3 within the Context of the Corinthian Correspondence.* Wissenschaftliche Untersuchungen zum Neuen Testament: 2 Reihe; 19. Tübingen: J.C.B. Mohr (Paul Siebeck), 1986.

Hanson, Anthony T. "The Midrash in II Corinthians 3: A Reconsideration." *Journal for the Study of the New Testament* 9 (October 1980): 2-28.

Héring, Jean. *The Second Epistle of Saint Paul to the Corinthians.* Translated by A. W. Heathcote and P. J.Alcock. London: Epworth, 1967.

Hickling, C. J. A. "Is the Second Epistle to the Corinthians a Source for early Christian History?" *Zeitschrift fur die neutestamentliche Wissenschaft* 66 (1975): 284-87.

_____. "The Sequence of Thought in II Corinthians, Chapter Three." *New Testament Studies* 21 (April 1975): 380-95.

Hill, E. "The Construction of Three Passages from St. Paul (Rom. 8:20-21, 2 Cor. 1:20, 2 Cor. 3:10)." *Catholic Biblical Quarterly* 23 (July 1961): 296-301.

Hooker, Morna D. "The Johannine Prologue and the Messianic Secret." *New Testament Studies* 21 (October 1974): 40-58.

_____. "Beyond the Things that are Written? St. Paul's Use of Scripture." *New Testament Studies* 27 (April 1981): 295-309.

Hughes, Philip E. *Paul's Second Letter to the Corinthians.* Grand Rapids: Eerdmans, 1962.

Jervell, Jacob. *Imago Dei: Gen. 1:26f im Spätjudentum, in der Gnosis und in dem paulinischen Briefen.* Göttingen: Vandenhoeck & Ruprecht, 1960.

Jones, D. R. *Haggai, Zechariah and Malachi: Introduction and Commentary.* London: SCM, 1962.

Josephus. *Jewish Antiquities,* I-IV. Loeb Classical Library, vol. 4. Translated by H. J. Thackeray. New York: Putnam's, 1930.

Käsemann, E. *New Testament Questions of Today.* Translated by W. J. Montague. Philadelphia: Fortress, 1969.

_____. *Commentary on Romans.* Translated by G. Bromiley. Grand Rapids: Eerdmans, 1980.

Kingsbury, Jack D. *Proclamation Commentaries: Matthew.* Philadelphia: Fortress, 1977.

Koenig, J. "The Motif of Transformation in the Pauline Epistles." Ph.D. Dissertation, Union Theological Seminary, New York, 1970.

Lambrecht, Jan T. "Structure and Line of Thought in 2 Cor.2:14-4:6." *Biblica* 64 (1983): 344-80.

Levenson, Jon D. *Sinai and Zion: An Entry into the Jewish Bible.* Minneapolis: Winston, 1985.

McDonald, James I. H. "Paul and the Preaching Ministry: A Reconsideration of 2 Cor. 2:14-17 in its Context." *Journal for the Study of the New Testament* 17 (Feb 1983): 35-50.

Marshall, I. H. *1 & 2 Thessalonians.* The New Century Bible Commentary. Grand Rapids: Eerdmans, 1983.

Marshall, Peter. "A Metaphor of Social Shame: Θριαμβεύειν." *Novum Testamentum* 25 (October 1983): 302-17.

Martin, Ralph P. *2 Corinthians.* Word Biblical Commentary, vol. 40. Waco, Tx.: Word, 1986.

Mason Rex. *The Books of Haggai, Zechariah and Malachi.* Cambridge: Cambridge University Press, 1977.

Metzger, B. M. *A Textual Commentary on the Greek New Testament.* London: United Bible Societies, 1975.

Moore, A. L. *1 & 2 Thessalonians.* The Century Bible New Series. London: Nelson, 1969.

Murray, John. *The Epistle to the Romans. The English Text with Introduction, Exposition and Notes.* Vol. 1.Grand Rapids: Eerdmans, 1959.

Neugebauer, F. *In Christus: Eine Untersuchung zum Paulinischen Glaubens-verständnis.* Göttingen: Vandenhoeck & Ruprecht, 1961.

Newton, M. C. *The Concept of Purity at Qumran and in the Letters of Paul.* Cambridge: Cambridge University Press, 1985.

Noth, Martin. *Exodus: A Commentary.* Translated by J. S. Bowden. Philadelphia: Westminster, 1959.

_____. *Numbers: A Commentary.* Translated by James D. Martin. Philadelphia: Westminster, 1968.

Petersen, David L. *Haggai and Zechariah 1-8.* Philadelphia: Westminster, 1984.

Plummer, Alfred. *A Critical and Exegetical Commentary on the Second Epistle of Paul to the Corinthians.* New York: Scribner's, 1915.

Plutarch. *Plutarch's Lives: Aemilius Paulus.* Loeb Classical Library, vol. 6. New York: Putnam's, 1918.

Provence, Thomas E. "'Who is sufficient for these things?': An Exegesis of 2 Cor. 2:15-3:18." *Novum Testamentum* 24 (January 1982): 54-81.

von Rad, G. *Genesis: A Commentary.* Translated by J. H.Marks. Philadelphia: Westminster, 1961.

Richard, Earl. "Polemics, Old Testament, and Theology: A Study of II Cor. 3:1-4:6." *Révue Biblique* 88 (July 1981): 340-67.

Ridderbos, H. *Paul: An Outline of His Theology.* Translated by J. R. DeWitt. Grand Rapids: Eerdmans, 1975.

Rissi, Matthias. "The Brighter Splendor: Paul and the Old Testament According to II Corinthians 3. *Affirmation* 1 (July 1967): 59-87.

_____. *The Future of the World: An Exegetical Study of Revelation 19:11-22:15.* London: SCM Press, 1972.

Sanday, Wm., and Headlam, A. C. *A Critical and Exegetical Commentary on the Epistle to the Romans.* Edinburgh: T. & T. Clark, 1911.

Schutz, J. H. *Paul and the Anatomy of Apostolic Authority.* Cambridge:University Press, 1975.

Smith, Wm. H., Jr. "The Function of 2 Corinthians 3:7-4:6 in its Epistolary Context." Ph.D. Dissertation, Southern Baptist Theological Seminary, 1983.

Stockhausen, Carol K. *Moses' Veil and the Glory of the New Covenant: The Exegetical Substructure of II Cor. 3:1-4:6.* Analectica Biblica 116. Rome: Pontifical Institute, 1989

Suter, David W. "Fallen Angel, Fallen Priest: The Problem of Family Purity in I Enoch 6-16." *Hebrew Union College Annual* 50 (1979): 115-21.

_____. "*Mašal* in the Similitudes of Enoch." *Journal of Biblical Literature* 100 (June 1981): 193-212.

Theological Dictionary of the New Testament. S.v. "Δόξα,"by G. von Rad and E. Kittel. 2:232-55.

_____. S.v. "Εἰλικρίνεια," by Friedrich Büschel. 2:232-55.

_____. S.v. "Πνεῦμα," by E. Schweizer. 6:332-455.

_____. S.v. "Πεποίθησις" by R. Bultmann. 6:7-8.

_____. S.v. "Τόπος," by H. Koester. 8: 187-208.

Thrall, Margaret. E. *The First and Second Letters of Paul to the Corinthians.* Cambridge: University Press, 1965.

_____. "2 Corinthians 1:12: ΑΓΙΟΤΗΤΙ or ΑΠΛΟΤΗΤΙ?" In *Studies in New Testament Language and Text: Essays in Honour of G. D. Kilpatrick on the Occasion of his Sixty-Fifth Birthday,* Novum Testamentum Supplements, no. 44, pp. 366-72. Edited by J. K. Elliott. Leiden: E. J. Brill, 1976.

_____. "A Second Thanksgiving Period in II Corinthians." *Journal for the Study of the New Testament* 16 (1982): 101-24.

van Unnik, W. C. '"With Unveiled Face': An Exegesis of Corinthians 3:12-18."
   Novum Testamentum 6 (July 1963): 153-69.

_____. "The Semitic Background of PARRESIA." In *Sparsa Collecta: The
   Collected Works of W. C. van Unnik. Part 2.* Novum Testamentum
   Supplements, no. 30, pp. 290-306. Leiden: E. J. Brill, 1980.

Vielhauer, P. *Oikodome.* Munich: Kaiser Verlag, 1979.

Williamson, Lamar. "Led in Triumph: Paul's Use of θριαμβεύω." *Interpretation* 22
   (July 1968): 317-32.

Windisch, Hans. *Der Zweite Korintherbrief.* Göttingen: Vandenhoeck & Ruprecht,
   1970.

INDEX

I. GENERAL

II. AUTHORS

Achtemeier, P. J. 52, 89
Baird, Wm. 50
Barclay, Wm. 41
Barrett, C. K. 49, 50, 54, 57, 62, 63,
65, 71, 72, 75-80, 83, 85, 89, 92, 96,
98, 100, 118, 120, 125, 127, 130, 132,
136-138, 142, 146, 151, 155
Black, Matthew 6, 37, 49, 71
Bowker, John 8
Brandenburger, Egon 38
Breech, Earl 38
Brockington, L. H. 99, 100, 103, 104
Bruce, F. F. 54, 57, 63, 72, 75, 79, 83,
113, 125, 128, 130, 136, 139, 146
Brueggemann, W. 32, 45, 48, 143
Bultmann, R. 44, 49, 50, 57, 62, 63,
65, 72, 75-77, 79, 83, 86, 88, 96, 100,
102, 104, 105, 110, 123, 125, 126, 128,
130, 132, 134, 136, 146, 147, 152, 155
Calvin, John 71, 147
Carrez, M. 79, 133
Charlesworth, J. H. 35-37
Childs, B. S. 111, 112, 142, 143
Clements, R. E. 25-27, 29, 30, 40
Collange, J.-F. 44, 48-50, 74, 75,
79-81, 83, 96, 99, 102, 105, 118,
123-125, 132, 136, 146, 151, 152
Cook, M. J. 5, 8, 18
Cranfield, C. E. B. 71
Crenshaw, J. L. 32, 33
Davenport, G. L. 34
Delcor, M. S. 37
Denis, A. M. 37
Dodd, C. H. 71
Dunn, J. D. G. 142, 151, 155
Egan, R. B. 76, 77
Eichrodt, W. 155
Eissfeldt, Otto 37
Fitzmyer, J. A. 45, 55, 134
Frizzell, L. E. 26
Furnish, V. P. 44, 45, 47-50, 54, 56,
62, 63, 65, 72-77, 79, 83-85, 87, 88, 99,
105, 110, 111, 113, 118, 120, 123-125,

128-130, 132, 136-140, 147, 148,
151-153, 155, 160
Georgi, D. 44, 55, 89, 105, 137, 138,
140, 143, 146
Gilbert, M. 34
Greenwood, D. 71
Hafemann, S .J. 49, 77, 79, 88, 89,
96, 140
Hanson, A. T. 44, 138, 139, 142, 148,
155
Haran, M. 26
Headlam, A. C. 71
Hengel, M. 33
Héring, J. 49, 62, 126
Hickling, C. J. A. 44, 45, 98, 99, 110,
133, 134, 136, 138, 147
Hill, E. 29, 111
Hooker, M. 45, 92, 98, 107, 113, 120,
133, 136, 137, 142, 148, 149
Hughes, P. E. 72, 96
Jaubert, A. 34, 37
Jeremias, J. 6, 8, 20
Jervell, J. 100, 102
Jones, J. R. 114
Josephus, 6-12, 14, 18, 19, 51, 55,
64, 143
Kee, H. C. 38
Kingsbury, J. D. 42
Klinzing, G. 39
Knibb, M. A. 38
Koenig, J. 53, 54, 99, 137
Lambrecht, J. T. 113, 136, 138, 146
Lane, Wm. 6
Lauterbach, J. Z. 12, 13
Levenson, J. D. 55, 98
Levine, B. 22, 25
Lightstone, J. 13
MacKenzie, R. A. F. 34, 71
Maier, J. 39
Marbock, J. 33
Marcus, R. 5
Marshall, P. 77
Marshall, I. H. 102

III. LITERATURE

www.ingramcontent.com/pod-product-compliance
Lightning Source LLC
Chambersburg PA
CBHW031257090426
42742CB00007B/487